ESSAYS IN MONETARY THEORY

ESSAYS IN MONETARY THEORY

BY

D. H. ROBERTSON

Professor of Political Economy in the University of Cambridge

And so she went on, taking first one side and then the other, and making quite a conversation of it altogether.

Alice in Wonderland.

HYPERION PRESS, INC.

Westport, Connecticut

Published in 1940 by Staples Press, London and New York
Hyperion reprint edition
Library of Congress Number 78-20487
ISBN 0-88355-864-5
Printed in the United States of America

Library of Congress Cataloging in Publication Data
Robertson, Dennis Holme, Sir, 1890-1963.
Essays in monetary theory.
Reprint of the 1940 ed. published by Staples Press, London and New York.
1. Money—Addresses, essays, lectures. 2. Interest and usury—Addresses, essays, lectures. 3. Business cycles—Addresses, essays, lectures. 4. Keynes, John Maynard, 1883-1946—Addresses, essays, lectures. I. Title.
HG221.R557 1979 332.4 78-20487
ISBN 0-88355-864-5

CONTENTS

Page

I. MR. KEYNES AND THE RATE OF INTEREST 1

II. THEORIES OF BANKING POLICY 39

III. THE 1931 CRISIS 60

IV. SAVING AND HOARDING 65

V. INDUSTRIAL FLUCTUATION AND THE NATURAL RATE OF INTEREST 83

VI. A NOTE ON THE THEORY OF MONEY 92

VII. THE FUTURE OF TRADE CYCLE THEORY 98

VIII. THE SNAKE AND THE WORM 104

IX. EFFECTIVE DEMAND AND THE MULTIPLIER 114

X. THE TRADE CYCLE—AN ACADEMIC VIEW 122

XI. A SURVEY OF MODERN MONETARY CONTROVERSY 133

XII. BRITISH MONETARY POLICY 154

XIII. SIX REVIEWS:—

Robbins: The Great Depression 168

Röpke: Crises and Cycles 173

Harrod: The Trade Cycle 176

Bresciani-Turroni: The Economics of Inflation 181

Hawtrey: A Century of Bank Rate 184

Guillebaud: The Economic Recovery of Germany 187

XIV. NOTES ON INTERNATIONAL TRADE 191

I. The Terms of Trade 191

II. The Transfer Problem 197

XV. THE FUTURE OF INTERNATIONAL TRADE 209

XVI. A VISIT TO THE LACCADIVE ISLANDS 227

PREFACE

THIS collection was (in the main) prepared for publication before the outbreak of war (and hence, incidentally, before I received an appointment in the Civil Service). It now looks a little dusty; but, after a short sojourn in my bank, it is offered, as my first book was offered in 1915, to those who can find time for an antiquarian interest in the problems and controversies of a vanished age.

The first and longest item conserves pretty closely the form of a course of lectures delivered at the London School of Economics in the summer term of 1939, but embodies also some material already printed in the *Economic Journal* and the *Quarterly Journal of Economics* (referred to throughout the book as *E.J.* and *Q.J.E.* respectively). The remaining items have already appeared in print in their present form (except that in one or two cases I have done a little excision): their reappearance is not to be taken to indicate that I stand by everything in them. Numbers II and XIV were included in the volume of *Economic Essays and Addresses* by Professor Pigou and myself, and are re-included here, on the suggestion of a colleague, for the convenience of students. The original place of appearance of each item is indicated in footnotes; and my thanks are due for the courteous manner in which my desire to reprint has been met by those concerned.

I owe an apology to students for my failure to present my thoughts on these matters in more architectural form. They will find, I fear, a certain amount of repetition, and doubtless also some inconsistency, in the pages which follow. Apart from natural indolence, I may perhaps offer as an excuse that I lived for twenty years at Cambridge under the pre-natal shadow of a series of large books by my two masters, from each of which in turn I hopefully awaited that definitive clearing up of the matters at issue which should make any further struggle towards systematic treatment on my own part superfluous. By way of attempt to give some unity to the present collection, I was tempted to confer upon it the rather highly-coloured title which stands above, and is explained in, the eighth essay. For so far as any single theme may be said to be illustrated by the collection as a whole, it is the difficulty of finding a just mean between regarding industrial depression as a mere phase of a symmetrical oscillation and regarding it as a symptom of mortal disease.

In this long and intricately worked terrain, the problem of acknowledgment has become a nightmare. I have tried to solve part of it *ambulando* in the text, but much remains. Among the many published appraisals of Mr. Keynes' latest work, I have, I think, derived most benefit from those by Mr. Hawtrey and Mr. Hicks; among many conversations on the same theme, those with Mr. Sraffa stand out in memory as most inevitably ending in theft. But it would be easy to add to both these short lists. Among lesser-known writers, a possible debt to Señor Bernacer of Alicante in the matter of "sequence analysis" will be recorded in *Economica*, February 1940: and I wish I could atone for an unaccountable failure to mention in my first book (1915) the mark which had been (and remains) imprinted on my mind by the account of "shortage of capital" contained in a brilliant and still almost unknown pamphlet, *Autour de la crise américaine de 1907*, by M. Marcel Larbordère.

I have left till nearly the last my most difficult task.

Fas est et ab hoste doceri—one learns even from one's friends. How am I to express my debt to Mr. Keynes in terms which, in view of the fact that no small part of this book consists of somewhat acid criticism of his work, shall not seem insincere? I find I have made one such attempt on p. 116, to which I invite the reader to turn at this point. In the badinage of correspondence, Mr. Keynes has accused me of being a bad snake, unapt at sloughing its old skins; while I have presumptuously claimed in reply to be a good glow-worm, shedding its feeble light fairly consistently and impartially on all the phenomena in its neighbourhood, by contrast with the powerful searchlight which launches a penetrating but distorting beam on a number of different objects in succession, obscuring the rest in temporary darkness. And there we must leave it.

My excuse for including the last item in the book must be that it contains references to the theory of taxation and the theory of international trade.

D. H. R.

LONDON.

January, 1940.

I

MR. KEYNES AND THE RATE OF INTEREST[1]

I. WORDS AND THINGS

§ 1. The purpose of these lectures is to restate in a more coherent and positive manner certain criticisms which I have felt impelled to make of the doctrines regarding the rate of interest put forward in recent years by Mr. Keynes.

I find it necessary in self-defence to start with a few words on the distasteful subject of methodology. In the course of one of our brushes, Mr. Keynes has suggested that I am a recent and reluctant convert to the view that the rate of interest is "in some sense a monetary phenomenon."[2] This is, I am afraid, a misapprehension. Obviously in a money-using world the rate of interest, in what Marshall calls[3] its "strict sense" of the price paid in money for the use of a sum of money, is "in some sense a monetary phenomenon"; and nobody can ever have supposed otherwise. The fact is, surely, that in expounding any branch of economic theory, there are two courses open to us. We can start with a situation simplified to the greatest possible extent by abstraction, and then gradually build up our theory by introducing successively the complications of real life. Or we can start by facing boldly all the complications of a momentary market situation, and then seek to discard the accidentals and distil the essentials. So it is with interest: we can begin by showing how it would emerge in a Crusoe economy, then introduce exchange, then money; or we can start with the actual world, with its (far from perfect) loan markets and its (far from

[1] See Preface, p. vii.
[2] *E.J.*, June 1938, pp. 318, 323.
[3] *Money, Credit and Commerce*, p. 73.

orderly) monetary systems. The danger of this latter method is that the same motive which leads us to adopt it, namely the desire to show ourselves at all costs "in touch with real life," will tempt us to seek to produce an apparently simple result in circumstances in which simplicity involves the exaggeration of incidentals and the obscuring of fundamentals. So anxious, however, am I to avoid the reproach of "classicality," that I am ready to follow Mr. Keynes by starting the analysis at the most difficult end. Until near its close, however, I propose to allow myself the same simplification as he has frequently done, namely, that of speaking as though there were only *one* rate of interest determined in a single market.

§ 2. If we start in this way, the natural course seems to be to describe the rate of interest as the market price of the hire of something which Marshall called "free or floating capital," which others have called "capital disposal" or "command over capital," and which recent writers seem to have settled down into calling "loanable" or "investible funds." This price, like other market prices, can be conceived as emerging from the interaction of schedules of supply and demand, showing the amount of loanable funds which, at given hiring-prices, people are respectively willing to put on to, and to take off, the market during the slice of time selected for observation. Since we have decided to start by facing all, or nearly all, the complications of the real world, we must not be surprised to find that these schedules are complicated things. In analysing their constitution, it is to some extent arbitrary whether we enter certain elements as additions to the demand side or deductions from the supply side, and *vice versa*. The classification which follows is no doubt only one of many possible ones; but it seems to bring out the main points requiring attention.

The amount of loanable funds which people are willing to put on the market at any price consists of the following elements, some of which may of course be negative:—

(i) current savings effected during the period:

(ii) "disentanglings," *i.e.* savings which have been made in the past and are being currently released from embodiment either in fixed capital (buildings, instruments, etc.) or in working capital (goods in process or in store) and so becoming available for re-embodiment either in the same or in different forms:

(iii) "net dishoardings," *i.e.* previously saved, or previously disentangled, money now being withdrawn from store and placed on the market, less money which is being currently saved, or currently disentangled, and withheld from the market:

(iv) net additional bank loans (including of course investments, since we are not distinguishing at this stage between different markets), *i.e.* the gross amount of new bank loans during the period less repayments to banks out of current disentanglings or current savings.

The amount of loanable funds which people are willing to take off the market at any price may be analysed according to the purposes for which the funds are required, as follows:—

(i) funds destined for expenditure on building up new increments of fixed or working capital:

(ii) funds destined for expenditure on the maintenance or replacement of existing fixed or working capital:

(iii) funds destined to be put into store:

(iv) funds destined for expenditure on consumption, whether individual or collective (*i.e.* through State doles, etc.), in excess of current income.

§ 3. This analysis, which is substantially identical with that of Professor Ohlin,[1] requires some comments.

(1) To some extent as regards the first, and to a greater extent as regards the second, item on both lists, the demanders and suppliers are likely to be the same persons, *i.e.* they do not appear on the market properly

[1] *E.J.*, Sept. 1937, pp. 423 ff.

so called, and the assumption that their actions are highly sensitive to the current behaviour of the rate of interest is not entirely realistic. In other words, up to a point there is probably a measure of automatism, especially as regards the re-entanglement of *working capital* disentanglings, in the conduct of business firms. But it would be a mistake to exaggerate the degree of this automatism, *i.e.* to overlook the extent to which disinvestment even in working capital is an ever-present possibility.

(2) The analysis shows that there is no difficulty, as it has sometimes been suggested that there is, in dealing by this market supply and demand method with the phenomenon of the offer of existing money stocks in exchange for securities, or existing security holdings in exchange for money. Still less is there any difficulty in dealing with the case [1] in which no exchanges of this kind are in fact occurring, the rate of interest having already moved sufficiently to prevent them: in this case the relevant elements of the supply and demand schedules are simply equated at zero.[2]

(3) Since the analysis deals in terms of the way in which people are willing to act at a particular time it is evidently necessary to interpret the terms used in a sense which makes it possible to relate them to the choices which are open to people at that time. Thus we must exclude both from "savings" and from "hoardings" (or from their opposite terms) those undesigned increments (or decrements) in people's money stocks which occur, as Mr. Lutz has well put it,[3] "after the transactions on the capital market are over," and as an unforeseen result of the behaviour of the flow of total expenditure which is consequential on those transactions. Whatever may be said in other connections for an "ex-post" definition of money savings which

[1] Specially mentioned by Mr. Keynes (*Q.J.E.*, Feb. 1937, p. 211) and Mr. Townshend (*E.J.*, March 1937, p. 158).

[2] But to ensure the occurrence of this result in any particular market it is usually, I imagine, necessary that dealings should be conducted through a class of middlemen who are in a position to choke off transactions by quoting *different* prices to potential lenders and potential borrowers.

[3] *Q.J.E.*, Aug. 1938, p. 612.

makes them necessarily identical for any period with the money value of the increments of real capital created ("investment"), it is clearly inappropriate to an analysis which seeks to distinguish between the origin of the various streams which people choose to place in a given interval upon the capital market. And for a definition of "hoardings" which makes them necessarily identical with the increase in the total stock of money, thus divorcing the concept entirely from the volitional processes of the public, I can see nothing to be said for any purpose whatever.[1]

§ 4. Since this saving-"investment" identity has played such a large part in the discussions of the last few years, I must be forgiven for a brief digression on it here. I wish I could feel that its expositors were *continuously* as conscious as at times they profess themselves to be that it is completely nugatory (to use a favourite word of Mr. Hawtrey's) for purposes of causal analysis as distinct from statistical calculation. But they are, in my view, inclined to forget [2] that these troublesome English words in -ing sometimes denote a process (requiring translation into Latin by an infinitive or gerund) and sometimes denote the object to which the process has been applied (requiring translation by a neuter past participle passive). And thus, since they are conscious that they have not perpetrated the absurdity (of which no one has ever accused them) of portraying the process of saving as identical with the process of "investing," they are tempted to forget that they *have* so defined their terms that aggregate amount saved is irretrievably identical with aggregate amount "invested." Hence they are enabled to close their eyes to the absurdity of even enquiring what the forces are which "ensure equality" between the two magnitudes which, in Mr. Harrod's words, "are but

[1] Mr. Lerner, in a recent geometrical fantasia (*E.J.*, June 1938, pp. 211 ff.) appears to me to have overlooked these considerations. Starting with an apparatus designed to register human choices, he proceeds to graft on to it concepts from which choice is excluded, and expects us to share his naïve glee at the confusion which results.

[2] See especially Keynes, *E.J.*, June 1937, p. 249.

one magnitude," causing the one to "elicit" the other or the other to "accommodate itself" to the one. To proceed thus is, I suggest, as though one were to define an elephant's trunk and its proboscis in identical terms, and then to enter upon a complicated discussion of the biological principles which ensure that the trunk is always equal to the proboscis. This lack of firmness in the handling of their own concepts convinces me that Mr. Keynes and his expositors are not altogether comfortable in the terminological garments which they have elected to wear.[1]

In any case I find myself in agreement with Professor Ohlin[2] that in the analysis of the market for loanable funds it is some kind of intentional or "ex-ante" concept of saving that is required. But there is a difficulty here which I must not attempt to conceal.[3] In Professor Ohlin's analysis, "planned saving" is the difference between "expected income" and planned, which can be taken to be identical with actual current, expenditure on consumption. In my own attempts at analysis, "saving" has been identified with the difference between *previously received* income and current expenditure on consumption. Now I am far from denying that people's current expenditure on consumption is influenced by their expectations as regards future income, or from supposing, as Mr. Hawtrey has imagined me to do,[4] that their capacity for present expenditure is

[1] The *locus classicus* of this two-mindedness is to be found in Mrs. Robinson's exposition of the principle of the "multiplier" (*Introduction to the Theory of Employment*, p. 22). Having a few pages earlier explained the necessary equality of saving and "investment," she proceeds to expound how an act of "investment," *e.g.* an outlay of money on house-building, generates a progressive increase in money income by giving rise to successive "rounds" of expenditure. "If the whole of the outlay on house-building were added to saving at the first round," she writes, "there would be no second round." But according to her own definitions it has inevitably been so added! Again, "the increase in incomes must necessarily continue up to the point at which there is an addition to saving equal to the additional outlay on house-building." But on her definitions this point is reached instantaneously, whether there is any increase in incomes beyond the original outlay on house-building or whether there is none!

[2] *E.J.*, June 1937, p. 237; Sept. 1937, p. 424.

[3] I should like, but am unable, to persuade myself that it is solved by Mr. Lutz, *Q.J.E.*, Aug. 1938, p. 605.

[4] See *E.J.*, Dec. 1933, p. 702, and a welcome defence by Professor Hansen, *Journal of Political Economy*, Oct. 1936, p. 674. Mr. Hawtrey's own position

limited by the amount of their immediately preceding income. But I have a twofold difficulty in assimilating my terminology completely to that of Professor Ohlin. In the first place, as Mr. Hawtrey has insisted,[1] expected income is necessarily a somewhat nebulous concept, since expectations are seldom precise. Secondly, let us suppose that people expect what is in fact going to occur, *i.e.* intuit rightly the change in the size of the income stream which will eventuate from the current transactions in the capital market. In this event, identity, in Professor Ohlin's terminology, between ex-ante and ex-post saving could coexist with change, indeed with extreme instability, in the stream of money income. This seems to me inconvenient; though since in this case the amount of the ex-post saving which will be withheld from the market will also be correctly foreseen, and therefore figure as a negative item among "dishoardings," the validity of the supply and demand analysis set forth in § 1 is not affected.

§ 5. I turn to the rival formulation of the immediate determinants of the rate of interest which has been given by Mr. Keynes. Instead of enquiring into what happens on the markets during an *interval* of time, it focuses attention on the position reached, as a result of previous market transactions, at a *moment* of time; and portrays the rate of interest as the child of a marriage between the amount of money which the monetary authority permits to be in existence at that moment and a schedule exhibiting the amounts of money

on this matter is highly individual. He speaks of savings over any short period as being supplemented by additional bank loans (*A Century of Bank Rate*, p. 175)—a conception which to the Keynsian is "purely mythical" (Mrs. Robinson, *E.J.*, June 1938, p. 236). Yet he does not appear to feel the need for a definition of savings of my type, and does not even accept Prof. Ohlin's distinction between designed and undesigned savings (*E.J.*, Sept. 1937, p. 439). The explanation appears to be that in his scheme additional bank loans devoted to capital outlay are only to be regarded as a supplement to savings in so far as they lead to a decumulation of stocks of goods.

My own approach, involving as it does the parcelling of time into significant intervals, entails admitted difficulties which may be incapable of a completely tidy solution: but the same, after all, is true of various other concepts, such as the general price-level or "keeping capital intact," which the workaday economist is rightly not willing on that account to abandon.

[1] *E.J.*, Sept. 1937, *loc. cit.*

which, in the light of their knowledge of the existence of various rates of interest, people would wish to hold at that moment. Before examining the relation of this apparatus to that which we have just discussed, I must allude briefly to three respects in which, as it seems to me, its author has at various times erected obstacles in the way of its clear comprehension.

(1) In the first place, he shifts about in his book between using the word "money" to *mean* "money" and using it to mean something which in ordinary monetary theory is sharply contrasted with money, namely the real resources over which command is kept in monetary form (whether such resources are better regarded as measured in "wheat," as by Marshall and Pigou, or in "labour," as by Keynes, is a secondary issue). The inconvenience of this latter usage is that if the price of real resources falls, we have to represent the consequence not, as in ordinary monetary theory, as a decrease in the quantity of money demanded, but as an automatic increase in the quantity of "money" supplied—the "supply of money" is no longer something which only the monetary authority can alter. I do not of course contend that this double meaning of the word "money" is illegitimate, but only that it is liable to cause confusion unless very carefully handled.

(2) Secondly, in one of several alternative formulations of the theory given in his book,[1] Mr. Keynes includes among the reasons for the downward slope of the curve by which the demand (in his sense) for money (in the ordinary sense) can be portrayed, the reason that at lower rates of interest the level of output and prices will be higher, and require therefore the holding of larger stocks of money. This is, to my mind, to confuse the amount of money which people will wish to hold in the face of a given rate of interest now existing with the amount of money which they will wish to hold as an indirect consequence of a given rate of interest prevailing at some previous time, and

[1] *General Theory of Employment, Interest and Money* (hereafter referred to as *G.T.*), pp. 171-2.

to ignore the overwhelming evidence to the effect that rising output and prices are usually in fact associated with rising rates of interest. This misleading formulation has, however, now been generally discarded [1] in favour of one in which the quantity of money demanded at any given moment is regarded as divided into two parts, the one dependent on the level of output and prices and virtually independent of the rate of interest, the other inversely related to the rate of interest.

(3) In certain more recent writings, to which I shall allude further later, Mr. Keynes has again rendered clear discussion difficult by introducing a number of hybrid concepts, such as "the supply of finance" and the "supply of liquidity," which are neither identical with the "supply of money" in his sense, since others than the banks are conceived of as contributing to them, nor identical with the "supply of loanable funds" in my sense, since he attempts to bring them into touch not with a flow of demand during an interval of time but with a state of demand existing at a moment of time. As in the case of the definition of savings (*supra*, § 4), I cannot but regard these verbal monstrosities as evidence that Mr. Keynes is not altogether comfortable in his own suit of clothes.

Nevertheless, when we have picked our way through these verbal tangles we are left, I think, in no doubt about the relation between the two methods of approach. Essentially they are two different ways of saying the same thing. Mr. Keynes' long-maintained determination to treat them as "radically opposed" [2] has been to me from the beginning the most baffling feature of this whole controversy.

As regards the relative merits of the two formulations there is doubtless much to be said. *Prima facie* the main advantages of the method set out in § 2 are two in number. (i) It accords with the ordinary language of

[1] It has, however, been revived by Mr. Lerner, *E.J.*, June 1938, p. 224, without any recognition of the difficulties involved.

[2] *E.J.*, June 1937, p. 241.

the market-place; I do not believe that the bill-broker or the impecunious schoolboy will ever believe that, whatever be the deeper causes of its behaviour, the rate of interest *is* anything other than what people have always supposed it to be—the price of the use of loanable funds. (ii) It accords with the general tendency of modern theory to emphasise the unity pervading economic phenomena; the rate of interest appears as a special case of the general theory of pricing. On the other hand it is quite possible that I have under-rated the merits of Mr. Keynes' formulation, which is apparently found the more convenient to handle by mathematicians. I remain, however, of the opinion that its use entails certain dangers, which can be classified according as we are (1) still taking the momentary market point of view with which we agreed to start, (2) proceeding to examine the course of events in a "short period" of monetary expansion or contraction, (3) proceeding further to examine the development of economic phenomena over long stretches of time. To a consideration of these dangers I will now pass.

II. THE MOMENTARY VIEW

§ 1. Already, before we leave the momentary market situation, the Keynsian formula, in its quest for an unattainable simplicity, obscures the part played in the determination of the rate of interest by the "classical" forces of productivity and thrift.

It cannot be too clearly stated that there is nothing whatever wrong with the common-sense view that a raising of the schedule of the marginal productivity (in terms of money) of loanable funds, *i.e.* of the net money yields which entrepreneurs expect from using various quantities of them, will raise the demand schedule for such funds in the market and so tend, *ceteris paribus*, to raise the rate of interest. This is true whether the raising of the productivity schedule is due to reasons of physical productivity or to reasons of price.

In spite of its temporary concession to the validity of the "loanable funds" concept, elsewhere so emphatically rejected, I still regard as a monument of confusion the sentence in which Mr. Keynes appears to challenge this common-sense conclusion. "The schedule of the marginal efficiency of capital," he writes, "may be said to govern the terms on which loanable funds are demanded for the purpose of new investment; whilst the rate of interest governs the terms on which funds are being currently supplied" (*G.T.*, p. 165). The schedule of the marginal utility of tea may be said to govern the terms on which tea is demanded: whilst the price of tea governs the terms on which tea is being currently supplied! From the fact that to the *individual* borrower the hiring price of loanable funds is a thing to be taken for granted, Mr. Keynes appears to proceed, in a way in which he would never do if he were speaking of an ordinary commodity, to the inference that that price is independent of the level of the collective demands of the *whole body* of borrowers; those who reject this inference are regarded as guilty of some kind of circular reasoning and as the victims of some kind of elementary confusion between a schedule and a price, between a curve and a point on a curve (*ibid.*, p. 184).

Of course Mr. Keynes never really succeeded in banishing the influence of marginal productivity; it crept in again at the back door under the wing of the "demand for money" for purposes connected with the conduct of business and the disbursement of income. Such apparent success as he achieved was due to a strange inconsistency in the scheme of his book, on which I commented at the time.[1] In that scheme "active money" could generally only grow as a result of a previous growth in income, so that the banks could only operate by increasing "idle money": yet at the same time it was apparently contemplated that, even if "idle money" were zero, there would still be some (unexplained) way for total money to be

[1] *Q.J.E.*, Nov. 1936, p. 181 *n.* 7.

increased and the rate of interest to fall, the growth of incomes following as a consequence.[1] Common sense suggests that the natural way for this to occur is by the banks performing the primary function of banking, *i.e.* lending money to people who want to make productive use of it. But in those days Mr. Keynes was so taken up with the fact that people sometimes acquire money in order to *hold* it that he had apparently all but entirely forgotten the more familiar fact that they often acquire it in order to *use* it.[2]

In later articles [3] Mr. Keynes has regained his memory of this simple truth. He has recognised that entrepreneurs often desire to be in possession of money which they will subsequently disburse—directly or indirectly—to the factors of production. He has even recognised that this money, which he calls by the name "finance," is often, though not of course necessarily, obtained from the banks.[4] And he has conceded that if there is an increase in the demand for "finance" there will, other things being equal, be a rise in the rate of interest. Thus he has not only remedied the inconsistency pointed out above, but also, as it seems to me, made a far longer stride back than he yet realises towards the orthodox view of the status of the schedule of marginal productivity of loanable funds as a principal determinant of the rate of interest. For it is evidently the height and shape of that schedule—in other words their profit-expectations—which guide the decisions of entrepreneurs as to how much "finance" they shall demand, these decisions in turn helping, as

[1] Cf. *G.T.*, p. 197, with p. 200 (bottom) and p. 209 (top).

[2] Some memory of this familiar fact seems to inspire the curious statement (*ibid.*, p. 195) that some money "is held to bridge the interval between the time of incurring business costs and that of the receipt of the sale-proceeds; cash held by dealers to bridge the interval between purchase and realisation being included under this heading." These are just the intervals during which the persons in question do *not* hold money, but have parted with it!

[3] *E.J.*, June 1937, pp. 246-8, Dec. 1937, pp. 663 ff., June 1938, pp. 318 ff. The page references in § 2 below are to these articles.

[4] It was a poor reward for adhering religiously to Mr. Keynes' peculiar use of the word "finance," and to his own simplifying assumption that " 'finance' is wholly supplied by the banks," to be accused of muddling up the quite distinct concepts of "finance" and bank loans! (*E. J.*, June 1938, *loc. cit.*)

Mr. Keynes admits, to determine the rate of interest.[1]

§ 2. The passages in which Mr. Keynes elaborates the concept of "finance" are, in my view, exceedingly confused; since they illustrate well the trouble in which the "demand for money" approach is liable to land those who employ it, unless checked by explicit reference to what is going on in the capital market, I must digress upon them at some length. My digression is based on the hypothesis that like the Book of Genesis they are an attempt at conflation of the works of two earlier writers, whom, following precedent, I will call by the initials J and E.

" 'Finance,' " Mr. Keynes insists (1937, p. 666) "is essentially a revolving fund": the money absorbed by one entrepreneur in preparation for an act of investment is subsequently released and becomes available for similar employment by another entrepreneur. Provided therefore that something remains constant the requirements of "finance" have no tendency to make the rate of interest rise. What is that something? and what is the act by which money which has been absorbed by one entrepreneur to serve as "finance" is released to another for similar employment? It is to these questions that the writers J and E give conflicting answers. According to J the condition for stability in the rate of interest is constancy in the rate of investment, *i.e.* in the rate at which the stock of capital is increasing. "In the main the flow of new finance required by current planned investment is provided by the finance released by current actual investment. When the flow of investment is at a steady rate, so that the flow of planned investment is equal to the flow of actual investment, the whole of it can be provided in this way without any change in the liquidity position" (*ibid.*, p. 666).[2] Consistently with this approach,

[1] On this subject I am indebted to writings by, and discussions with, Dr. E. S. Shaw; see his article in *Journal of Political Economy*, Dec. 1938, p. 838.

[2] In this and the following quotation I have ventured, to avoid confusion, to substitute the words "planned" and "actual" for the words "ex-ante" and "ex-post," which Mr. Keynes uses, at any rate as applied to investment, in an entirely different sense from Professor Ohlin.

the releasing process is conceived as the purchase of a new issue by some saver from entrepreneur A which enables the latter to repay the money which he has borrowed for "finance," thus permitting this money to become available as "finance" for entrepreneur B.[1] "There will always be *exactly* enough actual saving to take up the actual investment and so release the finance which the latter had been previously employing" (*ibid.*, p. 669). Provided this actual saving-and-investment in any period does not fall short of the planned investment in that period, there is no reason for the rate of interest to rise.[2]

Intertwined with this analysis we have that of the second writer E. According to E the condition for stability in the rate of interest is constancy, not in the rate of investment, but in the outstanding volume of working capital. Here we have to take account of a subsidiary confusion: for two different accounts have been given by E of the date and nature of the releasing process. According to the earlier account, "as soon as ,finance' is used in the sense of being expended, the lack of liquidity is automatically made good and the readiness to become temporarily illiquid is available to be used over again" (*ibid.*, p. 666). This was indeed a hard doctrine; for it is hard to see how the act of parting with money to the factors of production puts the entrepreneur in a position to part with more money in repayment of a loan. And indeed E has been induced to admit that this account of the matter was a mistake (1938, p. 320), since, when the "finance" is expended, the demand for money for "finance" purposes is im-

[1] I continue to adhere to Mr. Keynes' own simplifying assumption that A has provided himself with "finance" by borrowing from a bank. The argument can easily be re-stated for the case in which he has obtained "finance" by selling securities to the public.

[2] The J theory reappears in Mr. Keynes' discussion of the problem of Government borrowing, *Times*, July 24, 1939. "The clue to the solution of the Treasury problem lies in the Treasury's ability to wait until the new savings have had time to become available in an investable form. If the Treasury waits just long enough for the market to become greedy for stock the weight of savings seeking investment will force the rate of interest downwards." So the rate of interest *does* depend on the volume (or at all events the weight) of savings after all!

mediately replaced by a demand for income purposes. Accordingly, in the revised version of E, it is not in the disbursement of money by the entrepreneur, but in its subsequent recapture by the sale of goods to the consumer, that the releasing process consists.

Now taken by itself either J's account or E's (in the revised version) would be quite intelligible. What is not intelligible is the later editor's conflation of the two. For not having clearly perceived that they *are* two, he attempts the impossible task of formulating a conclusion which shall be appropriate to them both. That conclusion is the astonishing one that to afford relief to congestion in the capital market either an act of thrift or an act of consumption will in all circumstances do equally well; the purchase of a new issue and the purchase of consumption goods are indistinguishable in respect of their influence on the rate of interest. The comforting doctrine that an act of investment necessarily breeds equivalent acts of saving by other persons becomes for the moment transmuted into the even more comforting doctrine that it doesn't matter whether it does or not!

Clearly something has gone wrong: Dr. Shaw and I think we know what it is. The purchase of consumption goods from an entrepreneur enables him *either* to maintain his scale of output and the volume of his working capital *or* to repay a loan, *but not both.* If (being perhaps engaged in a seasonal trade such as farming) he elects to repay a loan, thus enabling the lender to provide another entrepreneur with new "finance," it is not indeed the consumer's act of consumption *per se* that has prevented a rise in the rate of interest, but the first entrepreneur's act of temporary disinvestment; nevertheless, in this case as in the other, the act of consumption may perhaps be said to have played a part in maintaining intact a given aggregate stock of capital without a rise in the rate of interest (the kind of stability envisaged by E). The purchase of a new issue from an entrepreneur, on the other hand, enables him to repay a loan *without* performing an act of disinvestment; it thus contributes to maintaining a given rate of increase in the aggregate stock of capital without a rise in the rate of interest (the kind of stability envisaged by J). The two acts are far from being equivalent; on the contrary, in circumstances in which the one will preserve equilibrium, the other will destroy it.

§ 3. In discussing Mr. Keynes' concept of "finance" I have already been led into my next theme. His formula seems to be apt to lead those who use it into uncertainty as to the part played in the determination of the rate of interest by thrift,[1] *i.e.* by the decisions being currently made to save a certain part of income.

In the first place it seems to be suggested that the proposition that the marginal convenience of holding money is equated with the rate of interest necessarily excludes and invalidates the proposition that the marginal inconvenience of refraining from consumption is equated with the rate of interest. Such phrases as that interest is not the reward of not-spending but the reward of not-hoarding [2] seem to indicate a curious inhibition against visualising more than two margins at once. A small boy at school is told that if he wins a race he may have either an apple or an orange: he wins the race and chooses the orange. When his mother asks him how he got it, must he reply "I got it for not eating an apple"? May he not say proudly "I got it for not losing a race"?

The inhibition just alluded to was not shared by earlier Cambridge writers. "These three uses," writes Pigou,[3] "the production of convenience and security, the production of commodities, and direct consumption, are rival to one another." "The quantity of

[1] I prefer this word to Mrs. Robinson's "*thriftiness*" or Mr. Keynes' "propensity to save," partly because it conveys a suggestion of *action*. Changes in -nesses and propensities do not in themselves exercise any effect on the external world. Nor does a decision to get up early necessarily indicate a reduction in the propensity to lie in bed—it may rather indicate an increased determination not to indulge that propensity! Cf. Miss Curtis, *Q.J.E.*, Aug. 1937, pp. 619-20.

[2] See *G.T.*, p. 174.

[3] *Essays in Applied Economics*, p. 181.

resources," writes Lavington,[1] "which he holds in the form of money will be such that the unit of resources which is just and only just worth holding in this form yields him a return of convenience and security equal to the yield of satisfaction derived from the marginal unit spent on consumables, and equal also to [2] the net rate of interest." It should be added that my own statement of the matter [3] "decumulation, as well as keeping-hoarded, is an alternative to keeping-invested" is not entirely appropriate to a world in which capital is growing, *i.e.* in which the "representative man" is in fact saving. To such a man the alternatives which present themselves may better be described as adding to hoards, adding to invested resources and (not decumulating but) failing to accumulate. There are inevitable difficulties in expressing in statically-framed terms the situation existing *at a moment of time during a period of change;* it is precisely for this among other reasons that Mr. Keynes' photographic formulation seems to me to need supplementing by a cinematographic one. But that does not effect the validity of the concept of a three-fold as contrasted with a two-fold margin of preference. Nor would the latter be destroyed, as Mr. Keynes seems to think,[4] if it should be true that on balance a rise in the rate of interest will diminish, and a fall increase, the proportion of a given income which people desire to save. For on the ordinary assumptions it remains true, of those whose response is of this kind, that they so act as to equate the marginal satisfaction derived from consumption with the marginal satisfaction derived from investing resources at the current rate of interest.

§ 4. I have not succeeded in discovering in Mr. Keynes' book any formal discussion of the effect of an

[1] *The English Capital Market*, p. 30.

[2] Lavington had better, I think, have written "measured also by."

[3] *E.J.*, 1937, p. 431.

[4] *G.T.*, p. 182. Contrast the interesting quotation from Marshall unearthed by Mr. Guillebaud (*E.J.*, 1937, p. 42): "my reasoning... would be valid even if we amused ourselves by supposing that a rise in the rate of interest diminished the supply of capital: provided that we also supposed that it ultimately diminished the demand for capital faster."

increase or decrease of thrift on the rate of interest; but I do not think the majority of readers can have failed to form, or can be blamed for forming, the impression that, in Mr. Keynes' view, the notion that an increase of thrift will tend to lower the rate of interest or to promote the growth of physical capital is, *except under the rarely-attained condition of full employment*, wholly erroneous.[1] Here too I venture to think there has been a greater change of front than Mr. Keynes himself has yet been able to realise; for it is now agreed that, *whether employment is full or not*, an increase of thrift *will* tend to lower the rate of interest. But, it is urged, this result will only occur to the accompaniment of depression and increased unemployment.[2]

Let me state in my own language what I believe the Keynsian is trying to convey. Suppose that I decide to spend £100 of my income on securities, instead of as hitherto on fine clothes. My action destroys £100 of the income of my tailor and his employees and depletes their money balances by £100. It also raises the price of securities, *i.e.* lowers the rate of interest.[3] This fall in the rate of interest tempts some people to sell securities and to hold increased money balances instead. Thus the fall in the rate of interest is checked, and not all of my £100 succeeds therefore in finding its way,

[1] Thus it is, I think, suggested that the question posed on *G.T.*, p. 213, namely, why a "fresh act of saving" should affect the factors on which the rate of interest has been asserted to depend, admits of no answer. On p. 185 discredit is cast on the "economic principle" which "has assumed, in effect, that, *cet. par.*, a decrease in spending will tend to lower the rate of interest." At the end of the book (p. 372) we are reminded that "we have seen that, up to the point where full employment prevails, the growth of capital depends not at all on a low propensity to consume but is, on the contrary, held back by it; and only in conditions of full employment is a low propensity to consume conducive to the growth of capital."

[2] For a meticulous statement by Mr. Keynes of his present position, see *E.J.*, Sept. 1938, p. 555.

[3] Debate on this matter has sometimes been hampered by the ghost of an old argument, dating from the days of the *Treatise on Money*. According to this argument the loss-making tailor, in order to avoid restricting either his personal consumption or the scale of his business, will sell securities to the same amount as I buy them. Obviously, so long as such a situation continues, the rate of interest will not fall nor the formation of capital equipment be stimulated; but neither, so far as the mere maintenance of total income (other than the tailor's) and employment goes, is it necessary that they should. Evidently, however, this can only be a transitional situation and it is not instructive to stop short at it.

through the markets for old securities and new issues, on to the markets for labour and commodities. Thus owing to the existence of this siding or trap, my act of thrift does not succeed, as "classical" theory asserts that it will, in creating incomes and money balances for builders and engineers equal to those which it has destroyed for tailors. The net result of the whole proceeding is a fall in the rate of interest and an increase, perhaps, in capital outlay,[1] but a net decrease in the total of money incomes and (probably) of employment.

The argument is formally perfectly valid; and the practical inference that, if existing money is going to ground in this way, it is *prima facie* the duty of the banking system to create more money, is quite consistent with the arguments of those who have expressed themselves in terms of "neutral" money, or of a "constant effective circulation," or of the maintenance of equality between the market and the "natural" rates of interest.[2] To the quantitative importance of the factors at work I will return later. Here I will only say that it seems to me a most misleading way of expressing the causal train of events to say, as is sometimes done, that the act of thrift lowers the rate of interest *through* lowering total incomes. I should say that it lowers the rate of interest quite directly through swelling the money stream of demand for securities; that this fall in the rate of interest increases the proportion of resources over which people wish to keep command in monetary form; and that this increase in turn is a cause of there being a net decline in total money income, *i.e.* of money incomes not expanding in one sector to the extent that they are contracting in the other.

Let us, however, be grateful for such measure of concordance as has been achieved. We need no longer attempt to believe in a crazy world in which, at some exceedingly elusive point of "full employment," the

[1] Even this is not certain, since the demand of the tailor, weaver, etc., for machines will decline.

[2] Cf. Cassel, *International Labour Review*, Oct. 1937, p. 443.

opposite of all that we have hitherto been saying suddenly becomes true. We have returned to a rational world, where the outcome of events is a matter of degrees and elasticities—a world which has been so tidily set out by Dr. Lange[1] that Mr. Keynes, at all events, believes it to have been the world of his own book.[2] And especially we may compliment Mrs. Robinson, who in her *Introduction to the Theory of Employment* has effected the transition within the compass of a few pages. For having told us quite categorically on p. 12 that "the desire to save does not promote investment," and explained at some length why she believes this to be so, she has decided by p. 47 that "it is thriftiness which makes investment possible" and even that "in an age of expansion, thriftiness appears as a cause of investment." Only Mr. Kahn remains, apparently, distressed[3] by Dr. Lundberg's desire to "restore to the will to save a determining influence on the rate of interest."

III. LONGER VIEWS

§ 1. Further dangers of the Keynsian formulation are brought to light when we pass from considering the situation at a moment of time to considering the behaviour of the rate of interest during a cumulative process of expansion or contraction.

According to ordinary doctrine an increase in the quantity of money and an increase in its velocity of circulation, due to a diminished desire on the part of the public to hold command over resources in monetary form, are broadly similar in their effects. But there is this difference, that while the latter need not, the former must normally, operate through a fall in the (*i.e.* in *some*) rate of interest, since banks do not give money away but lend it at interest. This appears to give rise, as

[1] *Economica*, Feb. 1938, pp. 12 ff.
[2] *E.J.*, June 1938, p. 321 *n.*
[3] *Ibid.*, p. 267.

already mentioned,[1] to a paradox, since rising prices and activity are commonly found to be associated with rising rates of interest. Marshall's explanation of the paradox is given in a famous sentence[2]: "the increase of currency increases the willingness of lenders to lend in the first instance, and lowers the rate of discount. But it afterwards raises prices and therefore tends to increase discount. This latter movement is cumulative." This result can, no doubt, be reached by shifting the Keynsian schedule with the progressive growth of the demand for money for "finance" and "transaction" purposes. But one at least of Mr. Keynes' expositors seems to have suffered from lack of resolution in applying this process. Mrs. Robinson has formed the view[3] that while in the course of a monetary expansion the rate of interest may be "driven back towards" the level at which it stood before the expansion started, it can never actually reach that level. Interest will always be lower at the end of a period of inflation than at the beginning! Never surely has theory, or pseudo-theory, flown more brazenly in the face of history.

That at one stage of his thought Mr. Keynes himself suffered from a similar inhibition seems to be suggested by his curious misunderstanding of Professor Fisher's celebrated proposition about the influence of price movements on the rate of interest. That proposition may be stated as follows. Owing to the imperfection of markets, and to inequality of foresight and bargaining power between borrower and lender, there is likely during an upswing to arise a divergence between the marginal productivity of investable funds *to the user* and the rate of interest "in the strict sense" which he is compelled to pay in the market. If however the former is rising, it is unlikely that the frictions will be so great as to prevent altogether the competition of borrowers from raising the rate of interest "in the strict sense." "Not only will lenders require, but borrowers can afford to pay higher interest in terms of money, and to

[1] Above, p. 9.

[2] *Money, Credit and Commerce*, p. 257.

[3] *Introduction to the Theory of Employment*, pp. 76-8.

some extent competition will gradually force them to do so. Yet... we reluctantly yield to this process of adjustment, thus rendering it very slow and imperfect."[1] "The money rate of interest, while it does change somewhat, does not usually change enough to fully compensate for the appreciation or depreciation."[2] Thus there occurs an increase in trade activity; but "as soon as the interest rate becomes adjusted, borrowers can no longer hope to make great profits, and the demand for loans ceases to expand."[3] In view of these passages, it is impossible to agree with Mr. Keynes that Professor Fisher has made "the mistake" of "supposing that it is the rate of interest on which prospective changes in the value of money will directly react, instead of the marginal efficiency of a given stock of capital."[4] Still less is it easy to understand why Mr. Keynes apparently believes him to have argued that it is the rise in the rate of interest "in the strict sense," and not its failure to rise more rapidly, which exercises a stimulating effect on the entrepreneur.[5]

§ 2. But there is a further point. As stated in § 1, according to ordinary theory it is only an increase in the quantity of money, not a decline in the desire to hold money, that need operate on prices and activity through a preliminary dip in the rate of interest. The entrepreneur who holds an idle balance which he desires to activise need not lend it in the market, but can use it directly for the purchase of commodities or the hire of labour: so far therefore as cumulative processes are generated by swings of entrepreneur confidence rather than of bank policy, there is not even a *prima facie* paradox in the positive association of rising interest with rising prices. The Keynsian analysis, with its special emphasis on the relation between money and bonds, at first sight appears to cast doubt on this result.

[1] Fisher, *Purchasing Power of Money*, p. 57.
[2] Fisher, *Theory of Interest*, p. 493.
[3] *Purchasing Power of Money*, p. 64. [4] *G.T.*, p. 142.
[5] *Ibid.*, bottom of page.

Why should the fact that commodities[1] have become more attractive as compared with money lower the attractiveness of bonds as compared with money and thus raise the rate of interest? Indeed, must not the same forces of increased confidence which make some people desire to part with money for commodities make other people desire to part with money for bonds and so *lower* the rate of interest?

These questions can perhaps be answered, at any rate partially,[2] in terms of "finance" or some such concept; or, which I imagine comes to the same thing, in terms of "complementarity"—one cannot do business without some money, but one can without any bonds. The same answer can be arrived at more simply by looking at the bond market and observing that, at a certain stage of revival, the amount of money which people are willing to take off that market in order to reinvest it in commodities exceeds, at the hitherto current rate of interest, the amount which other people are willing to put on to the same market out of their hoards. Let us use what form of expression we please, so long as the right result, namely, that the rate of interest tends to rise, is established.

But having recognised that a rising rate of interest is normally an accompaniment, and indeed a symbol, of an increase of confidence, we must not then proceed to advocate treating such a rise on lines which would only be appropriate if it were a symbol of collapse of confidence. Yet this is precisely the trap into which, on at least one occasion, the Keynsian method of thought has caused its own author to fall. "If the public is deprived of its normal supply of idle balances by the demand for active balances," he wrote during the boom of 1936-7,[3] "or if it gets nervous about the prospects of the gilt-edged market, then I feel strongly that, unless we deliberately desire to raise the rate of interest, this demand

[1] On this whole topic see Hicks, *Value and Capital*, ch. XXII, and Lerner, *E.J.*, June 1938, pp. 227 ff.

[2] This is not, I believe, the whole answer: see below, p. 27 *n* 1.

[3] *Economist*, Feb. 6, 1937, p. 302.

for idle balances should be satisfied for the time being, the extra idle balances being subsequently withdrawn as a change in the atmosphere or the circumstances permits." In other words, the monetary authority should create money freely during the boom, and destroy it drastically during the slump! "It is not easy," wrote Mr. Keynes in a supplementary letter,[1] "to get used to the idea of trying to avoid booms and slumps": it is not made any easier by muddling up two possible causes [2] of a rise in the rate of interest and advocating an inflammatory policy under the guise of a compensatory one.

§ 3. I have suggested that even from the momentary market point of view the Keynsian formulation tends to obscure unduly the parts played by Productivity and Thrift. Much more is this true when we pass to consider the trend of events over considerable stretches of time. I remain of opinion that from the long period point of view the most important things to be said about the rate of interest are not things about "liquidity preference" and the supply of money, but things about what Marshall calls productiveness and prospectiveness.[3]

In this connection the first thing to be said is that in one important respect Mr. Keynes has understated his

[1] *Economist*, Feb. 13, 1937, p. 359.

[2] Contrast Marshall, *Money, Credit and Commerce*, p. 254: "The rate of interest often rises rather high, under the influence of hope, in an ascending phase of industrial and commercial activity and prosperity: but it seldom rises very high for that reason. On the other hand, it may be raised to a vast height by fears that commercial or political disturbances may soon restrict the operations of credit."

[3] *Principles*, pp. 81-2. If this opinion is one of the "past misdeeds" of which Mr. Keynes wishes me to disembarrass myself (*E.J.*, June 1938, p. 319), I have made, I am afraid, but little progress towards the light! In riposte I may perhaps be forgiven for recalling how in 1930 an attempt (even more muddled, I freely admit, than appears from the printed record) to interest the Macmillan Committee in the short run relation between the state of confidence and the long term rate of interest came to grief against the rocks of his sturdy Johnsonian classicalism! See *Committee on Finance and Industry*, Minutes of Evidence, vol. I, pp. 334-5, especially Q. 4834 and Q. 4841. ". . . (*Witness*). What it comes to is this, that a large part of what appears to be the rate of interest on long-dated securities is now really a premium for risk, or believed risk, and the long rate of interest remains high compared with Bank rate because it contains a large element of what are really profits, the reward for real or imaginary risks. (*Mr. Keynes*) I should have thought the reason why the bond rate was high in London was that there were rows and rows of foreigners who were very willing to pay extremely high rates for the money. . . ."

own case. While there are hints here and there of a broader treatment, in the main his plan is to set the rate of interest in a direct functional relation only with that part of the money stock which is held for what he calls "speculative reasons," *i.e.* because it is expected that the rate of interest will subsequently rise. Thus the rate of interest is what it is because it is expected to become other than it is; if it is not expected to become other than it is, there is nothing left to tell us why it is what it is. The organ which secretes it has been amputated, and yet it somehow still exists—a grin without a cat. Mr. Plumptre of Toronto, in an unpublished paper, has aptly compared the position of the lenders of money under this theory with that of an insurance company which charges its clients a premium, the only risk against which it insures them being the risk that its premium will be raised. If we ask what ultimately governs the judgments of wealth-owners as to why the rate of interest should be different in the future from what it is to-day, we are surely led straight back to the fundamental phenomena of Productivity and Thrift.

In this respect the older Cambridge theory is kinder to "liquidity preference" than is Mr. Keynes himself. For it explicitly links up the rate of interest with what Mr. Keynes, including it somewhat paradoxically under the heading of "active" money, calls the money held for "precautionary" purposes—because people do not know what is going to happen, because they are afraid that debts owing to them may not be paid at the due date, because (as Marshall emphasises) they might otherwise miss a sudden chance of making an advantageous purchase. Thus neo-Marshallian theory elevates the relation between the desire to hold money and the rate of interest to the dignity of a long-period phenomenon, not dependent on the temporary expectation of change in a particular direction, but only on those chronic uncertainties of personal and business life which, while they may find no place in "equilibrium analysis" of the Continental type, have never, I think, been ruled out from the looser Marshallian concept of the long period.

In estimating, however, the long period degree of this dependence of K, the proportion of resources over which people wish to keep command in monetary form, on the rate of interest, there is an important consideration to be borne in mind. The satisfaction derived

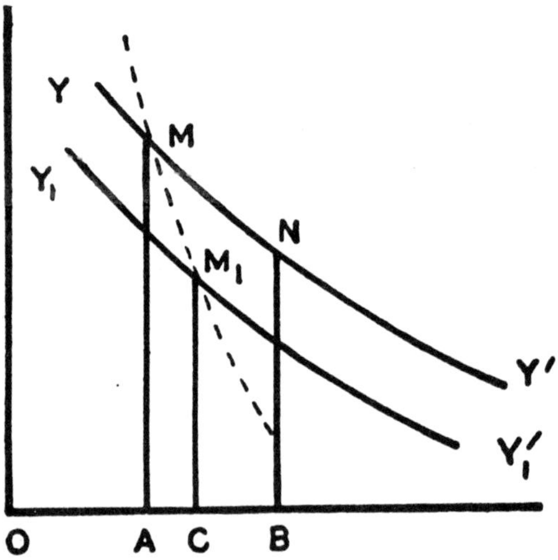

at the margin by wealth-owners from holding money is equated not directly with a given rate of return from invested resources, but with the satisfaction derived at the margin from that rate of return; and the satisfaction derived from a given rate of return is not a thing which can plausibly be regarded as remaining eternally fixed while fundamental change is occurring in the whole economic conjuncture. Thus as, with the succesful embodiment of thrift in physical capital, the rate of return on invested resources progressively declines, a given *n*th dose of "convenience and security" derived from holding money may be expected to be balanced up against, and measured by, a progressively lower rate of interest. In geometrical language, the curve connecting the desire to hold resources in monetary form with the rate of interest appears as a highly unstable object, liable to continuous displacement downwards as the volume of invested wealth grows. While a casual fall in the rate of interest from MA to NB may lead to a movement along YY' and an increase in "monetary resources" from OA to OB, a permanent fall will necessitate the re-drawing of YY' as Y_1Y_1' and an increase of "monetary resources" only to OC. And the locus of the points M, M_1, etc., may well exhibit an inclination so steep as to indicate, so far as the influence of this factor goes, virtual constancy in K, whatever the level to which the growth of wealth has attained and the rate of interest fallen. Thus even if we give a more extended interpretation than Mr. Keynes himself has done to the concept of the desire to hold money as a function of the rate of interest, we may well remain reluctant to attach to it any very great importance in determining the secular trend of events.[1]

The most obvious difference between the Keynsian and the neo-Marshallian approaches still remains, however, to be examined. In the former the schedule of liquidity preference is exhibited as one of the determinants of the rate of interest; in the latter the rate of interest is exhibited as one of the determinants of the proportion K, K in turn helping to determine not the rate of interest at all but the general level of prices and money incomes. The instructiveness of this latter approach depends of course on the assumption of the ultimate plasticity of the price and income structure in face of changes in the stream of money demand. It still appears to me that for the purpose of broad

[1] It seems to me likely that the solution of the short-period puzzle discussed in III, § 2, above, must also be reached partly on these lines. A nominal yield of 4 per cent. on a fixed interest security comes to weigh less heavily in the scales against a given parcel of convenience and security if 8 per cent. can be obtained by direct investment than if only 6 per cent. can be obtained. Even in the short run, YY' may be a tenuous and unstable creature, the ghost rather than the equal partner of the curve of marginal productivity of investable resources.

comparisons between different societies, or the same society at different stages of its history, this assumption is one that can fruitfully be made. In the making of such comparisons it would be rash indeed to conclude that unemployment of resources is likely to be specially great, or even the rate of interest specially high, in societies where a high estimate is placed on the convenience of keeping command over resources in the form of money.[1] Only if the hunt for liquidity eventuates in the successful devotion of resources to the acquisition of the precious metals will a high "liquidity preference" be inimical to an abundance of income-yielding instruments and therefore to a low rate of interest. India, for instance, is no doubt less well equipped, and has higher rates of interest, than if she had not dedicated so much of her thrift to the acquisition of gold.[2] But that conclusion is old-fashioned Ricardo, not new-fashioned Keynes!

IV. SHORT AND LONG RATES

§ 1. I have so far evaded, with an uneasy conscience but with good precedents, one of the most puzzling aspects of the whole problem, namely the relation between the rates of interest on loans of different periods, or (still to simplify unduly) between the short rate and the long. On this topic I present myself as little more than *a rapporteur* of what has been written

[1] Still less does there seem any reason why a high prestige-value for *land* (*G.T.*, p. 241) should make the rate of interest rule high. What it does is to keep the purchase price of land high, *i.e.* the net yield from buying it low, and to make the mortgage rate of interest seem high by comparison; but the mortgage rate (*e.g.* in India) is presumably *lower* than it would be if the land pledged had less prestige-value. Indirectly, of course, the opportunity to sell land at high prices or to borrow on it at relatively low rates may well encourage extravagant consumption and thus raise interest rates and retard the growth of wealth; but Mr. Keynes cannot be thinking of that, for it is an explanation which he specifically rejects (*ibid.*, p. 242).

[2] Thus from a long period point of view Mr. Keynes' conclusion (*G.T.*, p. 230) that inelasticity in the supply of the money metal helps to keep the rate of interest high seems to be the reverse of the truth. If the supply of moons is manifestly incapable of increase (*ibid.*, p. 235), no resources can be wasted in their production.

by others. My own understanding of the matter, such as it is, derives rather from the older studies by Lavington, and from a single highly-condensed page of Pigou, than from the more recent discussions by Hawtrey, Hicks, and others; but I have endeavoured to profit from the latter as well.[1]

If all long lending were really long, *i.e.* if the lender had to part with his money for the full currency of the loan, one would expect the long rate to be, in equilibrium, somewhat above the short; for it is both more convenient to borrow, and less convenient to lend, for long periods than for short. Through the agency of the organised market, however, the long lender can transfer his function to others by the sale of a security, while the long borrower can, to some extent, utilise successive short lengths of lending pieced together for his benefit. Nevertheless, the costs and imperfections of the market are such that we should, in my view, still expect the long rate to stand normally somewhat above the short, even when we have eliminated from the former all risks of total or partial default by finding (if we can) something which really is absolutely gilt-edged.

Lavington, however, concludes that "for many decades up to the end of the war the yield on consols and the three-months bill rate, when averaged over a period of a few years, were substantially identical." He attributes the persistent gap which developed after the war, and which has become more pronounced since he wrote, to a permanent loss of confidence by bankers, etc., in the eligibility of long-term debt, coupled with the emergence of a permanent new supply of eligible short-term investments, namely Treasury Bills.

§ 2. Given the normal relation between Rate and Yield (as following Lavington we can conveniently call

[1] See the following: Lavington, *English Capital Market*, pp. 91-7, and article in *Economica*, 1923-4, pp. 299 ff.; Pigou, *Industrial Fluctuations*, p. 276; Hawtrey, *A Century of Bank Rate*, chs. V and VI; Hicks, article in *The Manchester School*, 1939; Makower and Marschak, article in *Economica*, 1938, pp. 263 ff.; Kalecki, *Essays in the Theory of Economic Fluctuations*, pp. 107-15.

the short and long rates) there is at any moment a further possible reason for divergence between them. The rate is both more spontaneously volatile and more amenable to monetary action than the yield. For any given movement in it there will be an appropriate movement in the yield, depending on how soon and how far the rate is expected to move back again. Thus if the rate falls the yield must theoretically fall enough to establish an appropriate relation between the reward of the man who invests short and that of the man who invests long, facing the depreciation of his bond which will occur when the rate rises again to its normal level. Making some simplifying assumptions, namely simple interest and identity of normal rate and yield, the formula[1] may be given thus:—

Let p = normal rate = normal yield (expressed as a fraction),
q = actual rate,
n = number of years for which the rate is expected to be q before returning to p,
x = actual yield, so that the price of a bond bearing interest p becomes $\frac{p}{x}$ instead of 1.

The net return to be gained by holding such a bond for n years is np interest plus $\left(1 - \frac{p}{x}\right)$ capital appreciation.

This must equal the return from investing $\frac{p}{x}$ short for n successive years:

i.e. $$np + 1 - \frac{p}{x} = nq.\frac{p}{x},$$

whence $$x = p\frac{nq + 1}{np + 1}.$$

Of course this theoretical relation, implying as it does complete mobility of lenders and/or borrowers

[1] Of which Pigou's arithmetic (*loc. cit.*) is an illustration.

between the two markets, is not always achieved. But there is a curious lack of unanimity between students as to the direction in which it tends to be departed from during cyclical movements. At the one extreme stands Hicks, who pronounces the yield to be "quite extraordinarily insensitive to the cycle": in this he is joined by Kalecki—in certain circles the doctrine that the yield is infinitely malleable seems to be being rapidly superseded by the doctrine that it never moves at all! Hicks does, however, find a close relation between the movements of the yield and those of the "normal" rate, as represented by the average of the rates of the preceding ten years; this relation fails for recent years, owing (according to Hicks) to the dimming of the conception of a normal during these disturbed times, but is partially restored by reweighting the average of rates so as to give greater importance to the current and quite recent years.

As regards the cyclical relationship, Hawtrey occupies an intermediate position. He finds, in contrast to Hicks, that "there is quite clearly a cyclical movement" in the yield as well as in the rate, but that often when the rate moves the yield does not, or not perceptibly. Lavington, at the other extreme, claims to have established that, at any rate in times of boom, the movements of the yield are *greater* than the theoretical relation would lead us to expect, *i.e.* in boom the price of bonds falls unduly low. This he attributes to the fears of further capital depreciation generated at such a time. Certainly his figures seem to afford little support to those who argue that the yield is virtually immune from cyclical influences.

At any rate, whether over-realised or under-realised in practice, this theoretical relationship between rate and yield serves to show how the yield can stand now below what it is expected to be in future—a fact which is sometimes denied; and to show also that it is to the *difference between* [1] the rate and the yield, and not to the

[1] Cf. p. 24 *n.* 3.

yield as such, that the Keynsian notion is relevant of ven the gilt-edged yield being a compensation for a particular sort of "risk," *viz.* not the risk of the yield on the sum invested now varying in future years, but the risk of a bigger yield being obtainable on a given sum invested at a future date than is obtainable by investing it now.

§ 3. Bearing in mind this analysis of the repercussions of movements in the rate on movements in the yield, let us turn back to the gap, if such there be, between their normal levels. Must we say that this too is due to risk of a peculiar kind, *viz.* the risk of "undisentanglability"—of having to dispose of an asset on a market which is imperfect? In this event, only the shortest of short rates can be regarded as "the cost of waiting", every other rate containing a larger or smaller element which must be regarded as the cost of some kind or other of risk-bearing. Lavington in the end appears to adopt this standpoint; but I do not find it altogether acceptable. It seems to me more reasonable to regard the gilt-edged yield as being *the* rate of interest *par excellence*, the satisfaction of obtaining which is balanced at the margin against the satisfaction enjoyed from consumption; and to regard shorter-dated claims of various kinds as yielding various amounts of a *positive* benefit which can, if we like, be called liquidity, but is perhaps more illuminatingly described as freedom of manœuvre. Lavington's method seems to permit this positive benefit to emerge only in the extreme case, namely that of some kinds of money, in which no interest is paid at all. The alternative method, namely of starting from the gilt-edged rate, brings out that there is a whole range of claims yielding *some* interest and *some* freedom of manœuvre. And this range may well include some kinds of "money"; *i.e.* there is no need (as under both Lavington's method and Keynes') to make the non-yielding of interest the criterion of whether an asset (*e.g.* a current account) is or is not money: the latter term can be defined in the usual way as including anything that is widely or generally acceptable in discharge of business obligations, whether or not it is clever enough to yield its possessor some interest as well.

§ 4. Two of the writers—namely Lavington and Hawtrey—who have expounded the theoretical impact of changes in the rate on the yield have nevertheless emphasised—as I think rightly—that in the main their movements must be interpreted as the results of a common cause, namely changes in the demand for the use of loanable funds, both for short term purposes and for long. Marshall—again, as I think, rightly—goes further and assigns, from a trend or long term point of view, seniority in the chain of causation to the yield. "It is obvious that the mean rate of discount must be much under the influence of the mean rate of interest for long loans; which is determined by the extent and the richness of the field for capital investment on the one hand, and on the other by the amount of capital seeking investment."[1] Hicks' correlation analysis, which makes the present yield reflect the average rate of the last ten years, would, if it is regarded as convincing, cast discredit on Marshall's causal thesis, which is also apparently rejected by Hawtrey.[2] I must confess that I should myself require very strong inductive evidence to make me abandon what seems to me so plausible an account of the normal relationship, and that I find Hicks' treatment[3] very defective on the side of demand.

V. CONCLUSION

§ 1. What is the bearing of the "liquidity preference" view of interest on the problem of the preservation of monetary equilibrium in a progressive world? What I have to say on this must be much condensed, and itself forms part of a larger story, the earlier chap-

[1] *Money, Credit and Commerce*, p. 255.

[2] *Op. cit.*, p. 207.

[3] *Op. cit.*, p. 23.

ters of which must be taken as told. I take for granted that the social function of banking is to procure the effective utilisation of the community's thrift, and that the effective fulfilment of that function requires the execution of a certain policy with regard to the magnitude of the flow of total monetary demand. Should that policy be to cause that flow to increase in proportion to the increase in production? or in proportion to the increase in population? or in proportion, in some sense, to the increase in the aggregate stock of all factors of production? On these problems there is much to be said, and I doubt if they are capable of a perfectly clear-cut answer. But granted we have solved them in theory in some compromise fashion, we can go on to ask the further question, how far is the existence of the liquidity trap for thrift likely to hamper the banking system in its long run task of executing the chosen policy, and so bringing the fruits of thrift to birth?

The question falls conveniently into three parts:—(1) Under what conditions does the effective utilisation of thrift require a progressive fall in the rate of interest? (2) If such a fall is required, how serious is the influence of the liquidity trap in inhibiting it? (3) How responsive is capital outlay likely to be to such a fall?

(1) Whether a fall in the rate of interest is required depends on whether the rate of invention,[1] including the "invention" of new or resuscitated countries, keeps up with the growth of thrift, accentuated by the coming stagnation and decline of population in the west. On this last subject there is nowadays much anxiety, which I partly share. The excogitation of means to meet new wants requires more initiative than the reduplication of means to meet existing ones; and some of the new wants, *e.g.* for the services of manicurists and mediums, may not be of a very capital-using kind. During the nineteenth century the fundamental deformity of the Marshallian "short period"—the fact that it is not the

[1] See the illuminating discussion by Durbin, *Purchasing Power and Trade Depression*, esp. p. 76 and note.

same length at both ends, since most instruments take longer to wear out than to construct—was largely concealed from view by the growth of population, which increased the chances that the tail of each slump would be bitten off prematurely, as it were, by the head of the next boom. From many points of view the most satisfactory kind of population would doubtless be one which, while never getting any bigger, was always growing; but it is not very easy to see how that is to be achieved.

Nevertheless it is possible, I think, to be too gloomy. At no point has it been possible to divine just *where* the springs of "demand for waiting" would gush forth in the coming years. Marshall, giving evidence in the eighties,[1] set forth, in a striking passage which might almost be mistaken for one of Mr. Keynes' presidential addresses to the National Mutual Assurance Society, the most persuasive reasons why the rate of interest should drop rapidly in the future to 2 per cent.: yet within a few years the tide had turned.

(2) The upshot of our earlier discussion of this point may be conveyed by saying that so far as the desire for liquidity is due to the "speculative" motive, *i.e.* the belief that the rate of interest will rise, it does not seem reasonable to expect it to be proof against a prolonged fall due to a successful accumulation of capital wealth; while so far as it is due to uncertainty in a broader sense, there are reasons for supposing the curve representing it to be much more inelastic in the long run than the short. To an enormous extent the contemporary troubles of the world are due to the prolonged prevalence of a state of affairs that is neither peace nor war; real peace would do more than anything—more even than real war—not only to raise the curve of marginal productivity of investable funds, but to rotate and stiffen the roof of the liquidity trap into a straight line as vertical and rigid as Mr. Chamberlain's umbrella.

§ 2. (3) How responsive will capital outlay be to such fall in the rate of interest as the liquidity trap permits to

[1] *Official Papers*, p. 49, Q. 9678.

occur? Can we expect the response to be at all buoyant in a community in which, owing to the rapid growth of wealth, the producers of consumption goods are continually finding their livelihood threatened by the growth of thrift? On this there are three things to be briefly said.

(i) It is as well to remind ourselves, if necessary by an arithmetic example,[1] that a decline in the *proportion of income consumed* does not necessarily mean a decline in *the rate of growth of consumption*, still less of course in the absolute amount of consumption. It is not mathematically inevitable that, in a progressive society, the producers of consumption goods as a body should live in perpetual fear of extinction.

(ii) Even if particular groups of producers find the demand for their wares sluggish, so that they have no motive to undertake what Mr. Hawtrey has called the "widening" of capital, their best course may yet be to promote its "deepening"—*i.e.* mechanisation may be the best response to a sagging market. From the point of view of labour this is of course a double-edged conclusion.

(iii) As I have said in the course of commentary on Mr. Harrod's exposition of the "principle of acceleration," [2] some of the quantitatively most important forms

[1] Total Income	Consumed	Percentage Growth of Consumption	Percentage of Income Consumed	"Marginal Propensity to Consume"
10,000	8,000	—	80	—
11,000	8,400	5	76	40
12,100	8,820	5	73	38
13,310	9,261	5	70	36

I am in debt to Professor Hansen (*Monetary Policy and Economic Stagnation*, p. 39) on this point.

[2] See below, p. 179; and, for a revised statement of Mr. Harrod's position, *E.J.*, March 1939, pp. 14 ff.

of capital outlay in the modern world—the basic instruments of power, transport and business accommodation—are not very closely geared to the demand for particular types of consumption goods, but depend rather on largely and broadly conceived estimates of the potential progress of whole regions. And fortunately it is precisely these forms of capital outlay which, because of their durability, *are* reasonably sensitive to the rate of interest; for while the difference between 5 per cent. and 4 per cent. may make little difference to a manufacturer contemplating the installation of rapidly obsolescent machinery, whose rate of depreciation is large relatively to either rate of interest,[1] nobody really doubts that it does make some difference to a railway company contemplating electrification or an estate company contemplating the development of a seaside resort. It is certainly not impossible to conceive a community devoting a growing proportion of a growing income to such things without reducing the producers of consumption goods to bankruptcy—and that even though our chosen monetary policy should be one which permits the prices of finished goods to fall with the progress of technical efficiency. Indeed it is evident that broadly speaking this is what happened in that remote century which followed Waterloo—a period which even Mr. Keynes seems sometimes ready to treat as an exception to the general law of entropy[2] which he regards as governing human economic affairs.

§ 3. One goes up and down in one's outlook on this matter, as on so many other things. In 1932, between the births of Mr. Keynes' two big books, I find I was taking him to task for expressing in his *Treatise* a view, as I thought, too cyclical and not sufficiently secular of the problem of industrial malaise.[3] I suppose I am a little hard to please, for I now find myself in reaction against the pessimism as to the future of enterprise which has been spread, especially apparently in

[1] For some interesting arithmetic, see article by Bauer and Marrack in *E.J.*, June 1939, p. 237.
[2] See *G.T.*, p. 242.
[3] See the essay on *The Future of Trade Cycle Theory* in this volume, pp. 98 ff.

certain circles in the United States,[1] by his later book. To me, as I have said, it now seems that our present difficulties are very largely political; and that so far as they are not political, they are largely *institutional* rather than fundamental, and connected above all with the fact that our banking systems grew up in a world in which there seemed to be a natural harmony, which has proved to be illusory, between the desire of the public to keep money easily accessible in a bank and the desire of commerce and industry to borrow for *working* capital purposes. But that is a story for another occasion.

[1] See especially the able *Economic Programme for American Democracy* by a group of Harvard and Tufts economists.

II

THEORIES OF BANKING POLICY[1]

I THINK our chairman will bear me out that one cannot set up, even in the most modest way, as a writer on monetary affairs, without becoming the target for a continuous stream of documents—manuscript, typed and printed—designed to show that the ills of the human race are all due to monetary mismanagement, and all curable by monetary manipulation. In the back streets of London suburbs and northern industrial towns, on the plains of India and the prairies of the Middle West, those who have Found the Light about Money take up their pens and write, with a conviction, a persistence and a devotion otherwise only found among the disciples of a new religion. It is easy to scoff at these productions: it is not so easy always to see exactly where they go wrong. It is natural that practical bankers, vaguely conscious that the projects of monetary cranks are dangerous to society, should cling in self-defence to the solid rock, or what they believe to be so, of tradition and accepted practice. But it is not open to the detached student of economics to take refuge from dangerous innovation in blind conservatism. He must assess with an equal eye the projects of reformers and the claims of the established order; and to this end he must build up for himself a theory of money—a critical analysis of the nature and results of the processes by which, under a modern system of banking, money is manufactured.

[1] A lecture delivered at the London School of Economics and Political Science on February 13, 1928, and published in *Economica*, June, 1928. One or two passages from this lecture have been incorporated in my book *Money* (Nisbet & Co., 1928). See also Preface, p. vii.

Obviously, I cannot put a complete theory of money before you in an hour. My aim is the more modest one of making a critical comparison, from certain limited and selected points of view, between three broad principles which have been advocated, at one time and in one quarter or another, as the proper basis of a modern banking policy. I shall call these principles, for brevity, the Gold Standard Principle, the Principle of Productive Credit and the Principle of Price Stabilisation. But before I can examine them, I shall have to build up a rather elaborate scaffolding; and it follows that both the comparison itself and the argument that leads up to it will have to be skimped and bony and inadequate. I shall have to simplify and select and dogmatise—to suppress important complications and to eschew tempting controversies. I shall trouble you with few figures, though I shall make some illustrative references to a topic which is rightly attracting more and more attention in this country—the achievements, and not less the difficulties, of the Federal Reserve Banking System of the United States. Nor shall I make any but the most sparing use of even the elementary mathematics of which alone I am capable—though the chairman, under pressure, has permitted me two simple equations, which at the critical moment I shall inscribe on that board. Again, even at the risk of blurring the clear edge of thought, I shall eschew the use of certain strange and barbarous language for employing which elsewhere I have been severely taken to task.

My main preliminary propositions are five in number, but some of them are subject to qualifications almost as important as themselves: so that it is up a pyramid of eight steps that I must try to conduct you if we are to reach a secure platform from which to take our hurried survey of the three selected principles of banking policy.

I do not think my *first proposition* need delay us long, provided we are prepared to forego the delight of quibbling about words. It is that the preponderant form of money in the countries which it is most profitable for us to study consists in bank deposits subject to cheque: and that for the most fundamental purposes of monetary theory, we can, without serious risk of error, speak as though these deposits were the *only* form of money, ignoring the existence of paper notes and metal coins.

My *second proposition* is the time-worn one that this bank-money comes into existence mainly as the result of loans and investments made by the banking system, and that consequently, in most circumstances, the proximate force determining its amount is a series of decisions made by some person or persons situated within the banking system. Historically, there seems to me no question that the bulk of the bank-money in existence has come into existence in this way. Even, for instance, if we ignore the war-period, the main reason why in the previous half-century the supplies of bank-money in England increased some 2½ times was not because individuals were carting cash into the banks, but because, owing to amalgamation, owing to the perfection of clearing-house arrangements, owing to the importation of gold, the banking system found itself enabled, consistently with its principles, to expand its loans and investments to a corresponding extent. I should not have thought it worth while to assert this truism in the shape of a formal proposition, were it not that a widespread feeling among bankers that they are being "got at" in some way by orthodox teaching on this matter has induced even so eminent an authority as the late Walter Leaf to use language which is cloudy and misleading. If anybody retains any lingering doubts on this matter, whether these doubts arise from consideration of the multiplicity of banks or from some less rational cause, I commend to him the careful and patient article of Mr. Crick on "The Genesis of Bank Deposits" in *Economica*, June 1927. Here time forces me to treat this particular controversy as closed.

But there is *one important qualification* to be made. I

should admit, and indeed insist, that while a banking system can always prevent the quantity of bank-money from rising *above* any assigned limit, there may arise conditions of falling prices and failing confidence in which it is exceedingly difficult for it, without the help of allies, and without a revolution in banking practice, to prevent the volume of bank-money from falling *below* some assigned limit. The reason for this is that banks create money predominantly by way of loan: and just as the White King required two messengers, one to fetch and one to carry, so custom requires two parties in a loan transaction—one to lend and one to borrow. It is arguable that the Federal Reserve System, by the support which it has given in recent years to the practice of instalment-buying, has already inaugurated such a revolution in banking practice as I have in mind: but until we see bankers giving away money with both hands, I personally shall be prepared to admit that the control which a modern banking system can exercise over the volume of money may prove under certain conditions to be incomplete.

My *third proposition* leads us into more difficult country. In the form in which I shall state it first, it is not the complete truth, but a first approximation to the truth. "The real value of a country's bank-money is the same thing as the amount of real savings which the public has put in the past at the disposal of industry through the medium of the banks, and its amount lies in the discretion of the public and not of the banks." The banks determine how much money shall be outstanding, but it is the public which determines, through the habits which it adopts as regards the hoarding and spending of money, what that amount of money shall be worth. And since the balance-sheets of the banks must balance, it is broadly true that the real value of their industrial assets at any time is governed by the real value which the public is embodying at that time in its holdings of bank-money. It is presumably some half-perception of this half-truth which leads bankers to make such statements as that "they can only lend what the public has deposited with them."

Once more I must refer you to the recognised authorities—such as Pigou's essay on the Exchange Value of Legal Tender Money—for an account of the forces which determine the public's habits with regard to the hoarding and spending of money, and determine therefore also the amount of real saving which is so to speak crystallised in its holdings of bank-money at any moment of time. It is more important for me to press on and explain the *two serious qualifications* which reduce my third proposition to the status of a half-truth.

First, there is no question that, for a period of time, the banking system, by creating new money and handing it over to its nominees, can continuously extract from the public more savings than the public spontaneously decides to provide, and can hand the disposal of these savings over to its own nominees. I wish to avoid the ambiguous word inflation, but it is such a process as is commonly called by that name that I have in mind. Rightly analysed, it seems to consist of two elements, which have not in the past been sufficiently distinguished. First, the newly created money in the hands of the banks' nominees is continually pouring on to the markets in competition with the existing money in the hands of the public, raising prices against the public, and depriving it of consumption which it had expected to enjoy. Secondly, this rise of prices entails a diminution in the real value of the public's holdings of money: and it is at least possible that some of them will seek to restore this real value towards its old level, and to that end refrain from consumption to which they are legally entitled, thereby performing an additional act of saving beyond that to which they are actually compelled by the action of the banks. This additional saving on their part is *in a sense* voluntary: but since they are induced to do it by the consequences of the previous action of the banks, we may fairly include it for our purposes under the general term of "forced savings," which I propose to apply to the resources diverted in this way from the general consumer to the nominees of the banks.

At the close of such a period of forced saving, it may quite well happen, if the public's habits about saving have not permanently altered, that the real value of the outstanding volume of bank-money, and the real value of the industrial assets by which it is balanced in the books of the banks, are exactly what they were before the whole process began. In such a case, our third proposition would lead us to infer that the public had, in the interval, made no contribution of savings through the banks to industry: but such an inference would be entirely false. The mere fact that a bank's balance-sheet balances throws no light on the question whether, in the past—even the quite recent past—the bank has been acting as an intermediary for spontaneous investment or as a burglar. The pious protestations of bankers about "being unable to lend more than has been entrusted to them" seem often to ignore this important point!

The second qualification of my third proposition is equally important, and much less generally understood. While apart from the cases of compulsion just discussed, the public decides the amount of real savings which it is prepared to put at the disposal of industry through the banks, it needs the co-operation of the banks to make its decision effective. If, in the face of an increased willingness on the part of the public to perform this particular kind of saving, the banks fail to take appropriate action, then the potential saving will go to waste. It will be dissipated in the form of lower prices and increased consumption by the public at large. The bank can prevent this undesigned result if, and only if, it makes new loans or investments on a sufficient scale to prevent prices from falling and ensure that the public really does the saving which it intends to do. By acting in this way the bank is behaving not as a burglar but as a benefactor: it is not imposing unsought burdens on the people, but enabling their thrifty intentions to bear fruit.

In case this matter is not yet clear, consider what actually happens if I decide to save £50 in the form of bank deposit instead of buying, say, a set of gramophone records. I do not, under modern conditions, carry fifty pound notes into the bank: indeed, it is broadly true that under modern conditions nobody can put anything into a bank that is not there already. (The necessary qualifications to be made in the case of such people as shopkeepers and railway booking clerks will occur to everybody.) The only action which I have to take is the negative one of failing to draw a cheque in favour of the gramophone company. If, as we will assume for the sake of simplicity, the gramophone company banks at the same bank, the only obvious effect of my masterly inactivity on the banker is to absolve him from the need of making an entry in his books. But, in fact, it has a much more far-reaching effect: it enables him to make a new loan of £50 to some worthy trader without producing the price-raising consequences which such a loan *would* entail if I had not decided to put a chain round the neck of my £50 deposit.

If bankers only realised that against additional loans created in such circumstances there is no theoretical objection, they would perhaps be less nervously anxious to deny their ability to "create credit." And it is fair to add that the language of some economists, by failing to distinguish clearly the circumstances in which additional loans are created, has given the bankers some excuse for their nervousness.

But to this olive-branch to the bankers I must hastily append a warning. Conditions such as I have described, in which the public is anxious to increase the amount of its real saving done in monetary form, are very easily confused in practice with conditions in which there is a tendency for prices to fall, and therefore for the commodity value of the public's money-holdings to rise, for quite a different reason. That reason is a growth in the effectiveness of human labour—an increase in the quantity of goods and services which a day's labour of given quality can turn out. To say that in such circumstances a fall in commodity prices is "natural" is not, I think, as it is sometimes represented to be, a mere retreat into mystical and question-begging language. It is an expression of the truth that if in such circumstances the banks counteract the threatened fall of prices by expanding the supply of money, they *will* be extracting forced savings from the public no less than if, in normal circumstances, they expand the supply of money in such wise as to drive prices upwards. This distinction between a fall in prices due to increased productivity, and a fall in prices due to an increased desire on the part of the public to perform monetary saving, is, I think, of the highest importance for a right theory of banking policy: and it is not the less important because the two phenomena may be exceedingly difficult to disentangle in the actual world.

My *fourth proposition* is a rather complicated one, and I shall break it up into a lot of little sentences. The first part takes us away for a moment from the banks altogether, and bears on the nature of industrial capital. The real circulating capital of a country at any moment of time consists in the whole mass of goods, from the seed-corn in the ground to the loaf in the baker's shop, which at that moment are at some point on their journey through the process of production. This process of production consists in the gradual addition of saleableness to goods by the exercise of human effort and ingenuity. The value of the circulating capital bears a certain definite relation to the length of time over which this process of production is spread: and so as not to indulge in too great refinement or use symbols where figures can be made to serve, we may say that the circulating capital is equal in value to one-half the output during a period of production. If, for instance, we conceive of the process of production as a vast sausage-machine which it takes ten minutes to traverse, and which turns out one sausage per minute, one of the potential sausages in the machine will have been there for nine minutes and one only for one: but on the average they will have been there for five minutes, and their average value is that which is conveyed by five minutes' laceration, *i.e.* the value of half a completed sausage. The aggregate value of the ten amorphous objects is therefore that of five completed sausages, that is, of five minutes' output.

Now some of this circulating capital has been built up out of the savings made by business men and corporations themselves, or borrowed by them directly from the public: while some of it has been built up out of savings put at their disposal by the banks. Again, some of the real savings which the public puts at the disposal of the banks have been crystallised in this circulating capital, while some have been crystallised in the form of bricks and mortar, machinery and gold reserves, and some again have been embodied in the form of shells long since fired and mules long since deceased.

Now we come at last to my terrible equations which I will first write up in all their naked horror, and then attempt to clothe with life.

When the industrial and banking systems are in equilibrium,

$$aKR = bC$$
$$C = \tfrac{1}{2}DR$$
$$\therefore aK = \tfrac{1}{2}bD$$

R is the community's real annual income in terms of goods.

K is the proportion of this income over which the public wish to keep command in the form of bank-money, so that KR = the real value of the aggregate of bank deposits.[1]

a is the proportion of KR which the banks have crystallised in the form of circulating capital as contrasted with instrumental capital, bank premises, Government debt and reserves.

[1] In view of the criticisms advanced against this mode of statement by Keynes (*Treatise on Money*, vol. I, p. 232) it is as well to make it plain that while the magnitude KR can always be *expressed* as a fraction of R, it is not necessarily *determined upon* with reference only to the size of R [1931.]

C is the circulating capital, b the proportion of C which has been built up with the aid of the banks as contrasted with that supplied by the business world itself or by direct public subscription.

D is the proportion of a year which is covered by a period of production, so that DR is the real income or output during a period of production.

Then these two equations follow from our preceding discussion. As a rough approximation, we may guess that both for England and U.S.A., $D = 1$, $a = b = K = \frac{1}{2}$.

I now reach the climax of this part of my discussion. Provided there is no change in the relative magnitudes of the proportions a and b, or in those of the proportions K and D, a uniform rate of growth in population and output can be sustained without rupture of equilibrium. But to this end it is necessary that the banking system shall add to the supplies of bank-money at the same rate.[1] Once more, therefore, in the case of the normal processes of progress as in the case of an increase in the desire of the average member of the public to perform monetary saving, the creation of additional money by the banks is seen to be not merely blameless, but a positive duty.

My *fifth and last proposition* concerns occasions when this even rate of growth is interrupted. If for any reason the rate of industrial growth is accelerated, and still more if industry is passing through the first phases of recovery from deep depression, the various factors in

[1] This matter is explained, clumsily but at length, in my *Banking Policy and the Price Level*, pp. 66-70, and more briefly in *Money* (1928), ch. V, § § 5, 8. So far as I can see, though some have tried to persuade me otherwise, it is for a constant *arithmetic* rate of growth of population that my equation is valid. Put broadly, provided that $aK = \frac{1}{2}bD$, the batch of new workers drawn into employment in a production-period D_1 are to be conceived of as doing, sooner or later, enough monetary saving to justify the banking-system in financing the drawing into employment of an equal batch of workers in some subsequent production-period D_2. To maintain equilibrium with a constant *geometrical* rate of growth, we must, I think, have $aK = \frac{1}{2}bD(1 + x)$, where x is the rate of growth of population per production period. But I wish the whole matter could be explored thoroughly and carried much further by an expert mathematician (cf. the suggestive remarks of Mr. R. W. Souter, "Equilibrium Economics," *Quarterly Journal of Economics*, Nov. 1930, p. 90). [1931.]

our equations are thrown out of gear. First, it is of the essence of Circulating Capital that it must begin to grow *before* the rate of output grows, and *a fortiori*, therefore, before the new real saving in monetary form which the new output facilitates is done. Secondly, there is a strong tendency for the proportion b to grow—that is to say, a strong tendency on the part of the business world to urge that an abnormally large fraction of the new Circulating Capital required should be provided with the aid of the banks. The first occurrence is, so far as I can see, a physical necessity. The second is dependent on business habit and banking policy. The effect of the first occurrence, in terms of our equations, is to make C = something more than $\frac{1}{2}DR$, and the effect of the two combined is to make bC considerably more than aKR. The resulting disequilibrium involves the imposition of forced saving on the public by the banking system and a rise in the price-level.

The condition of strain thus set up is what is known as a trade-boom. I must resist the temptation to describe even in outline the various secondary factors by which the strain is aggravated and prolonged, or the various expedients—some real, but some only illusory—to which the banking system may have recourse to tempt the public into economy and so mitigate the element of compulsion in the burden which is placed upon them. The bare bones of the analysis already in our hands are sufficient for my purpose of a broad comparison of banking policies.

For that, our main task, we have none too much time; but it will, I think, be good economy to use a little of what remains in a brief recapitulation of the steps we have already taken. First, we decided that to elucidate that part of the theory of money which concerns us to-night, we can concentrate our attention on bank deposits. Secondly, we decided that the magnitude of these bank deposits lies mainly within the discretion of the banking system, though it is not certain that in all conceivable circumstances the system will find it easy to create as much of them as it might have reason for desiring to create. Thirdly, the real value of these bank deposits, which must balance the real value of bank assets held against them, lies within the discretion of the public and not of the banking system; so that there is a broad apparent correspondence at any time between the amount of saving which the public has been willing to do in monetary form and the power of the banks to assist industry and trade. But there are two things which make this correspondence more apparent than real: the first is the power of the banks to extract forced savings from the public over a period of time by the creation of new money, without impairing that apparent equilibrium between saving and investment which is suggested by the fact that their balance-sheet balances. The second is the possibility that the banks, by failing to create *sufficient* new money, will permit individuals to increase the real value of their bank balances without transforming this new saving into new real industrial assets—a process which, again, will leave no trace of disharmony in the balance-sheet.

Our fourth step led us through an analysis of the purposes to which the banking system devotes its resources to the conclusion that a uniform expansion of population and production calls for a uniform expansion of bank deposits, and that such an expansion involves no fraud upon the public. But our fifth step led us to the conclusion that an exceptionally rapid rate of industrial growth *does* throw the relation between the banking system and the public on the one hand and the race of industrial borrowers on the other out of equilibrium, and set up a strong tendency to the extraction of forced saving from the public.

We come now at last to our three alternative principles of banking policy. I do not, as I have said, propose to examine them from every possible point of view, but only to ask about each of them three questions, suggested by the course of my previous analysis. First, can it be relied upon not wantonly to extort forced savings from the public? Secondly, can it be relied upon efficiently to transmute all real saving offered to it by the public into industrial capital? Thirdly, is it likely to respond readily to the genuine requirements of industry for exceptional supplies of savings in exceptional circumstances?

(1) Let us take first the Gold Standard Principle, by which I mean the principle of banking as understood in England before the war. Let me admit at once that a good deal of what I have to say is not applicable without qualification to the present day, when gold is passing more and more into the position of a Merovingian monarch, with Governors Norman, Strong and Schacht as joint Mayors of the Palace. But from a theoretical point of view the pure pre-war system is still worth considering. From our present standpoint its distinguishing features were two. The first was its preoccupation with its legal tender—that is, ultimately, of its gold—reserves, which made the rate at which it created new money depend on accidental circumstances, and not on either of the two fundamental underlying realities—namely, the rate at which the public is willing to perform new saving in monetary form, and the rate at which the requirements of industry and trade for circulating capital are increasing. Hence it might occur, and it did occur, that owing to a heavy production and import of gold, the supplies of money were increased, regardless of the power of industry to make fruitful use at the moment of the resources thrust into its hands, and regardless of the burden imposed by rising prices upon ordinary folk. Or, again, it might occur, and it did occur, that owing to a shortage of gold reserves, the rate of increase of industrial output was retarded, though everything might be ripe for an industrial expansion and though the public might be bubbling over with the desire and intention to save and to put its savings, if only it knew how, at the disposal of traders and manufacturers through the medium of the banking system. That is the essence

of the case, now hardly disputed, against the uncontrolled gold standard.

The second feature of "gold standard banking" is the preoccupation of the banker with the "liquidity" of his assets, in the sense of the ready convertibility of them (or of the collateral by which they are protected) into what he calls cash, as contrasted with their "liquidity" in the sense of the extent to which they represent consumable goods rapidly approaching their final goal in the consumer's hands. I do not want to overstress this point. No doubt, as Mr. Leaf has told us, the six months or seasonal loan is the backbone of the banker's business, and a further part of his resources is embodied, directly or indirectly, in rapidly maturing bills of exchange. No doubt his desire that his loans shall be fairly regularly and frequently paid off works in the same direction as a rule that his resources shall be employed for preference in the building up of circulating capital. Nevertheless, bankers are never tired of telling us that provided they are satisfied with the credit standing of their borrower, it is not their business to enquire too closely into the purposes for which he uses his loan. The revelation by Lloyds Bank in 1927 that no less than 25 per cent. of its advances—as large a sum as went to agriculture, retail trade, the coal trade and the iron and steel trades put together—came under the heading "personal and professional," while its interpretation is not altogether clear, must have come, I think, as a surprise to many. There is, so far as I can see, no guarantee in the principles of banking as understood in England that the resources entrusted to the banks will not, under certain conditions, be used to an undesirable extent in building up fixed as contrasted with circulating capital, or in facilitating "speculation" in the sense of that ambiguous word which implies that the natural forward flow of goods on to the market is being impeded rather than promoted.

(2) The alternative Principle of Productive Credit presents at first sight a gratifying contrast. This principle claims our attention for several reasons.

First, it was openly proclaimed by the Federal Reserve Board in their celebrated Report for 1923 as being the guiding principle of their policy. Secondly, its assumptions seem to lie behind the provisions—found not only in the Federal Reserve Act but in the charters of many of the Central Banks founded in recent years on the American model—which prescribe the nature of the assets which the Central Bank is to keep against its note and deposit liabilities. Thirdly, it seems to embody a sentiment which is very widely entertained among traders and manufacturers as to what they have a right to expect the banking system to do for them.

"The Federal Reserve System," says the report for 1923, "is a system of productive credit. It is not a system of credit for either investment or speculative purposes." I have no time to examine with you in detail how far this principle is embodied, and how far it is deserted, in the actual regulations of the Federal Reserve System. I must press on to the implications which lie behind this theory of productive credit. They seem to be nothing less than this—that every person who can show reason to suppose that he is going to be able to sell £100 worth of goods within some reasonable space of time should be entitled to borrow £100 from the bank. And what *this* amounts to is the doctrine that the trader and the producer are entitled to depend on the bank for the whole of their supplies of circulating capital.

This doctrine is naturally very acceptable to the business world. Judged by the test of what is called "elasticity" and "responsiveness to the needs of trade," the principle of productive credit passes with very high honours. Its appeal to the tribunal of real activities and real values seems at first sight to give it an immense theoretical superiority over the rigid and mechanical illogicality of the gold standard principle. Yet can we be sure that it is really free from all the defects of the latter or from subtle dangers of its own? Is not the boasted elasticity and responsiveness a doubtful virtue? Do we really want our banking system to be a mere passive punch-ball for the pugilists of industry and trade?

"It is the belief of the Board," says the Report of 1923, "that there will be little danger that the credit created and contributed by the Federal Reserve Banks will be in excessive volume if restricted to productive uses." I am not sure, as I shall explain presently, that this view has been borne out by events: but even if it has, it may be conjectured that this result has been due rather to a happy combination of practical judgment and exceptionally favourable circumstances than to a correct theoretical basis. In other circumstances there seems no guarantee that the doctrine of productive credit may not lead to the extraction of forced savings from the public. For consider, in the light of our equation, what it means. Take a banking system which is in equilibrium with $aK = \frac{1}{2}bD$, and apply the doctrine of productive credit. What this means is that for all future increments of production, the fraction b is to be raised to 1. Unless some countervailing change is made in one or more of the other factors a, K and D, the conditions leading to the extraction of forced savings are present.

To put the same point in looser but perhaps more vivid language. The notion common to the American theory of 1923 and to a great deal of much less solid and respectable propaganda—indeed to 90 per cent. of the writings of monetary cranks—is that every batch of goods is entitled to be born with a monetary label of equivalent value round its neck, and to carry it round its neck until it dies. This notion is false and may be dangerous, because the label in fact does not remain tied round the neck of the goods, but goes off on a round of visits of its own. Nine out of ten advocates of "elastic" monetary systems neglect that phenomenon called the velocity of circulation of money which is epitomised in our symbol K; and not even the remaining one is aware of the danger of neglecting the numerical relation between this phenomenon and that independent but equally fundamental phenomenon, the period of production of goods, which is epitomised in our symbol D.

It is quite true that there has been no undesirable rise of prices in the United States. Indeed, as is well known, the danger there has been of a precisely opposite character. That brings me to my second count against the Principle of Productive Credit—that, if rigidly applied, it may in certain circumstances fail to transmute the thrifty intentions of the people into effective industrial savings. The power and desire of the American people to save has shown itself in many forms in recent years, and among others in an increased desire to leave their bank deposits untouched for considerable periods. While in the five and a half years between March 8, 1922, and September 7, 1927, the demand deposits in the "reporting member banks" of the Federal Reserve System increased by 29 per cent., the time deposits increased by 102 per cent. A corresponding change has come over the assets of the banks. Between the same dates the investments of reporting member banks increased by 63 per cent., loans secured by stock or bonds by 71 per cent., all other loans only by 18 per cent. These figures must be interpreted with caution, but it is undisputed that during the last few years the resources of the American banks have been used to a greatly increased extent in the provision of fixed as compared with circulating capital. On the principles of productive credit, this is very shocking: but the wary empiricists who run the Federal Reserve System have been too wise to be very deeply shocked. After all, if K is increasing, what more natural than to preserve equilibrium by a corresponding reduction in a?

(3) And so we hear less nowadays of productive credit and more of stabilisation of the price-level. The high priests of the Federal Reserve System show indeed a natural anxiety not to commit themselves too deeply in this matter—partly, it would seem, because they doubt the ability of the average Middle Western farmer to keep clearly in his mind the distinction between the

general price-level and the price of wheat. Perhaps they may even have been a little embarrassed by Mr. McKenna's recent unqualified assertion of their omnipotence in this respect. Nevertheless, a perusal of the exceedingly able and interesting evidence given by Governor Strong before the Financial Committee of the House of Representatives leaves, I think, little doubt that the conception of the stability of general prices plays at least a very important part in shaping his thoughts and plans. And it is well known that in England a number of eminent experts have been for years proclaiming the stabilisation of the price-level as the sole and sufficient objective of banking policy. Let us, therefore, in conclusion, direct our thoughts to the Principle of Price Stabilisation. Obviously we have no time to consider it from all the possible points of view. We must be content to ask about it our three selected questions—and one more, perhaps more searching still.

First, does it effectively debar the extraction of forced savings from the public? Yes, in most circumstances—but not in all. In America, factory output per head is said to have increased by 40 per cent. between 1919 and 1925; and though, of course, this figure does not correctly represent the growth in productivity per head for the population as a whole, there is no reason to doubt that this latter has been very considerable. I have already argued that it is by no means meaningless to say that in such conditions there is a natural tendency for general prices to fall, and that to keep them from falling is "inflationary" in the sense that it is extracting forced savings from the public. The Federal Reserve authorities have not, I think, been blind to this aspect of the situation. It is significant that the index-number of prices calculated for use in the New York Federal Reserve Bank is heavily weighted with the prices of retail goods and of labour, and does not therefore show the same tendency to fall as a result of increased productivity per head as does an index-number of wholesale prices. Nevertheless, in so far as the Federal

System has not gone all out for stabilising the price of *labour*, it cannot, I think, be wholly absolved from the charge of having burgled from the public in these years of rapidly advancing productivity. From one point of view the generous financing of instalment-buying, of which I shall have more to say in a moment, may be regarded as an attempt to sell back to the public with the left hand a purchasing power which is being filched from them with the right.

Does price-stabilisation ensure the transmutation into industrial capital of every genuine increase in the capacity and desire to save? Yes; from this point of view it gets, so far as I can see, full marks. Does it do all that it ought to do to furnish industry with the material means for taking those discontinuous leaps to a higher level of activity which, whatever their inconveniences, have hitherto seemed to be an inseparable part of the phenomenon of industrial progress? Well, here I have my own private heresy. I am not sure that a little forced saving now and again may not be the necessary price which we have to pay for what we call progress, and that a doctrinaire application of the principle of price-stabilisation in all circumstances might not be inimical to the rapid growth of aggregate economic welfare. But I do not wish, even if there were time, to develop that theme to-night. I must hurry on to the last question of all—is the policy of price-stabilisation practicable?

Now once more it would take me another hour to discuss this question adequately, and I must confine myself to pointing out those considerations which arise directly out of my previous analysis. It is true, as I have already said, that it is not quite clear *what* price-level, if any, the Federal Reserve System has been trying to stabilise, and that the fact that the wholesale price-level in America fell by 10 per cent. between mid-1925 and mid-1927 must not be too readily taken as evidence of its lack of capacity to achieve its ends with complete success. But it is clear, I think, that the situation has not been an easy one. If my interpretation of American conditions is right, there has been at work there an extraordinary concatenation of forces tending to lower the level of commodity prices. Industrial progress has on the one hand raised productivity per head and increased the desire of the people to perform monetary saving: while on the other side of the equation it may be conjectured that it has shortened the period of production and, by increasing the power of businesses to finance extensions of circulating capital for themselves, has diminished the degree to which they need to have recourse to the banks. Under such conditions Governor Strong has been hard put to it to affect the level of commodity prices in an upward direction. He pumps money into circulation, but instead of driving up commodity prices it hangs about the stock markets, driving up the price of industrial securities. Then, as we have seen in the last few weeks, he gets nervous, mops up money by the sale of securities in the open market and puts up his bank-rate.

There remains one more resource, and that too has been adopted on an enormous scale. When you have pumped into the producer all the money which he will absorb, you can try it on the consumer as well. According to recent estimates, a sum of about £450,000,000, say £4 per head of the population, is now outstanding on loans to consumers for the purchase of motor-cars, saxophones and other desirable commodities. There are many things to be said about this development from the broader social point of view: from our immediate standpoint it is chiefly interesting as a notable, and perhaps somewhat disquieting, oblation upon the altar of price-stabilisation.

And if these things are done in the green tree, what shall be done in the dry? There seems at present no limit to the growth of American business activity: but if that great country *should* ever become even temporarily saturated with 50-storey buildings and motor-cars, can we be certain that *any* purely monetary policy would meet the needs of the situation? In any case, can we be certain that the experiences of El Dorado are a safe guide to the policy of less favoured lands? The out-and-out price-stabiliser claims that he can always check a fall in prices and cure unemployment by monetary means, and that there is no need for such fancy palliatives of industrial depression as the deliberate spacing through time of governmental and other large demands for constructional work. I think the difficulties experienced by the Federal Reserve System even in times of raging prosperity should make us pause before admitting such extreme claims.

It has been my business to examine existing principles of banking policy, and not to elaborate new ones. But to escape the imputation of cowardice, let me suggest in conclusion that the ideal banking policy might be one which was founded on the principle of price-stabilisation as a norm, but which was ready to see the fruits of a prolonged and general increase in individual productivity shared in the form of lower prices, and perhaps to acquiesce in moderate price-rises in order that advantage might be taken of discontinuous leaps in industrial technique. And it would be a policy that did not claim omnipotence, or feel competent of its ability to cure the evils of uncertainty except in alliance with a much more comprehensive attempt to control and stabilise the desires and activities of the community than most monetary reformers—even, I think, most thorough-going Socialists—have yet visualised.

III

THE 1931 CRISIS[1]

"THE crisis" is the result of the repercussion on our national economy of an exceptionally severe international depression of trade. The *primary* cause of this depression, as of others in the past, is the difficulty of reconciling progress with stability, of ensuring that the provision of the world with increased capital equipment takes place at a steady rate. This aspect of the depression—the "glut" of capital goods—showed itself at its clearest in the United States and in the countries, including Germany, which up till 1928 were expanding their capital equipment with the aid of American savings. But on this occasion there have been special aggravating forces at work, namely (i) the rapid application of science to agriculture, leading to the ruin of whole groups of high cost producers and to a decline in the total receipts even of low-cost ones, (ii) the decline in the rate of growth of population, which means that the demand for prime necessities does not keep pace with the growth of wealth, and also that capital equipment gluts take longer to work off, (iii) the durable nature of some of the new objects of consumption (*e.g.* wireless sets). Owing to the difficulty experienced by consumers, producers and financiers in adapting themselves to changed situations, these changes express themselves in the form of an obliteration of money incomes and a catastrophic fall of prices. The "maldistribution of gold," often alleged as the cause of the fall in prices, is itself a result rather than a cause of the world depression, since the countries

[1] Abstract (printed in the *Cambridge Review*) of two public lectures given at Cambridge in October 1931.

in which the glut (whether of capital goods or of raw products) has become acute cease to be able to pay interest on their debts out of the sale of their produce and also to offer a reasonably attractive field for further investment. But it is true that the consequent flow of gold to America and France has been aggravated by high tariffs and by the exaction of war debt payments.

As regards the treatment of such depressions, the truth lies somewhere between the standpoint of the "boosters," who believe that cheap and abundant money and the generation of a spirit of optimism can lift us out of them, and that of the "penguins," who believe that high-cost and inefficient concerns must be eliminated before business can revive. Applied too soon or indiscriminately, the remedies of the former are likely to be futile or even harmful by leading to a further saturation of already saturated channels of investment (*e.g.* the operations of the American Farm Board). Applied too long or indiscriminately, the prescriptions of the latter drive even sound businesses into bankruptcy through the continuous fall in prices. International action is required; but the task set to it is much harder than the mere manipulation of technical rules about gold reserves, etc.—it is the discriminating canalisation of investment. At present the prospects of such action have been impaired by the development of a *secondary* phase of the depression, taking the form of an almost world-wide loss of confidence in banks whose assets have become illiquid, and a consequent tendency to hoard currency. This phase of the world's trouble has been aggravated by Britain's departure from the gold standard.

In considering the repercussion of these events on our national position, and assessing such statements as that "nationally we have for a long time past been living beyond our means and living to a considerable extent upon our capital" (Mr. Snowden), it is essential to distinguish between (i) our general position as a nation with regard to the provision we are making for the future by adding annually to our capital equipment,

(ii) our position as a nation as regards lending to, or borrowing from, foreigners, (iii) the position of our Central Government as regards paying for its expenditure out of current revenue. In the matter of (i) there is no great reason to be anxious, and it is certainly not true that "for a long time past we have been living on our capital." As regards (ii) it seems to be true that in recent months, owing mainly to a falling off in dividend and interest receipts from abroad, our payments due to foreigners on current account had come to exceed our claims upon them on current account by an amount which has been estimated at £2,000,000 a week, instead of (as in pre slump years) falling short of them by rather more than this figure. This is probably an unsatisfactory situation, but it does not mean that "the State is heading for bankruptcy" (Mr. MacDonald), nor would it have forced the Bank of England to suspend gold payments. This event was caused by a violent rush to withdraw *capital* from London, due partly to internal difficulties in the countries seeking to withdraw capital, partly to lack of confidence in the position of the Government's finances, partly to anxiety at the degree to which British financiers (with a mixture of rashness and nobility) were supporting the fabric of Central Europe. London was ill-fitted to cope with the loss of confidence, owing to the abnormally large volume of her short-term liabilities to foreigners, itself apparently the result partly of deliberate policy on the part of her banks, partly of a weakness in our exporting power connected with our high level of internal production costs, and dating back to the industrial troubles of 1926.

As regards (iii) the effect of the slump was naturally to increase the State's expenses and diminish its receipts. It is not necessarily wrong for a Government to borrow in time of trade depression, and it is almost certainly to the world's interest that the Governments of rich creditor countries should do so: but owing to the weakness in our balance of payments we were probably no longer in a position to serve the world in this manner. It is easy to show that the "cuts" exercise an influence adverse to employment: but it was, and remains, a matter of choosing the lesser evil. At the same time, now that with the lapse from the gold standard any attempt to bring down the general level of money incomes has presumably been abandoned, the "cuts" have lost a large part of their point and become an advanced guard without an army. We ought in the next few months to consider afresh whether we really wish certain classes of State servants and unemployed persons (both of whom pay the taxation relevant to their income-class) to lose gross income as compared with other persons (the calculations as to the relative percentage "sacrifices" of the various classes of taxpayers and recipients of State payments have mostly been devoid of meaning). Meanwhile the cuts have left an awkward problem in the form of a sense of patriotic guilt in the minds of well-to-do persons, who are apt to vent it in a form which was appropriate during the war but is inappropriate now—namely by reducing their own consumption of home-produced goods and services without ensuring that that of other persons is correspondingly expanded.

To turn to the fall in the pound. Its effect is to give a continuing stimulus to exports so long as (i) other countries do not do likewise and (ii) home costs do not rise. (i) So far the position is good—it is our customers and suppliers who have followed suit, not our competitors: but this situation may not last, especially as regards Germany. Further, other countries may reply to us (some have) not by exchange depreciation but by wage-cuts and tariff increases: and it might become worth considering whether a precarious exchange-advantage is not worth surrendering in favour of the formation of a limited "sterling-block" of countries within which attempts to galvanise investment into life might prove more successful than they have done in the gold-standard world. (ii) Meanwhile the danger of the "vicious circle" of rising prices, rising wages and falling exchanges is sufficiently serious to make it too dangerous to attempt to use our freedom to lighten substantially the real burden of internal private and public debts by allowing the general level of money incomes to rise: though it might perhaps be legitimate to use it to correct the disequilibrium between "sheltered" and "unsheltered" wages by allowing the latter to rise somewhat. In any case we ought not to be alarmed if we see the volume of credit and currency increasing sufficiently to finance the increased volume of export trade.

It is theoretically possible that, if left to itself, the exchange might fall so far as to make the vicious circle almost impossible to avoid. In this event restriction of imports might be necessary. But the immediate imposition of a high general tariff on the top of an "exchange-protection" of 25 per cent. would seem to be madness. Ultimately the "right" level of exchange depends partly on the amount of new annual foreign investment which we wish to promote or permit, and raises the whole question of the subjection of such investment to increased social control.

IV

SAVING AND HOARDING[1]

§ 1. IN a future article I hope to examine certain aspects of the relation between saving, the rate of interest and the course of industrial fluctuation. But since the first of these concepts is a troublesome one, I propose to devote a preliminary article to explaining and illustrating the meaning which is here attached to it.

I assume the existence of a period of time, to be called a "day," which is finite but nevertheless so short that the income which a man receives on a given day cannot be allocated during its course to any particular use. A man's disposable income—the income about which the question arises on any particular day as to whether it shall be "saved" or "spent"—is thus the income received not on that day but on the previous one. A man is said to be *saving* if he spends on consumption less than his disposable income.

The form of our analysis will be much simplified if we can bring ourselves to identify this "day" with the period during which, at the outset of our inquiry, the stock of money changes hands once in final exchange for the constituents of the community's real income or output. To do so, it is true, will not only take us out of touch with the facts, but will preclude us from considering the possibility of an increase in the velocity of circulation of money against output above that from which we happen to start: for our definition does not admit of a piece of money coming to do more than one job in a day. Nevertheless, in order to throw a broad light on certain situations in which this possibility is not relevant, this simplifying identification will here at first be made.

[1] *E.J.*, Sept. 1933.

§ 2. There are certain other concepts, akin to but distinct from Saving, which seem to be useful in considering these matters.

A man is said to *lack*, or to do Lacking, if his consumption on any day falls short of the value, at the time of its receipt, of the income which he has at his disposal on that day. It is thus clear that Saving may involve Lacking. Thus, if a man receives an income of £10 on zero day and spends only £8 on consumption on day 1, and if the general situation around him is unaltered, he is lacking the quantity of consumption goods which could be bought for £2. But it is also possible (1) that Lacking should occur without Saving, (2) that Saving should occur without Lacking. (1) Suppose that on day 1 our man spends the whole of his £10 on consumption, and is therefore not saving; but suppose that other people add to the flow of money expended on that day, thus competing with him for the flow of goods coming forward for sale and driving up their price, so that his £10 buys 8 units of goods instead of 10. Then he is lacking 2 units of goods. It is convenient to call Lacking arising from such a cause Automatic, to distinguish it from the Voluntary Lacking which arises out of Saving. (2) Suppose that on day 1 our man spends only £8 on consumption, but suppose that other people contract the flow of money expended on that day, so that his £8 buys 10 units of goods instead of 8. Then he is saving, but doing no Lacking at all.

It is important to have a separate name, or at all events a separate pigeon-hole in the mind, for this experience of consuming less (or more) than one would have done if other people had not altered their expenditure. For this experience does not itself *constitute* Automatic Lacking (or its converse): it only *entails* Automatic Lacking (or its converse) if, in accordance with the general definition of Lacking, consumption falls below (rises above) the value, at the time of its receipt, of the disposable income. The names which I have suggested, for want of better, for these experiences are

Automatic Stinting and Automatic Splashing. Thus in case (2) above, our man is experiencing Automatic Splashing, but is not doing any negative Lacking.

§ 3. A man is said to be *hoarding* if he takes steps to raise the proportion which he finds existing at the beginning of any day between his money stock and his disposable income. On our simplified hypothesis this proportion is, to begin with, unity: *i.e.* if the representative man's income received on zero day is £10, so also is his money stock at the beginning of day 1. If on day 1 he spends £8 on consumption goods and £2 on a tool or a security, he is saving but not hoarding; if he spends £8 on consumption goods and leaves £2 unspent, he is hoarding as well as saving, for he is taking steps to raise the proportion specified above from 1 to $1\frac{1}{5}$. Thus Saving does not necessarily involve Hoarding. But neither does Hoarding necessarily involve Saving. For suppose our man on day 1 spends £10 on consumption but adds to his money stock by selling a tool or a security worth £2. In this case also he will be taking steps to raise the proportion specified above from 1 to $1\frac{1}{5}$, and will therefore be hoarding: but he will not be saving.

The converse operations to Saving, Lacking and Hoarding may be called Dissaving, Dislacking and Dishoarding.[1] Hoarding (Dishoarding) may be alternatively defined as acting in such a way as to decrease (increase) the velocity of circulation of money against output.

§ 4. It will be useful to illustrate these concepts from a situation to which Mr. Keynes' work has attracted particular attention—an "economy campaign" on the part of consumers. It will be assumed that the com-

[1] On our simplified hypothesis the possibility of Dishoarding on day 1 is, at least for the representative man, ruled out. For he cannot spend on consumption more than his disposable income, unless indeed he borrows, or sells some property, to enable him to do so: and even in that case he cannot, from the definition of a day, allocate on day 1 any part of the income received on that day to repaying the loan or repurchasing the property. Nothing therefore can cause his money stock at the beginning of day 2 to fall short of his income received on day 1. This only shows, of course, that the simplification is unsuitable for dealing with some of the situations we may want to consider.

munity consists of two classes, "the public" (A), whose rates of money income are prevented by contract or custom from varying during such short periods of time as are here under consideration, and "entrepreneurs" (B), of whom this is not true. To bring out the essential points, it will be assumed that a decline in the demand for a group of commodities is met not at all either by a restriction of output, or by a restriction of sales and accumulation of stocks, but entirely by a reduction of prices sufficient to market the original output. It need hardly be emphasised that such a situation is unstable, and likely to generate an accumulation of unsold stocks and a restriction of output and employment. To simplify the argument still further, we can start by assuming that at the outset "Investment," defined as expenditure on new instrumental goods,[1] is zero, all net output consisting of consumable goods.

Let S be the expenditure, R the income received and T the output on any day, P the price-level of T, and M the money stock at the end of the day. Let us use subscripts to denote classes and days. Then we start with $S = R = PT$, $S_a = R_a$, $S_b = R_b$. Also, on our simplified hypothesis about the length of the day, $M_a = R_a$, $M_b = R_b$.

Now let us suppose the public decides to save, in the form of an addition to its money stock, an amount of money X per day. Then we have $S_1 = M_a - X + M_b$, $P_1 = \frac{M - X}{T} = \frac{M - X}{M} . P$, $R_{1a} = M_a$, $R_{1b} = M_b - X$, $M_{1a} = M_a + X$, $M_{1b} = M_b - X$. The public has both saved and hoarded: entrepreneurs, spending their previous day's income, have neither saved nor dissaved, neither hoarded nor dishoarded.

The public has intended to consume $\frac{M_a - X}{P}$ and to

[1] More strictly, as expenditure on non-available output, in Mr. Keynes' phrase (*Treatise on Money*, I, p. 127); but for the purposes of this particular argument we may ignore the fact that some Investment takes the form of increased expenditure on increments of working capital.

lack $\frac{X}{P}$, but it has in fact consumed $\frac{M_a - X}{P_1}$ or $\frac{M_a - X}{P} \cdot \frac{M}{M - X}$, *i.e.* it has experienced Automatic Splashing $\frac{M_a - X}{P}\left(\frac{M}{M - X} - 1\right)$ or $\frac{X}{P} \cdot \frac{M_a - X}{M - X}$, and has lacked $\frac{X}{P}\left(1 - \frac{M_a - X}{M - X}\right)$ or $\frac{X}{P} \cdot \frac{M_b}{M - X}$. Entrepreneurs have experienced Automatic Splashing $\frac{X}{P} \cdot \frac{M_b}{M - X}$. Thus the whole of the Saving of the public has gone to waste in the form of increased consumption either by itself or other people.

If on day 2 entrepreneurs spend their previous day's income $M_b - X$, they are, in accordance with our definitions, neither saving nor dissaving,[1] neither hoarding nor dishoarding. If the public again saves and hoards X, we have $S_2 = M_a - X + M_b - X = M - 2X$, and the price-level continues to fall. The excess of $\frac{M_a - X}{P_2}$ over $\frac{M_a - X}{P_1}$ is consumption accruing to the public through Automatic Dislacking, the excess of $\frac{M_a - X}{P_1}$ over $\frac{M_a - X}{P}$ is consumption accruing to them through the fact that, in Professor Pigou's words, past contracts have been doctored in their favour. The former type of benefit is enjoyed in common with entrepreneurs, the latter type is enjoyed at their expense.

It will be seen that the cause and extent of the fall in the price-level on any day can be defined alternatively in terms of the Hoarding done on that day, or in terms of the excess of Saving over Investment on that day—Investment remaining zero throughout.

§ 5. What happens if the monetary authority sets out to counteract the economy campaign by a daily injection of new money of amount X into the system? The answer varies according to what supposition we make

[1] In Mr. Keynes' terminology, they are saving.

about the method of injection: to fit our simplified world in which Investment is normally nil, it will be most convenient to suppose that the new money is issued through the hands of a body of dole-drawers, whose expenditure on any day, since they are innocent of the earning of income, must be accounted Dissaving. If the injection begins on day 1, we have $S_1 = S$, $P_1 = P$, $M_{1b} = M_b$. The Hoarding of the public has been successfully offset by the creation of new money: or (if we prefer) the Saving of the public has been offset by the Dissaving of the dole-drawers. This procedure can be repeated day after day as long as the economy campaign lasts: though it is open to the *prima facie* objection that it involves a misuse of the public's savings.[1]

If the authority delays the injection of X new money till day n, it will on that day prevent the price-level falling from $P.\frac{M - (n - 1)X}{M}$ to $P.\frac{M - nX}{M}$; it will not, of course, raise it to P. In other words, it will cancel with Automatic Stinting the Automatic Dis-lacking that would otherwise have been experienced, but will not effect any re-doctoring of past contracts. If it wishes to effect the latter, it must inject more than X per day, thus inflicting Automatic Lacking on all parties.

§ 6. We may turn now to a somewhat different case, to which Mr. Keynes has invited particular attention. In this case entrepreneurs, instead of reducing their expenditure to match the reduction in their disposable income, maintain it at its old level, having put themselves in a position to do so by selling securities to the public, whose Saving takes from the start the form of purchasing these securities and not of adding to its money stock.[2] In order to analyse this case, we must approach closer to real life by supposing that Saving and

[1] We must postpone to a later stage the question whether this *prima facie* objection is always justified.

[2] The supposition that the distress sale of securities begins simultaneously with the extra Saving of the public seems to me somewhat unrealistic; nevertheless, since it is not inconsistent with our definition of a day, and since Mr. Keynes appears to attach importance to it (*E.J.*, Sept. 1931, p. 417), I have thought it best to retain it.

Investment are normally positive, part of the income received by the public on any day being used on the following day in the purchase of new instrumental goods.[1] Let T, T' and T'' be total output, output of consumption goods and output of instrumental goods respectively; P, P' and P'' their price-levels; S, S' and S'' the expenditures upon them; and R_b, R_b' and R_b'' the incomes, M_b, M_b' and M_b'' the money stocks, of the entrepreneurs who produce them.

Then on day 1, $S_1' = S' - X$, $P_1' = P'.\dfrac{S' - X}{S'}$;

$S_1'' = S''$, $P_1'' = P''$; $S_1 = S - X$, $P_1 = P.\dfrac{S - X}{S}$.

$M_{1a} = M_a$, $M_{1b}' = M_b' - X + X = M_b'$, $M_{1b}'' = M_b''$. As in the previous case, entrepreneurs neither save nor dissave, and the fall in P may be attributed to the excess of the Saving of the public ($S'' + X$) over Investment (S''). But the sale of securities by consumption entrepreneurs indicates that they realise that their income received on day 1, and at disposal on day 2, will only be $M_b - X$; their action, therefore, in insuring, by the sale of securities, that their money stock at the beginning of day 2 shall be M_b' constitutes Hoarding $\left(\text{for } \dfrac{M_b'}{M_b' - X}\right.$ is greater than $\left.\dfrac{M_b'}{M_b'}\right)$. Thus the fall in P may equally be ascribed to the Hoarding of consumption entrepreneurs. There is, I think, no paradox about this way of looking at the matter. For if consumption entrepreneurs had not sold securities, while the public had remained unwilling to let its extra Saving take the form of Hoarding, the latter would have had to devote the extra sum saved X to the purchase of new instrumental goods, thus increasing the incomes of some

[1] At the cost of further complicating our algebra, we could approach closer still to real life by assuming that part of the Saving and Investment is normally done by consumption entrepreneurs. We could also take account of the fact that if Investment is normally positive, the output of consumption goods is presumably continuously increasing and their price falling as a result of more efficient methods of production.

entrepreneurs as much as it diminishes those of others, and causing the price-level of output as a whole to remain unchanged. It is the Hoarding by consumption entrepreneurs which prevents this result from occurring.

Thanks to their Hoarding on day 1, consumption entrepreneurs are enabled on day 2 to repeat their old expenditure M_b'; in so doing they are now dissaving, since their expenditure M_b' exceeds their disposable income $M_b' - X$. But in again selling securities worth X to the public on day 2 they are no longer hoarding, since their action is not calculated to raise the proportion of money stock to disposable income above $\frac{M_b'}{M_b' - X}$, but only to keep it at that level. Hence, since there is no Hoarding, or (if we prefer) since the Dissaving of entrepreneurs cancels the Saving of the public so that total Saving $= S'' =$ Investment, there is no further movement of any of the price-levels ($S_2' = S_1' = S' - X$; $S_2'' = S''$).

§ 7. In real life there are, of course, intermediaries in the form of an organised stock market between the public and the entrepreneurs who make new instrumental goods. So also are there intermediaries in the form of merchants, etc., between the public and the entrepreneurs who make new consumption goods; and it seems reasonable in a first approximation to abstract from both. But it will perhaps be well, at the cost of temporary departure from our simplified hypothesis about the length of the day, to digress here to examine the situation which arises if the chain of intermediaries is longer in the one case than in the other. Suppose that if at the outset I am spending £10 on consumable goods on any day I hand it direct to an entrepreneur, while if I am saving—but not hoarding—£10 I hand it to a dealer in securities (C), who on the same day is handing £10 in exchange for a new issue to a company promoter or local authority (D), who on the same day is handing £10 to a purveyor of instrumental goods (E). This picture, though still, of course, highly simplified, seems to represent fairly the essential facts of a capital market in equilibrium.[1]

If now on day 1 I save more without hoarding, *i.e.* if I switch over £5 from the purchase of consumption goods to the purchase of securities, and if there are no distress sales of securities by entrepreneurs, while C and D make the same disbursements as on the previous day, the price of consumption goods falls and the price of instrumental goods fails to rise. What has happened? Either C has sold me the usual volume of securities at an enhanced price, or he has drawn upon a reserve pool of securities to meet my demands—probably the two happenings have been combined, the latter preponderating. In the former case the price of a certain service, which ought to enter into an index-number of output, has gone up.[2] In the latter case C has hoarded, for by selling for money an asset other than money he has taken steps to increase the proportion of his money stock to his disposable income.

If, by a further departure from our simplified hypothesis about the length of the day, we assume that C has a reserve of money in excess of his daily turnover, there arises the possibility that C should on day 1 preserve his pool of securities from depletion by buying more new issues from D. This action will doubtless occasion some rise in the price of a particular type of output—the services of D; but for the most part it will involve Hoarding by D, who under the impact of C's demand creates new securities, the sale of which increases the proportion of his money stock to his disposable income. Finally, if D also has a reserve of money, and concurrently with the creation and sale

[1] It involves, of course, the assumption that the average number of times which money is exchanged against output is less than once per day. The money stocks of C and D must be at least equal to their daily *turnover*, not their daily *income*.

[2] This seems to be the natural way of looking at the matter (and in consonance with British income-tax practice), so long as the rise in price is confined to the batch of securities which I buy from C. But if we must assume that through the sympathy of an organised market it is instantaneously transmitted to the securities which C buys, so that for his usual expenditure he can buy fewer of them, then in this case, as in the other, he must be regarded as hoarding. For he has substituted a certain amount of money for a certain volume of securities among his assets, and raised the proportion of his money stock to his money income.

of new securities increases his expenditure on E's products by a like amount, there is no Hoarding at all, and no fall at all in the price of output as a whole.

Thus in all cases such fall in the price of total output as occurs is seen to be attributable to Hoarding by *someone*—either the public, or the entrepreneurs of consumable goods, or the dealers in securities, or those who handle the proceeds of new issues.[1]

§ 8. What happens if, in the case set out in § 6, the monetary authority undertakes counter-action along the lines explained in § 5, *i.e.* by injecting new money X through the hands of a body of dole-drawers? If it takes immediate action, we have $S_1' = S'$, $S_1'' = S''$, and the price-levels do not move; $M_{1b}' = M_b' + X$. What happens on day 2? If entrepreneurs have reason to expect a repetition both of the economy campaign and of the counter-action—*i.e.* if, not distinguishing between a dole-drawer and a member of the public, they expect to receive the same income on day 2 as on day 1 and day 0—they have no need to sell securities in order to maintain their expenditure at M_b'. Hence, if appropriate arrangements can be made, the extra savings of the public become available for financing the counter-action of the authority. If consumption entrepreneurs neither save nor dissave, *i.e.* if they spend on consumption their disposable (which is also their anticipated) income M_b', we shall have $S_2' = S'$, $S_2'' = S''$, and again no movement in the price-levels. This situation can be repeated day after day: though it is open to the *prima facie* objection that it involves a misuse of the public's savings and presumably a burden on the public finances for interest payments.[2]

It does not seem, however, that we can assume that consumption entrepreneurs will acquiesce permanently in their money stock bearing an enhanced proportion to their disposable income.[3] For their object in taking

[1] Hoarding by this last class seems to have assumed great prominence during the later phases of the great American "boom" which broke in 1929.

[2] See p. 70, *n.* 1.

[3] It is to Mr. Maurice Allen of Balliol College that I am indebted for recognition of this point and its consequences.

steps to increase that proportion on day 1 was to put them in a position to maintain their old expenditure M_b'. The authority's action having removed the difficulty in the way of their doing this, it seems natural to suppose that on some day *n* (which may even be day 2) they will either (i) dishoard and dissave, thus raising S_n' to $S' + X$ and P_n' to $\frac{S' + X}{S'}.P'$; or (ii) dishoard without dissaving, thus swinging a sum X into the capital market and raising S_n'' to $S'' + X$ and P_n'' to $\frac{S'' + X}{S''}.P''$.[1]

If it wishes to avert this situation, the authority must not only refrain from creating additional money on every day except day 1, but must be ready to destroy on day *n* the money created on day 1—presumably in case (i) by intercepting and destroying the extra money saved by the public instead of arranging for its expenditure through the hands of dole-drawers, and in case (ii) by selling securities out of a reserve pool to consumption entrepreneurs. We shall then have $S_n' = S'$, $S_n'' = S''$, $M_{nb}' = M_b'$, and full equilibrium for the moment restored. On the following day, if the economy campaign continues, the creation of new money is again called for. Thus the neutralisation by such means of a perfectly steady economy campaign *of the character now under discussion* would seem to call for a great flexibility of monetary policy between the three courses of money-creation, money-canalisation and money-destruction.

§ 9. What happens if the authority, being concerned to maintain the stability not of P' but of P, counteracts on day 1 not in the way hitherto supposed, but by increasing Investment? In this case we get $S_1' = S' - X$, $P_1' = \frac{S' - X}{S'}.P'$; $S_1'' = S'' + X$, $P_1'' = \frac{S'' + X}{S''}.P''$, $M_{1b}' = M_b' - X$, $M_{1b}'' = M_b'' + X$. What happens on day 2 depends on the action of instrumental entre-

[1] Alternatively, the authority may divert this X into additional expenditure by dole-drawers, with results on S_n' and P_n' similar to those reached under (i).

preneurs, which cannot be predicted from our data: but *unless they are smitten with a desire to hoard*, they will disburse the accession X to their disposable income either (i) on consumption goods or (ii) in the capital market.

(i) In this case we get $S_2' = S'$, $P_2' = P'$. Consumption entrepreneurs can count on an income M_b' and therefore have no motive to sell securities: the savings of the public thus become available for maintaining S_2'' at $S'' + X$ and P_2'' at $\frac{S'' + X}{S''} \cdot P$, thus raising P_2 to $\frac{S + X}{S} . P$. If the authority wishes to avert this, it can do so only by destroying money, *e.g.* by selling to the public securities worth X out of a pool.[1] The events of days 1 and 2 can then repeat themselves in an endless cycle.

(ii) in this case we get $S_2' = S' - X$, $P_2' = \frac{S' - X}{S'} . P$. Consumption entrepreneurs are constrained to repeat their sales of securities to the public,[2] absorbing its extra savings. $S_2'' = S'' + X$—the X coming in this case from the instrumental entrepreneurs themselves—and $P_2'' = \frac{S'' + X}{S''} . P''$. To preserve the stability of P the authority need not reverse, but must not repeat, its counter-action. This situation can repeat itself day after day.

The slight difference between the results of case (i)

[1] The action of instrumental entrepreneurs in spending their disposable income $M_b'' + X$ constitutes neither Saving nor Dissaving, neither Hoarding nor Dishoarding. The action of consumption entrepreneurs in spending M_b', while their disposable income is $M_b' - X$, constitutes Dissaving and also Dishoarding (since its effect is to decrease their proportion of money stock to disposable income from $\frac{M_b'}{M_b' - X}$ to $\frac{M_b'}{M_b'}$). The public's extra Saving, unless absorbed by the authority, equals its extra Investment. Thus unless the authority deflates, there is an excess of Investment over Saving, or (in the alternative language) an uncompensated act of Dishoarding.

[2] Thus dissaving, but neither hoarding nor dishoarding (see § 6, *sub fin.*). Their Dissaving cancels the extra Saving of the public, while the extra Saving and Investment by instrumental entrepreneurs equal one another.

and case (ii) turns upon the fact that in the latter the motive of consumption entrepreneurs for keeping an enhanced proportion of money stock to disposable income remains throughout unimpaired, while in the former it does not. In this respect the case discussed in § 8 resembles case (i). But in all cases it will be seen that if secondary Hoarding of this type is the only kind of Hoarding at work, the total net counter-creation of money required, even in the face of a long-drawn-out economy campaign, is at most very small. To represent such distress sales of securities as a major cause of disturbance and of the need for counter-creation of money seems to be misleading. Their effect in this direction is negligible compared with that of primary Hoarding by entrepreneurs or public, *i.e.* a refusal to spend disposable income *either* on consumption goods *or* on instrumental goods or securities.

§ 10. In real life, the length of the average period of circulation of money against output is considerably greater than that which we can, with any show of plausibility, attribute to the "day" as defined in § 1. If we conceive of this period as consisting of K days, and define T as the output not during a day but during a circulation period, we can rewrite the equations of the second paragraph of § 4 as follows:—$S = R = \frac{T}{K} \cdot P$, $S_a = R_a$, $S_b = R_b$, $M_a = KR_a$, $M_b = KR_b$.[1]

For the sake of variety we may analyse the consequences of this complication in connection not (as would be easy) with an "economy campaign," but with the issue of new money by the banking system to draw a new batch of workpeople into employment and build up a new increment of working capital—that is, of goods in process of production. The new money may most conveniently be regarded as being spent on consumption goods, by the new workpeople, on the day of its crea-

[1] Assuming K to be the same for both classes of the community. The method can be extended to the case (presumably actual) in which

$$\frac{M}{K} = \frac{M_a}{K_a} + \frac{M_b}{K_b}.$$

tion, their own output not being of a type which is available for consumption and not entering, therefore, into the stream designated by T. If the banking system creates in this way $\frac{X}{K}$ units of money per day, we have, therefore, $S_1 = \frac{M+X}{K}$, $P_1 = \frac{M+X}{T} = \frac{M+X}{M}.P$; $R_{1a} = \frac{M_a}{K}$, $R_{1b} = \frac{M_b+X}{K}$; $M_{1a} = M_a$, $M_{1b} = M_b + \frac{X}{K}$. In contrast, therefore, to the case analysed in § 4, entrepreneurs' money stock, instead of continuing to bear the old proportion to their disposable income, has come to fall short of K times that income by an amount $\frac{X}{K}(K-1)$. There is, therefore, some *prima facie* case for supposing that they will perform Hoarding and Lacking with a view to restoring the proportion to its old level; and there is a certain simplicity, if no more, in supposing that they will aim at spreading this process over the remaining $(K - 1)$ days of the circulation period, thus saving $\frac{X}{K}$ per day, *i.e.* spending $\frac{M_b}{K}$ per day instead of their disposable income $\frac{M_b+X}{K}$. Thus on any nth day, where n is less than K, we get $S_n = \frac{M+X}{K} = S_1$, $P_n = P_1$. At the end of K days in all, $M_{Kb} = M_b + X = KR_{Kb}$, and the motive for further Hoarding disappears. Thus $S_{K+1} = \frac{M+2X}{K}$, $P_{K+1} = \frac{M+2X}{M}.P$, and the process begins anew.

In the "standard" case here analysed, the effect of this complication may be expressed by saying that the creation of new money tends to raise the average velocity of circulation of all money, this tendency being counteracted on days 2 to K of each circulation period by the Hoarding of entrepreneurs. Or, again, it may be expressed by saying that each piece of new money exercises an influence on the price-level on the day of its birth, and thereafter recurrently at the end of each K days.[1]

It is convenient to have a separate pigeon-hole in the mind for Saving which, while perfectly voluntary, is undertaken not, as it were, out of the blue, but in order to restore a proportion of money stock to disposable income which has been disturbed by an alteration in the rate of expenditure by other people (including the monetary authority). Such Saving (which is, of course, also Hoarding) and the Lacking which it entails may be called Induced, to distinguish them both from the spontaneous Saving and Lacking which are performed without any such provocation, and from the Automatic Lacking which is performed involuntarily. While there is no particular reason to think that the "standard" case analysed above is more likely than any other, there does seem to be reason to think that Induced Saving and Dissaving are often of importance in retarding the movements of prices and incomes generated by autonomous variations in the supply of money, or in its velocity of circulation against output.

§ 11. Definitions are, of course, a matter of taste and convenience, and must be judged by their fruits; but at the risk of seeming to indulge in barren controversy I may perhaps be excused for saying a little in defence of the apparatus here employed. The definition of Saving corresponds, I think, much more closely to the usage of ordinary life and is much less likely to cause confusion than the paradoxical definition employed by Mr. Keynes, according to which entrepreneurs are Saving if they contract their consumption to match a contraction in the income which they have received, and Dissaving if they expand their consumption to match an expansion in the income which they have received. Nor is it touched by the argument which Mr. Keynes[2] and Mr. Kahn have advanced in support of their terminology, namely that with a "simple-minded"[3]

[1] Cf. Pigou, *Theory of Unemployment*, p. 200.
[2] *E.J.*, 1931, p. 422. [3] The word is Mr. Kahn's, *E.J.*, 1932, p. 492.

definition of Saving, Saving and Investment are necessarily equal. For, so runs the argument, the former is (to the simple-minded) the excess of total income over income spent on consumption goods, while the latter is the excess of total income over income received from the sale of consumption goods. Now the money spent on consumption goods must necessarily equal the money received from their sale; hence the excess of total income over the one must necessarily equal the excess of total income over the other. But it is clear that this disconcerting result only follows if we insist on identifying the income received in any small slice of time with the income whose expenditure (*plus* or *minus* certain other items) generates the income received in this small slice of time, thus averting our eyes from what common sense proclaims (even to the simple-minded) to be the essence of the whole matter; namely the power possessed by the public and by the monetary authority to alter the rates of income flow—the former by putting money into and out of store, the latter by putting it into and out of existence. On my definition, Saving and Investment are *not* necessarily equal, and it is on the difference between them that the *movement* of the price level (not, as in Mr. Keynes' scheme, the *state* of the price-level as compared with some normal state) depends.

§ 12. It is, I think, a defect of Mr. Keynes' scheme that it fuses together two distinct types of burden inflicted on the public by an inflation of bank credit in the interests of capital-formation. These are, on the one hand, the Automatic Lacking imposed through the expenditure of newly created money by new work-people, etc., brought into employment to build up additional working capital; on the other, the diminution of consumption which results from the distortion of contracts occasioned by a rise in prices which has already occurred—a diminution which renders possible increased Saving and Investment by the entrepreneurs in whose favour contracts have been distorted. The former burden stops when the inflation stops: the latter does not. The former would be a feature of inflation in a community which consisted entirely of small independent farmers, craftsmen and dealers: the latter would not.

Professor Hayek's very interesting historical study [1] confirms me in the impression that it is the former type of burden which has been principally in the minds of most of those writers who have called attention, under one name or another, to the phenomenon of "Forced Frugality." "The additional banknotes," writes Mill, "are, in the ordinary course, first issued to producers or dealers; and though the stock of commodities in the country is no greater than before, yet a greater share of that stock now comes by purchase into the hands of producers and dealers." "L'émission de billets de banque pour une certaine somme," says Walras, "amène, pendant toute la période d'émission, une hausse du prix des produits consistant en revenus consumables et capitaux neufs qui se mesure approximativement par le rapport du montant de l'émission au montant du revenu social antérieur. Ce phénomène est transitoire: une fois l'émission terminée, la hausse en question disparait." Wicksell, in Professor Hayek's words,[2] taught that "the rise in the price-level... is in the first instance brought about by the entrepreneurs spending on production the increased amount of money lent by the banks. This process... involves what Wicksell now for the first time called enforced or compulsory saving."

Bentham's exposition is somewhat confused: for while it is only the *first spending* of the new money which is regarded as contributing to the formation of new capital, attention is also drawn to the *continuing* burden suffered by "fixed incomists" as a result of the rise in prices.[3] In Professor Hayek's own treatment both elements seem to be present, but not very clearly distinguished: thus, while it is the newly created money which is

[1] *Q.J.E.*, Nov. 1932, pp. 123 ff.—from which the following quotations are reproduced.

[2] *Prices and Production*, p. 21. [3] Hayek, *Q.J.E.*, *loc. cit.*, p. 125.

pictured as inaugurating the régime of "forced saving," it is on the encroachment of wages on re-investable profits that chief emphasis is laid as the factor which brings it to an end.[1] In Professor Mises' analysis the two elements are, I think, distinguished, but the term "erzwungenes Sparen" is confined, rather unexpectedly, to the second: the thing so named consists entirely of money saved and invested by entrepreneurs as a result of the expansion of their incomes, and is conceived of (also rather unexpectedly) as contributing, so far as it goes, to a fall in the "natural" rate of interest.[2] Until there is a greater measure of agreement as to what "Forced Saving" really consists in, I do not feel able to abandon my own inelegant terminology!

The relevance of these distinctions to the analysis of the trade cycle will appear, I hope, in the sequel. But it may be suggested at once that a rise in the rate of interest which renders unprofitable those extensions of capital equipment which have been paid for out of bank loans falling due for renewal,[3] will not necessarily have that effect on those extensions which have been paid for out of windfall profits.

[1] *Prices and Production*, esp. pp. 52-3. Cf. Haberler in *Gold and Monetary Stabilisation*, pp. 64-5.

[2] *Geldwertstabilisierung und Konjunkturpolitik*, pp. 45, 49.

[3] *Prices and Production*, p. 55, top.

V

INDUSTRIAL FLUCTUATION AND THE NATURAL RATE OF INTEREST[1]

"This must be the wood," she said thoughtfully to herself, "where things have no names. I wonder what'll become of *my* name when I go in? I shouldn't like to lose it at all, because they'd have to give me another, and it would be almost certain to be an ugly one. But then the fun would be, trying to find the creature that had got my old name!"—*Through the Looking-Glass.*

§ 1. THE following paragraphs are an attempt to bring together (1) the concept of Saving developed in my article in the *Economic Journal*, Sept. 1933, and (2) the attempts which have been made to analyse cyclical fluctuation in terms of a divergence between the "natural" and the "market" rates of interest.

As regards (1) I am not insensible to the force of the objections which have been made on the score of the vagueness of the length of the necessary minimum period of lag ("day") assumed. It is possible that there is greater justification than I have been ready to suppose for Professor Pigou's method of treating the period of lag as identical with K (the pre-existing circulation-period of money against real income), or at all events for treating it as having a fairly considerable minimum possible value dependent on the complexity of modern processes of production and sale. In any case *some* conception of a lag still seems to me necessary to protect us against the peril of confounding causes with results, and *processes* of change with *states* of abnormality.

As regards (2) I have not the knowledge of continental literature required for a critical and historical

[1] *E.J.*, Dec. 1934.

discussion of the concepts in question. A few introductory remarks must suffice. (i) Evidently neither of the rates concerned is a single one, but rather a family of rates for loans and investments of different kinds. In order to keep the schematic treatment which follows reasonably simple, we shall be obliged to concentrate on some central or representative rate in each case, ignoring the important complications which arise from the relative movements of rates for loans of different lengths and with different quantities of gilt on their edges. (ii) In some connections it is important to distinguish between rates charged by banks and "market" rates charged by outside lenders. Again, however, for our broad purposes it must suffice to deal in terms of a single "actual" rate, whose behaviour at any moment is to be pictured as dominated by the action of the banks. (iii) There are difficulties and disagreements about the exact meaning of equilibrium, and consequently of the "natural" rate which will preserve it in a progressive community.[1] They will be passed over here, with a view to concentrating on the much greater difficulties which attach to an attempt to give a meaning to the "natural" rate *when once equilibrium has been departed from*. It may be said, however, that the idea of equilibrium here adopted implies a state of affairs in which (1) wages and profits are at a "normal" level, (2) capital is growing, but (3) since the society has already become a prey to fluctuation, employment of the factors of production is not full but at a level which is in some sense the mean between those attained in boom and in depression. Under some conditions equilibrium will involve stability of the general level of commodity prices; under others, perhaps more probable, a progressive fall. Again, under some conditions it will involve constancy of the supply of money, under others (*e.g.* a growing population) a creation of some additional money in each unit of time. To avoid complicating the wording

[1] See my note in *Economica*, Nov. 1934.

of the following sections, in which attention is directed to the differences between equilibrium and other states, I shall write as though equilibrium implied constancy in the supply of money, leaving the necessary verbal amendments, for the cases in which it does not, to be made by the reader for himself.

§ 2. Starting with equilibrium in this sense, we have a curve DD' representing the declining marginal productivity of new lendings in industrial uses, in other words representing the rate per atom of time at which industry could employ new lendings at various rates of interest. And we have a curve SS' representing the rate of new available savings per atom of time—available, that is, after deducting new savings absorbed in financing consumption by governments or individuals. It would be misleading to say that the rate of interest "depends on" the intersection of these two curves, since there would be a rate of interest in a society in which no new capital was being formed, indeed even in a society in which capital was not productive and all borrowing was for consumption: nevertheless, in equilibrium the rate of interest PM is the rate at which the new lendings which can be absorbed by industry per atom of time and the new available savings per atom of time are equal. At this rate (*i.e.* at one of the family of rates typified by PM) the banks are continually renewing loans.

Now, owing to the discovery of the Diesel engine, South America, or what not, an industrial expansion sets in, and DD' is raised D_1D_1'. If the banks keep the rate of interest right down at PM ($= P_1M_1$), the initial rate of *lendings* per atom of time will exceed the rate of available new *savings*, and the whole of the excess MM_1 per atom of time will consist of newly created bank-money. If, however, the banks allow the rate of interest to rise somewhat, there is a complication in that the higher rate will stimulate the mobilisation of *past* savings existing in the form of bank deposits, and part of the excess of new lendings over available new savings will consist of these reservists. But there is a more important complication—the outpouring of MM_1 new or mobilised money per atom of time will progressively both increase total incomes and redistribute them in favour of entrepreneurs, *i.e.* in a manner on balance favourable to saving, so that SS' becomes displaced to the right (S_1S_1'). There is now a *quasi-natural* rate of interest P_2M_2 which would

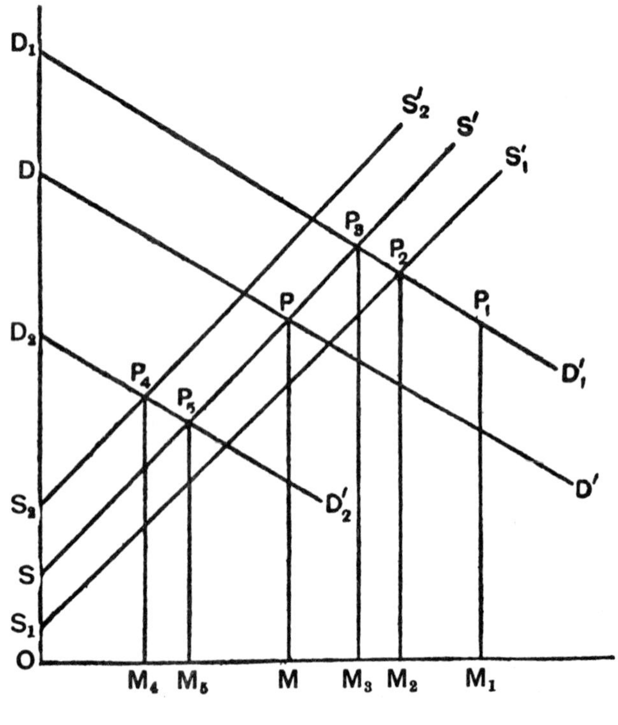

equate industrial requirements and available new savings under the new conditions, towards which the actual rate is likely to rise, and which if it is reached will give *quasi-equilibrium*, with no *further* money-creation or mobilisation of past savings.

§ 3. But this quasi-equilibrium is very unstable, for two reasons. (1) Wages, etc., are clambering up and eating into profits, thus causing S_1S_1' to relapse towards

SS', raising the quasi-natural rate, with the actual rate in pursuit, towards P_3M_3, and reducing borrowings towards OM_3. This, of course, shows itself primarily in a recession of the demand for instrumental goods, and is the feature of the "crisis" emphasised—in various terminologies—by Continental theorists. Work on the new Cunarder will be suspended.[1]

(2) But a more fundamental change is imminent. Owing to saturation with *existing* instruments, whose marginal productivity has fallen very low, the curve of marginal productivity of *new* lendings will be violently displaced downwards—say to D_2D_2'. This in turn involves the shrinkage of income and its redistribution in favour of non-savers, as well as some distress-borrowing by unemployed persons and loss-making entrepreneurs, so that the new quasi-natural rate will be P_4M_4—not P_5M_5. So long as the actual rate is kept above this there will be an excess in the rate of available savings per atom of time over the rate of industrial borrowings, showing itself in a progressive extinction of bank loans and a progressive immobilisation of savings in the form of bank deposits.

As I have argued elsewhere,[2] there is no necessary incompatibility between these two explanations of the "crisis." The first may be the actual spear-head of relapse, the second in practice coming up as a reinforcement, though it would have been capable of winning the battle by itself. The Cunarder suspended on the plea of high interest-rates remains suspended, with bank-rate at 2 per cent., because there are too many ships. The relative importance of the two causes (both of them describable as "over-investment") may vary on different occasions: it might be, for instance, that (1)

[1] The "Austrian school" seems to me to exaggerate the embarrassment which the raising of *current* interest-rates will cause to those who have taken in hand extensions financed out of windfall profits, or out of long loans raised at the lower rates: also to exaggerate the speed at which saving can be disentangled from fixed instruments, and therefore the danger that the boom-expansions of fixed capital will be lost—the railways built in the 'forties are still with us!

[2] *A Study of Industrial Fluctuation*, p. 241; *Banking Policy and the Price Level*, p. 90.

furnishes an almost completely satisfactory explanation of the sharp short set-back of 1907, while going a very little way towards explaining the conditions of 1929.

§ 4. If the rate of interest is reduced to P_4M_4, at which the rate of available new savings equals the rate of industrial requirements, the position of quasi-equilibrium so attained may be considerably more stable than its boom-counterpart P_2M_2. For (i) owing to the durability of fixed instruments, D_2D_2' is not likely to be jerked upwards as D_1D_1' was jerked downwards: (ii) owing to the greater resistance of wages, etc., against a fall than against a rise, S_2S_2' does not so easily relapse towards SS' as did S_1S_1'. Thus we "bump along the bottom."

If now the banking system, to promote recovery, contrives a lowering of the actual rate, say to P_5M_5, how are we (*a*) to describe, (*b*) to appraise its action? (*a*) It must, I think, be described as a lowering of the actual rate below the nearest thing to a natural rate which now exists, *viz.* the quasi-natural rate P_4M_4—involving, as it does, an initial rate of money-creation M_4M_5 per atom of time.[1] To call P_5M_5 a natural rate would be to assume that the expansion and redistribution of income which the lowering of the rate will admittedly promote will bring the savings curve right back to its "normal" position SS'—a thing which, with D_2D_2' at its existing height, is beyond the bounds of possibility.

But (*b*) it does not follow that the lowering of the rate is wrong policy. It produces *some* displacement of S_2S_2' to the right, and creates conditions favourable for an eventual rise of D_2D_2', while in the existing condition of the latter it can scarcely be considered dangerous. The objection[2] that when "normal" conditions are restored the natural and actual rates will be PM, and enterprises which have been initiated at the rate P_5M_5

[1] A greater rate of money-creation than this will be required if the method adopted is such as to promote the immobilisation in the form of bank deposits either of new savings or of past savings previously embodied in other kinds of capital asset.

[2] For an able statement of this objection, see *Economist*, March 17, 1934, p. 563.

will be in difficulties, is not convincing. For (i) it applies in some degree to all rates lower than PM, including the quasi-natural rate P_4M_4; but to resuscitate on these grounds the ex-natural rate PM would be to promote not merely a continuance of stagnation but a renewal of money-contraction and hoarding. And (ii) it seems reasonable to hope that the same forces which will eventually raise D_2D_2' to DD' will increase the profitability of enterprises which have been initiated at the rate P_5M_5 and enable them to pay the higher rate PM.

At the same time, fears that the new position of normality may be passed unawares must not be dismissed as baseless. For it would be an abuse of the method of abstraction to suppose that it will in all respects resemble the old, especially as regards the level of commodity-prices. In particular if, in a society which has already become a prey to fluctuation, full employment of the factors of production, in their existing distribution between consumption and construction trades, is taken as the objective of policy, there seems a virtual certainty that normality will be overstepped, and the ball of cyclical fluctuation set rolling again.[1] This *may* be a lesser evil than the continuance of present unemployment and the retardation of progress; but it is not a good.

§ 5. It remains to enquire briefly what the relation is between the doctrine that fluctuation is to be explained in terms of a gap between the *natural* rate of interest and the *actual* rate, and the doctrine that it is to be explained in terms of a gap between the *real* rate of interest and the *money* rate. The answer is, of course, to be sought in the fact that the so-called "real" rate is not really a rate of interest at all,[2] but a hypothetical charge which takes into account changes in the real

[1] See the stimulating discussion by Mr. Durbin, *Purchasing Power and Trade Depression*, pp. 167-72.

[2] See Adarkar, "Fisher's Real Rate Doctrine," *E.J.*, March 1934. The whole of this section is simply an attempt to bring Professor Adarkar's illuminating discussion into connection with the concept of the natural rate. It is assumed for the sake of simplicity of language that the situation is one in which equilibrium involves a stable price-level.

value of the money principal borrowed. The "capital windfall" transferred by a rise in the price-level to the borrowing entrepreneur from the lender is simply another aspect of the real or income windfall accruing to him at the expense of the other factors of production. It may appear at first sight, therefore, that to prevent trouble we ought to have raised the money rate just enough to obliterate the entrepreneur's "capital windfall," thus confiscating his real or income windfall and robbing him of the means and motive for misbehaviour. But to argue thus is to ignore that the rate of price-rise is itself the result of a given gap between the actual money rate of interest and the natural (real and money) rate. Any raising of the money rate will diminish the rate of price-rise and so narrow the gap between the money rate and the real rate. Let us, for instance, start in equilibrium and imagine a rise of DD'. It may be that if the rate is held at 5 per cent., a price-rise of 10 per cent. will develop in a year, so that the real rate turns out to be — $5\frac{1}{2}$ per cent., and it appears in retrospect that it would have taken a rise in the money rate to $15\frac{1}{2}$ per cent. to obliterate the windfall. But it may be that if the money rate had been raised immediately to 7 per cent., there would have been no price-rise and no windfall at all, *i.e.* that the new natural rate was 7 per cent. And it may be that now, prices having risen by 10 per cent. with a consequent expansion and redistribution of incomes, a rise in the money rate to 6 per cent. will be sufficient to prevent any *further* rise in prices, *i.e.* that the new quasi-natural rate is 6 per cent. On the other hand, it *might* be that it would have required a raising of the rate to 20 per cent. to prevent any rise in prices; and in this case to have raised it to $15\frac{1}{2}$ per cent., while it would have reduced the price-rise from 10 per cent. to (say) 3 per cent., would still have permitted the emergence of windfall gains to the entrepreneur.[1] Thus the "real rate"

[1] Professor Adarkar (*op. cit.*, p. 341) appears implicitly to rule out this contingency; but it seems a real if improbable one.

doctrine turns out to be less instructive as a guide to policy than it appears to be at first sight.

§ 6. The foregoing picture is, of course, over-simplified in a dozen ways.[1] It will not commend itself to those who regard the cause of relapse as purely monetary, nor to those who find the notion of a lag, and therefore of a possible divergence between the rate of industrial borrowings and the rate of available new savings per atom of time, superfluous and indeed misleading. But I venture to hope that there are some who will find in it a contribution towards clarifying the relation between diverse doctrines of the causes of industrial relapse, and between conflicting views of the duty of the banking system in time of depression (I have designedly avoided discussion of the duty of the consuming public, the Trade Unions and the Government).

[1] Among other things, as Mr. J. E. Meade has pointed out to me, it ignores such secondary displacements of *DD'* as may be due to the change in aggregate incomes induced by a divergence between actual and quasi-natural rates.

VI

A NOTE ON THE THEORY OF MONEY[1]

§ 1. In the course of his discussion of the "Cambridge" method of approach to the theory of the value of money (*Treatise on Money*, I, pp. 229-39), Mr. Keynes makes two propositions which may be paraphrased as follows: (1) It is not useful to bring the volume of real income or output R and its price-level P into relation with the total stock of money M by means of a factor K, denoting the proportion of R over which people wish to keep command in monetary form. It is only useful so to bring them into relation with that part of the money stock which is held for the purpose of facilitating the disbursement of *income*; for the remainder of the money stock is held for business and investment purposes not directly connected with the level of output, and is used to purchase things whose price-level may behave very differently from that of output. (2) The price-level proper to equations of the "Cambridge" type is a price-level in which the various items are weighted according to their relative importance in respect of the money balances which they cause to be held, and not (as in equations of the Fisher type, using the concept of velocity of circulation) according to their relative importance in respect of the transactions per unit of time to which they give rise.

I venture to suggest that neither of these propositions is well founded.

§ 2. (1) It is of course true (as is recognised in Marshall's own illustration of the "Cambridge" theory) that many people will have other quantities than their income in mind (for instance, their capital or their

[1] *Economica*, Aug. 1933.

business turnover) in deciding upon their monetary requirements. But from the fact that their money stock is not exclusively *determined* as a proportion of their income, it does not follow that it cannot usefully be *expressed* as such a proportion; still less that the real value of the whole community's total money stock cannot usefully be expressed (as in the equation $\frac{M}{P} = KR$) in terms of the constituents of real income or output. For the whole of M is *potentially* expendable against output, and if in any period of time more or less of it were to be so expended than was previously the case, P would alter. It is of the utmost importance that under certain conditions money which has been imprisoned in what Mr. Keynes calls the "savings deposits" and "business deposits" may seep out, raise the aggregate of incomes and "income deposits," and drive up P. Such a change is represented in the "Cambridge" approach by a diminution of K: it would not be represented by any change in a symbol which stood for the proportion borne to R by the real value of "income deposits" alone. Mr. Keynes' charge that "the equation entirely obscures disturbances ... arising out of a change in the proportion in which deposits are held for the different purposes distinguished above as Savings, Business or Income" seems to me exactly the reverse of the truth.

To give an example: If business becomes more closely integrated[1] than before, a certain amount of money which has been held for the purpose of making payments between firms will become redundant, and will (under normal conditions of trade) presumably be spent or invested in ways which will increase the aggregate of incomes and raise the price-level of output. There has been no change in the general velocity of circulation of money, or, in other words, in the proportion of

[1] In view of the attention attracted by Dr. Hayek's analysis, which tends to a confusion of the two things, it may be as well to state that there is no necessary connection between a change in the degree to which business is integrated, and a change in the degree to which it uses "capitalistic" or "roundabout" methods of production.

annual transactions which people wish to have enough money on hand to conduct; for the volume of transactions has diminished *pari passu* with the volume of business deposits. But there has been an increase in the velocity of circulation of money *against output*, in other words a decline in the proportion of annual output which people wish to have enough money on hand to purchase. The initiating change has been a change in business practice, not in habits regarding the disbursement of income; but that does not mean that there is no connection between it and the behaviour of the price-level of output. The "Cambridge equation" seems to me well designed to bring out this connection—and to suggest that a change of this kind calls *prima facie* for compensatory action on the part of the monetary authority.

§ 3. (2) Mr. Keynes' second proposition is concerned not with the *type of transaction-flow* which can properly be brought into relation with the stock of money, but with the *type of index number* which can properly be brought into relation with the stock of money and the flow of money respectively. We can therefore legitimately examine it by means of a simplified case in which the flow of transactions is identical with the flow of real income or output.

Let the annual output be 200 units of wheat and 200 units of cloth. A unit of each commodity is the amount which is sold for £1 in the base period. Let people desire to keep enough money on hand to purchase a year's output of wheat and six months' output of cloth. Then the money stock is £300, of which £200 is "held against" wheat and £100 is "held against" cloth. The Fisher equation ($MV = RP$) is $300 . \frac{4}{3} = 400 . 1$, and its Marshall counterpart ($M = KRP$) is $300 = \frac{3}{4} . 400 . 1$. The community's "real balances" KR are the equivalent of nine months' output.

Now, for some extraneous reason, let the price of wheat double, the monetary authority obligingly providing the community[1] with so much extra money as is needed to enable it to increase the money "held against" wheat in proportion, *i.e.* raising the money stock from £300 to £500. The price of cloth remains unaltered. If we weight our index number in the ordinary way, namely according to the relative magnitude of transactions in the two commodities in the base period, we shall weight them both equally, and the new price-level is $\frac{3}{2}$. The Fisher equation becomes $500 . \frac{6}{5} = 400 . \frac{3}{2}$, and its Marshall counterpart becomes $500 = \frac{5}{6} . 400 . \frac{3}{2}$.

What has happened? The average velocity of circulation of money has by common consent been reduced, because the new money is being devoted to a use in which money is relatively sluggish. But it is simply stating the same fact in other words to say that the proportion of annual output which people wish to have enough money on hand to purchase is correspondingly increased, or that the community's "real balances" (*KR*) have become the equivalent of ten months' output instead of nine. Our index number is perfectly designed to reveal this state of affairs.

According to Mr. Keynes we ought, for the purposes of the Marshall equation, to weight wheat twice as heavily as cloth in our index number, because in the base period it occasioned twice as big a holding of money balances. If we do this, the price-level will become $\frac{5}{3}$ instead of $\frac{3}{2}$, the Marshall equation will be $500 = \frac{3}{4} . 400 . \frac{5}{3}$, and the community's real balances will be unchanged, though its money balances would now buy ten months' output instead of nine. Here, surely,

[1] This seems to be the procedure visualised by Mr. Keynes. "A rise or fall in the price of certain articles causes a greater fluctuation in the amount of the cash-balances of the community than a similar movement in the price of other articles which give rise to an equal volume of cash-transactions" (*op. cit.*, pp. 77-8).

is a great and unhelpful paradox! I cannot resist the conclusion that Mr. Keynes' "cash-balances standard" is an unnecessary and confusing complication.

§ 4. Before, however, finally dismissing it as such, we must have regard to one use which Mr. Keynes makes of the distinction which he draws between it and the "cash-transactions standard," weighted in the ordinary way. There is, as he points out (*op. cit.*, pp. 237-9), an interval between the date at which a given price is quoted in the market and the date at which the transaction based on this quotation is actually performed. Since people's monetary requirements depend on the transactions to be performed in the quite near future, there is also an interval, but not such a long one, between the date at which a price is quoted and the date at which it affects monetary requirements. For instance, price quotations made in March may affect monetary requirements in June and monetary transactions in September; while in the last-named month monetary requirements are being influenced by price quotations made in June, which will influence monetary transactions in December. Hence, if prices are continually rising, the price-level which is relevant to the monetary requirements of September (*viz.* the price-level quoted in June) will be higher than the price-level relevant to the monetary transactions of September (*viz.* the price-level quoted in March). This is perfectly true: but it does not mean that we need to use an index number weighted on any other than the ordinary plan. It only means that if the P of our equations is derived from price *quotations*, we must be careful to bring it into relation with other quantities which are relevant to it, and not with other quantities which are not. As regards the Fisher equation, the best way seems to me to be to introduce the concept of "latent money"—money which does not exist but is affecting the quoted price-level as if it did exist—the equation referring to a period six months (in the case supposed) later than the date of the price quotation. As regards the Marshall equation, it seems simpler to bring P into relation with the *con-*

temporary stock of money only, the proportion of annual output (or other flow) over which people wish to keep present command in the form of money being reduced by the fact that they have a confident expectation of being able to get hold of more money by the time they require it. It is of great importance that the result of the intrusion of latent money (as of the increase of any other substitute for real money, such as barter or book-credit) is to destroy the identity which normally exists between a Marshall fraction of the K type and the inverse of the analogous velocity of circulation, causing the former to sink below the latter. But there is no need for, or help in, a specially constructed index number to show that this is so.

A numerical example may help to make the matter plain.[1] For simplicity the volume of transactions is taken as constant at 100 (in fact, of course, in such a period, it is likely to increase somewhat).

	Quoted price-level (previously 10)	Money Stock.	Value of Transactions	Recorded Velocity of Circulation	Marshall Fraction
March	10	100	1,000	10	$\frac{1}{10}$
June	15	100	1,000	10	$\frac{1}{15}$
September .	20	150	1,000	$\frac{20}{3}$	$\frac{3}{40}$
December . .	25	200	1,500	$\frac{15}{2}$	$\frac{2}{25}$
March	30	250	2,000	8	$\frac{1}{12}$

Equations relevant to June price-level and money stock (December transactions). M' = latent money.

$$(M + M')V = TP.$$

$$(100 + 100)\frac{15}{2} = 100 . 15.$$

$$M = KTP.$$

$$100 = \frac{1}{15} . 100 . 15.$$

[1] It is assumed (following Mr. Keynes) that the monetary authority is completely complaisant in conforming to and implementing the price-decisions made in the market.

VII

THE FUTURE OF TRADE CYCLE THEORY[1]

PARTLY no doubt as a result of the "world crisis" the last few years have seen a remarkable outburst of analytical and speculative discussion, by writers of first-rate reputation, of the fundamental problems of economic progress and economic fluctuation. These eminent writers have each followed their own train of thought and employed their own terminological apparatus: and it is therefore by no means easy for the contemporary student to discern the mutual bearings of their contributions or to decide whether they are leading us towards a greater or a less measure of agreement on the problems involved. In some cases, and over some part of the field of discussion, a difference of terminology seems to conceal an essential similarity of analysis. Thus, inspired by their common derivation from Wicksell, the teachings of Keynes and of Hayek, so different in their formal presentation, appear to agree in finding the distinguishing feature of the boom in a rate of formation of concrete capital which outruns the spontaneous saving available for embodiment in such forms. But these two writers differ radically in their analysis of, and prescriptions for, the ensuing slump. Hayek regards it as the ineluctable aftermath of debauch, whose worst consequences can only be obviated by fostering, through severe economy, those processes of spontaneous saving whose inadequacy has left us, so to speak, with a dead body of concrete capital deprived of its soul. Keynes, with equal appearance of logic, calls attention to the fact that the process of "forced saving" which occurs

[1] From the *Festschrift* in honour of Professor Spiethoff, 1933 (published by Duncker u. Humblot, Munich).

during the boom has its converse, a process of "wasted saving," during the slump, when the abstinences of individuals run to waste in uncovenanted consumption by the possessors of fixed money incomes, in borrowings by entrepreneurs to carry on production at a loss, and finally in the curtailment of output and employment. From this wastage, he believes, the banking system can rescue us by the relentless creation of money, thus forcing down the rate of interest, stimulating the creation of concrete capital and providing the homeless soul of saving with a corporeal body. Thus his practical standpoint differs little from that of a school of writers with whom, at first sight, he has analytically less in common than with the Austrians—the writers who find the whole cause of economic fluctuation in mishandling of the monetary machine.

Thus, if it is true that differences of terminology sometimes overlie similarity of analysis, it is also true that similarity of practical prescription sometimes overlies divergence of analysis. It is these artificial logomachies and artificial alliances which make it so difficult to assess just what degree of synthesis has been achieved and just where the crucial elements of unresolved controversy still lie.

It will, I think, assist us in penetrating towards the heart of the difficulty to turn once more to the dispute about right action in the slump which has been alluded to above. A course of action is under discussion which involves the placing of money on easy terms in the hands of producers, and the raising of prices against consumers, with the object of increasing the volume of concrete capital, both fixed and working, above its present level. This course of action is condemned by one party as an "artificial" interference with the "natural" course of events, bound to bring its own punishment; it is defended by the other as a restoration of a "natural" position which has been undermined by "artificial" pressures and phobias. How are we to frame a criterion of what is "natural" or "normal" and what is not? Keynes attempts to provide an answer by means of an ingenious and paradoxical definition of "saving" which, however, itself involves a conception of normality in the earnings of entrepreneurs which is difficult to reconcile with the conception of economic progress. Alternatively, it is tempting to try to define normality in terms of the fullness of employment of the factors of production. Yet it is by no means certain that this could be done even in a world in which "normality" was preserved and fluctuation absent: still less is it clear that it can be done in a world which has once become a prey to fluctuation, and in which therefore the level of factor-employment attained at the moment of greatest activity is substantially above the average or the most frequent level. Yet to accept a panic-stricken *status quo* as the natural or normal, with which all interference is vain, offends not only the conscience but the intellect. Thus the divergent prescriptions of the doctors direct our attention to the fundamental difficulty of handling the concept of equilibrium in harness with that of progress. Normality, and its symbol the "natural rate of interest," seem to be like a path which is plain enough to see while you are treading it, but which is exceedingly difficult to rediscover once you have strayed away from it.

And if the differences of the doctors draw our thoughts in this direction, so also do their agreements. For it will be observed that both the doctrines outlined above concur in this respect, that they hold it desirable to restore at the earliest possible date the high level of production of instrumental goods which has been attained, with the aid of "forced saving," during the boom. The one school seeks to attain this end by means of the expansion of bank credit, the other by means of the augmentation of spontaneous saving through the economy of consumers and the lightening of the charges upon entrepreneurs: but they are agreed upon the end itself. Yet the legitimacy of the end is by no means self-evident. For it seems conceivable that the preoccupation of both schools with the "excessiveness," during the boom, of capital formation *relatively* to saving, has led them to give insufficient attention to the possibility that *both alike* have been proceeding at a rate which, having regard to the technique of modern industry and to the nature of men's desires, cannot be continuously sustained without leading to *malaise* and disorder. If this be so, the question of whether the restoration of full activity in the industries making instrumental goods does or does not involve "forced saving" and a "warping of the structure of production" becomes secondary to the question of whether, within any reasonably short period of time and without far-reaching interference with the existing social order, it is practicable at all. Some suspicion of this disturbing possibility is betrayed by those champions of reflation who couple their advocacy of monetary expansion with an advocacy of constructional enterprise by public authorities, therein differing from their allies of the straiter monetary sect who hold that, in Mr. Hawtrey's words, public works are a "mere piece of ritual" enabling nothing to be achieved which could not be achieved by the unaided activities of an enlightened Central Bank. Yet, however desirable such *ad hoc* extensions of public activity during the slump, it has yet to be proved that they are capable, either quantitatively or qualitatively, of filling the gap in the order-books of the instrumental trades as a whole. For the truth seems to be that the processes of construction of the main modern instruments of production and transport are essentially discontinuous, so that so far as they are concerned it is hard to conceive of "progress" proceeding continuously rather than by a succession of fits and starts. And if some approach to an even rate of growth was attained in the nineteenth century, when both population and the area of effective economic intercourse were rapidly increasing, it may turn out (paradoxically enough) to be harder to attain in a planet which, thanks to the activities of the prospector and the pioneer and to the success of the propagandists of birth control, is rapidly ceasing to be a worthy member of an expanding universe.

If an admirable but inconvenient durability comes to characterise not only the instruments of production but also a considerable proportion of the goods upon which consumers spend their incomes (for instance motor-cars and wireless sets), and if at the same time the achievements of science in the domain of agriculture have slaked the thirst of the soil for the co-operation of fresh capital, it seems evident that the ship of economic life may be set a problem in re-orientation which transcends the capacities alike of its navigators and of its monetary steering-gear. Under such conditions the popular instinct which finds the root cause of dislocation in undigested plenty may be a surer guide than the laborious but one-eyed analysis which finds it in flouted scarcities and unjustified rigidities. As to the former, it may be conceded that it is often, if not always, a "shortage of saving" in some sense which precipitates the crisis, but it may be doubted whether even a plethora of saving would have enabled full activity to continue for long unbroken. As to the latter, when I am killed by a motor-car in the streets of London, my slayer will maintain that the accident happened because I was too slow in getting out of the way: but my indignant relatives will probably remain of the opinion that it happened because the motor-car came too fast.

Would a drastic redistribution of income be of service towards preventing the emergence of these temporary but devastating bewilderments as to how next to use our powers of giving orders to Nature? If so, some slackening in the rate of growth of those powers would no longer, I think, seem to most people too heavy a price to pay. But is such a redistribution, involving for millions of people a permanent divorce between their reward and their economic worth, compatible with efficient conduct of the world's affairs? But again, if private enterprise remains sovereign, can it, at its most successful, find any way of countering slumps save by the perpetual stimulation of increasingly meretricious wants and increasingly hectic habits of life? Can it, consistently with its own nature, succeed in the more subtle task of transmuting into diffused leisure the concentrated unemployment of to-day?

Such are, I think, the larger problems which press upon the mind once the trade cycle is properly envisaged not as a passing rash on the fair face of a static equilibrium but as a deep-seated functional disorder of the endocrine glands which control the rate of organic growth. They cannot be discussed here. I will rather end by suggesting that the very uncertainty of the possibility of steady progress may perhaps serve as a bridge for reconciling opposing schools in respect of less ambitious courses of action. For once it is recognised that in mid-slump the speedy restoration of full activity in the instrumental trades is in any case out of the question, the alleged objections to the maintenance of consumption at the maximum possible level seem to crumble away. Under such conditions a policy of reflation designed to maintain the purchasing power of consumers seems to contain little danger of a pernicious "warping of the structure of production"; and at the same time to offer the best hope of eventually restoring "rentability" to the capital structures left stranded by the receding tide. How can such a policy be applied? How can we loosen (yet not beyond the possibility of restoration) the queer nexus which has come to subsist between the creation of money and the business of commercial lending and borrowing, in such wise as to keep our emergency largesse free from the possible defects of loans at a zero rate of interest? This seems to be one of the most fruitful fields of enquiry for practically-minded theorists at the present day.

VIII

THE SNAKE AND THE WORM[1]

It seems a little mad to attempt to discuss in half an hour the vast theme of the rôle of the State in the control of economic fluctuation. Madder still to make the attempt on one's first visit to the great country which has been the scene of the boldest and most enormous experiments in this field. Maddest of all, perhaps, to speak on this subject in the presence of Professor Copland, that skilful designer of cunningly mixed cordials for depressed economic systems. But I must fulfil my promise.

Let me state in a few words what I shall try to maintain. It seems to me that the problem consists, in theory, of an easy half and a difficult half; that the difficult half would be difficult even in a world in which fluctuation was the only significant kind of economic movement: and that its difficulty is increased by the circumstance that fluctuations in fact occur against a background of secular and structural change, from which they are not always easy to disentangle.

The easy half of the problem concerns the rôle of the State in the face of pronounced economic depression. When I say that it is easy, I do not mean of course that it is easy to handle in practice: on the contrary, its solution is attended with the most formidable practical difficulties. I do not even mean that, in most countries, there is any close agreement, either among economists or among practical persons, as to the particular

[1] A paper read, under the more prosaic title "The State and Economic Fluctuation," at a symposium of the Harvard Tercentenary Conference of Arts and Sciences, Sept. 1936, and printed in the volume *Authority and the Individual* (Harvard University Press).

measures which would be effective towards the end sought, still less as to the degree to which each of them can be usefully applied. But I do mean that there is a measure of general agreement—a much greater measure, I think, than prevailed only a few years ago—both in the diagnosis of what, in this phase of the story, has gone wrong and consequently also as to the ends which public action should seek to promote. Whatever the cause of the original recession of trade, and whether or no it has been an inevitable or even a salutary occurrence, it seems evident that after a certain stage it is apt to degenerate into a purposeless and obscene orgy of destruction, like a snake eating its own tail—a process "devoid," as Professor Röpke has recently put it, "of every necessary function and therefore without sense." It seems clear that in such circumstances it is right and reasonable to use the manifold powers of the State to reverse the evil process of cumulation, and to restore what I will call for the moment by the question-begging name of a normal level of activity. Nor, under such conditions, is there necessary opposition between measures helpful to consumption and measures helpful to the formation of capital equipment. For re-employed bricklayers and engineers will buy boots; and rehabilitated bootmakers will, eventually, buy buildings and machines. We can usefully start at either end, or at both.

The difficulties in the way of framing effective action along these lines are well known: it would take me the rest of my half-hour even to catalogue them. I must content myself with posing—alas! not answering—two questions under which a great many of them are subsumed. That they are questions, ultimately, not only of economics but also of ethics and psychology only illustrates the hard lot of the economist, masquerading as a man of science in a universe not of cells and atoms but of passions and volitions.

The recovery measures open to a national state may be classified broadly into those which, if successful, will benefit the world at large, and those whose direct effects, at all events, are merely to enable the country which applies them to hoist itself up on the shoulders of its neighbours. A successful public-works campaign by a large creditor country is an example of the former, the introduction or elevation of a protective tariff of the latter. How far—this is my first question—can a given country wisely or decently go with measures of this second class? The question is complicated by the fact that attention cannot always be fairly confined to the direct effects of such measures, apart from their setting in a whole complex situation. Take for instance what is, from some points of view, the deadliest card in the whole pack with which the game of international beggar-my-neighbour is played—the card of currency devaluation. To many Continental observers the depreciation of the pound in 1931 seemed, and I think still seems, an unforgivable stab in the back, a prime cause of the final agonies of the depression in Europe, with all that they have involved of economic disintegration and political menace: to most Englishmen it appears in retrospect as an inevitable preliminary to the creation of a centre of recovery whose healing influence has spread far beyond the confines of England and even of the British Commonwealth. Again, the freeing of the dollar in 1933 was condemned as a wanton act by many who had found excuse in *force majeure* for the depreciation of the pound: but a good case can be made for the view that the freedom of manœuvre so obtained was essential to give a fair chance to America's great constructive and world-assisting experiment. Finally, almost everyone outside the European gold countries has agreed for some years that the writing-down of their monetary units, however inconvenient to special interests elsewhere, would amply pay its way from the world point of view in the release of confidence and the removal of fear.

Thus selfishness is not always as selfish as it seems. Nevertheless, if we are concerned rather with prescription for the future than appraisal of the past, there can be no doubt, I think, of the general lines of the answer to my first question. It seems clear that the combating of depression could be made immensely more effective in the future than it has been in recent years if nations were more concerned to defeat the common enemy and less concerned to steal a march on one another, less anxious about their balances of payments, less ready to be shocked at one another's budgetary difficulties. And evidently this is a matter where *noblesse oblige*: acts of self-denial and self-restraint which would be useless quixotry on the part of weak and isolated and indebted nations may not be too much to demand from the concerted wisdom of powerful creditor States.

I turn to my second question—remember I am still dealing with the easy half of my subject! How far is the taking of effective action against developed depression compatible with popular government on the one hand and private capitalism on the other, or how far must it always come to grief against the rocks of loss of public confidence, especially the giant rock of the distrust of the organisers of employment and the owners of wealth? In particular, what type and degree of disequilibrium in the public finances will popular opinion stand? Will it permit local governments to incur debt, as long as the national budget balances? Or will it acquiesce in the existence of an extraordinary national budget which does not balance, as long as there is also an ordinary budget which does? Will it countenance a large volume of public loan expenditure as long as there are bricks and mortar to show for it, but stick at the financing of pensions or unemployment relief by similar methods? Will its wealth-owners suffer the Government to borrow almost gratis from the banks with nothing worse than a shaking of heads, but, at the very mention of an expansion in the issue of legal tender money, will they, like the sea-blooms in Shelley's poem,

> . . . suddenly grow grey with fear
> And tremble and despoil themselves?

Who can tell? The problem would seem to be one for the psycho-analyst rather than the economist: yet the economist if he wishes to be listened to, no less than the statesman if he wishes to be re-elected, will neglect it at his peril. There are said to be, in the far north and the far south, happy lands where economists all give the same advice, where the Government listens to it, where the public understands why the Government has listened —and where, the cynic might add, the very prices of timber and wool play, as though by magic, their appointed part in the harmonious scheme. But we cannot all live in Sweden or Australia. Perhaps in darker but nevertheless not yet totalitarian lands the solution for the present lies in the rigid separation of professional economists into two classes—a class of economic advisers, who must subdue their hand to the material it works in, and never forget that there is nothing either good or bad but thinking makes it so; and a class of pure economists, who are licensed to think what the Japanese call dangerous thoughts and even to think them aloud, but who in return must suffer themselves to be burnt at the stake rather than ever be trapped into giving advice to anybody about anything.

In England of late years the thinker of dangerous thoughts has looked out upon a varied scene. He has watched, with a sort of melancholy and negative satisfaction, some foreign governments which have made "Sound Finance" their prime objective find themselves ever further and further from their aim, like Alice in the garden of live flowers, when she tried so obstinately to reach the Red Queen by the old-fashioned method of walking towards her. He has watched with mixed feelings the rulers of his own country handling with extreme skill some of the weapons of recovery, and condemned by the aftermath of their own somewhat misty economy propaganda to leave others rusting and unused. He has watched, as through a glass darkly, the dictatorships wielding those rejected weapons with apparent effect, but at a cost in freedom which seems to him too high to pay. And finally he has watched a government which the laws of hospitality forbid me to name, lengthening its own journey, perhaps, by straying into strange and gaily coloured flower-beds, but destined, as he hopes, through turning its back so firmly on the Red Queen of "Sound Finance", in time once more to meet her face to face.

I must hurry on to the second, or difficult, part of my subject, or I shall never reach it. Granted that the State, working through its control of the public finances as well as its ultimate authority over the mechanisms of money and banking, should initiate measures of recovery, how far should it press them, and when if ever should it reverse the engines? Is there an evil symmetry between boom and slump, and virtue in the middle course? or does the symmetry stand revealed as illusion, the golden mediocrity as cowardice and defeatism, when we reflect that the mean level between boom and slump is a mean level not merely of prices and profits or even of output but also of employment, and that to stop short at any but the highest possible level of activity means to turn a deaf ear to the claims of individuals for reabsorption into the economic machine? It is here, I think, that a real cleavage of opinion still persists.

Let me try to summarise the opposing viewpoints. So long, one party urges, as there are men who can be drawn back into employment by an enlargement of the stream of money demand, drawn back they ought to be. That prices may rise substantially in the process is no argument against its legitimacy, in the later any more than in the earlier phases of expansion: it is merely the consequence of living in a world where certain elements of equipment are limited, temporarily or permanently, in supply. Not until unemployment is conquered can inflation in any damaging sense be said to begin.

"Yes," say the other side, "but consider the character of the employment created in the high boom. We do not, most of us, maintain, as some of us did a few years ago, that all the capital equipment then called into existence is doomed to melt away irretrievably like the snow. On the contrary we admit that in the main it contributes in the long run to the permanent enrichment of the world. But we still think that to press on so rapidly with its formation is a mistake, because it sets before the economic system problems in digestion and readjustment which it cannot possibly solve. And we still think that the process by which you propose to achieve your ends, namely the unreasonable enrichment of the entrepreneur class, is fairly and illuminatingly described as the infliction of a system of forced levies on the rest of the community, including the working class as a whole, and that sooner or later their effort to react against this system will play its part in inducing crisis and collapse. This way of looking at things does not, as you seem to suppose, depend on an unfounded assumption that there is no unemployment left. For by attempting to abolish the residuum of unemployment to-day you are making it worse for to-morrow; whereas by acquiescing in its temporary continuance you would be promoting a tempo of industrial progress, and an eventual distribution of labour between industries, more appropriate to the modern world—a world which has no need to be in such a hurry since, as you admit yourselves, the devil which Malthus unchained has been hooked up again."

"You are a defeatist!" cries Party A.

"You are a Communist," replies Party B, "or if you aren't you ought to be. For nothing short of a completely authoritarian State could cope with the immense problems of transfer and readjustment, let alone fiscal embarrassment, in which your policy will land you if you carry it out to the bitter end."

I must not attempt to carry the debate further, or I should have to make the parties fall at loggerheads over the nature of that central mystery of the economic scheme—a theme too intricate for the closing minutes of my half-hour, the theory of the rate of interest. But I have said enough, perhaps, to indicate what seems to be emerging, with increasing clearness, especially since the publication of my colleague Mr. Keynes' latest book, as the true issue. It is not so much a conflict between different views of the most effective method of controlling cyclical fluctuation. It is rather a conflict of view between those who still believe that cyclical fluctuation is the worst enemy which controlled capitalism has yet to subdue, and those who think that they detect, lurking beneath the coils of the cyclical snake, a more insidious enemy still. This alleged enemy is a chronic and endemic tendency towards the stifling of enterprise, the leakage of thrift, and a consequent running-down of the whole system—a sort of worm seated at the very heart of the institutional and psychological bases of our society, and battening on the very growth of wealth which he strives unavailingly to prevent. Is he a real worm, or is he the figment of generous imaginations tortured by the tragedies of the worst and deepest slump of history?

I dare not swear he is an unreal worm; but I may conclude by offering one or two reasons why he might be thought to exist even if he does not—in more prosaic language, why the problem of the control of cyclical fluctuation may be complicated by the fact that such fluctuations are apt to occur against a background of structural change. If it is always hard to know where to stop in a policy of expansion, it is hardest of all in a country in which large numbers of persons have lost their employment through a permanent decline in the demand for their labour. And if, as was the case in Britain, these persons happen to be found partly in the instrumental trades which are liable anyhow to be specially affected by cyclical depression, the difficulty becomes acute of distinguishing between unemployment which it is sensible to try to remove by expansionist measures, and unemployment which, in so far as it can be removed at all and not merely relieved, calls for the less spectacular but more difficult treatment of gradual industrial and local transfer. It is not surprising that, in recent months, Rearmament should have seemed to come as a *deus ex machina*, to solve, or rather postpone the solution of, the dilemma. Neither is it surprising that, in the years preceding 1929, Restriction, the paradoxical twin brother of Expansion (for Boost and Bolster are the father and mother of them both), should have been invoked to ease the problem of excess capacity in a number of leading raw materials. Yet it can hardly be doubted that those attempts, in high boom, to resist the process of structural change contributed to the violence of the ensuing collapse: and the spectacle of governments—in order to implement what is, let us pray, a temporary and gluttable demand—unbalancing gaily in the boom of 1936-7 those budgets so meticulously balanced in the slump of 1931-2, may well make us uneasy about what is to follow.

Finally, I must mention very briefly another type of secular change which may confuse the course of cyclical policy. It may be—there are signs of it, I think, in England as well as in the United States—that, with the growth in the average size and strength of individual firms, there occurs a decline in the demand for that type of service which the virtuously brought up banker is most ready to render—the provision of working capital by short-term loans. In this event the banking system may lose efficiency as a conduit for the transmission of thrift into industry, and a super-cyclical tendency towards deflation and the waste of saving may develop, bearing a certain resemblance to the phenomena of epidemic slump and even suggesting the presence of endemic worm. Yet it does not follow, I think, that anti-slump measures of the regular kind—cheap money, open market purchases, budget deficits—are an adequate or appropriate response. Structural faults call rather for structural remedies—in this instance, perhaps, for the devising of new types of financial institution to fill the gap left by the old.

I have left you, I am afraid, with a picture somewhat negative and confused. Perhaps if I were to attempt to sum up in two sentences what I have tried to suggest it would be thus. The advocates of energetic State action against developed depression have had in all

IX

EFFECTIVE DEMAND AND THE MULTIPLIER [1]

I. EFFECTIVE DEMAND

§ 1. THERE is a verbal obscurity in Mr. Keynes' exposition of his central apparatus (pp. 23-32) which may have troubled others besides myself.

Income (later called Y) is the proceeds which result from giving a certain amount of employment; aggregate demand price (D) is the proceeds which are *expected* to result from giving that amount of employment; aggregate supply price (Z) is the proceeds the expectation of which will just make it worth while to give that amount of employment, and for simplicity may be regarded as made up of factor-cost (F) and associated profit (P) (pp. 24-5).

Suppose we are in equilibrium, *i.e.* with $D = Z$, at a level of output R entailing less than "full" employment. Why is not output increased to $R + \Delta R$? Because if it were, then, since part of the increase in individual incomes would not be spent,[2] sales-proceeds would fall short of the sum which makes the production of $R + \Delta R$ worth while (ΔY would be less than ΔZ).

But suppose that entrepreneurs (perhaps having heard at their last Rotary Club luncheon a lecture on J. B. Say) expand output in the *belief* that ΔY will equal ΔZ. Their disappointment must surely not be represented, as is suggested in these pages, as due to a

[1] Being the first two sections of an article on Keynes' "General Theory of Employment, Interest and Money" in *Q.J.E.*, Sept. 1936, pp. 168 ff., parts of the third section of which have been utilised in the essay on *Mr. Keynes and the Rate of Interest* printed in this volume.

[2] I am not here examining the conditions under which this is probable.

countries a hard fight to wage against the forces of apathy and despair. Let us salute them everywhere, in their victories or in their honourable defeats: but let us beg them, whether flushed with success or saddened with failure, to think again before concluding that cheap money and Government deficits, still less trade restriction and exchange manipulation, are the right diet for all phases of the trade cycle or the right remedy for all the economic ills of the world.

divergence between aggregate demand price and aggregate supply price; for in the case supposed these two are equal. It must be represented (as Mr. Keynes first discloses much later, on p. 78) [1] as due to a divergence between aggregate demand price and income. Mr. Keynes, in fact, oscillates between using "aggregate demand price" to mean what he has defined it to mean, *viz.* what entrepreneurs *do* expect to receive, and using it to mean (p. 30, line 5) what they "can expect" to receive, *i.e.* what they can legitimately expect to receive, because that, whether they expect it or not, is what they *will* receive. In a world in which errors of anticipation are common, the distinction is not unimportant!

§ 2. Suppose, for instance, that ΔY, while less than ΔZ, turns out to be greater than ΔF—as will happen, *e.g.* if factors spend all their increments of income and profit-receivers even a small fraction of theirs. Then ΔP is positive; the general mistake has promoted the general gain. Z, it is true, exceeds Y, *i.e.* for the representative entrepreneur marginal cost exceeds marginal receipts, and if he expects the situation to be repeated he would be wise to contract output. But he is doing better than he was; hope springs eternal; may not the mistake be repeated, and on a larger scale? If it is, ΔP will again be positive; indeed on these lines, even though Z continues to exceed Y, output will be in unstable equilibrium at any point short of "full employment" in the consumption trades. But perhaps, as output grows, Z will not continue indefinitely to exceed Y, for consumption breeds investment, as well as investment consumption. The mistake will turn out not to have been a mistake after all.

It is tempting to interpret along these lines Marshall's famous account of the automatic process of trade re-

[1] The contrast here (rather suddenly) declared to be "vital for causal analysis" is, indeed, not between aggregate demand price and income but between effective demand and income; but "effective demand" is simply that particular value of the aggregate demand schedule at which aggregate demand price is equal to aggregate supply price (and in the real world therefore is something of a Cheshire cat?).

covery, with its suggestion of the need for, and ultimate occurrence of, a sort of plot.[1] A precarious and dilatory process, perhaps, and one that we may well fortify by contrived investment. But in assessing so low the natural recuperative powers of the economic system, has Mr. Keynes taken full account of the potentialities, for good as well as evil, of that contrast between the realised and the expected which, at some moments "vital for causal analysis," at others seems forgotten?

§ 3. Since Mr. Keynes' final statement (p. 78) of the contrast between effective demand and income is made in the course of some comments on an apparatus of my own,[2] it may be convenient to some readers if I add one or two notes. I should like to preface them by saying that at every stage, from the prehistoric days of "induced lacking" and its converse onwards, my own thoughts about the increased or diminished "abstinence" done out of enlarged or curtailed incomes have largely derived from his, even though latterly both our methods and our practical inferences have tended to diverge.

(i) Mr. Keynes inadvertently says that I called "income" what in fact I called "disposable income" to distinguish it from income, *i.e.* from income received.

(ii) His "day" (p. 47) is not the same as mine. For my clock struck midnight with income in the hands of its final disposers, while his strikes midnight with proceeds in the hands of entrepreneurs. Thus if we start in equilibrium with income Y, and if entrepreneurs (having read J. B. Say) "to-day" expand employment

[1] *Principles*, p. 711. "If all trades which make goods for direct consumption agreed to work on and to buy one another's goods as in ordinary times, they would supply one another with the means of earning a moderate rate of profit and of wages. The trades which make fixed capital might have to wait a little longer; but they too would get employment when confidence had revived so far that those who had capital to invest had made up their minds how to invest it. . . . There is of course no formal agreement between the different trades to begin to work again full time, and so make a market for each other's wares. But the revival of industry comes about through the gradual and often simultaneous growth of confidence among many various trades."

[2] *E.J.*, Sept. 1933, p. 399.

by ΔN, to-day's income, according to my clock, is necessarily at least $Y + \Delta Y$, and it is not until to-morrow that income may fall to a lower figure.

(iii) It does not seem to me quite true that if I say that there is an excess of saving over investment, in the sense of my article, I mean "literally the same thing" as Mr. Keynes means when he says that income is falling. For I am trying (as I cannot but think the author of the *Treatise on Money*[1] was originally trying) to formulate in a convenient phrase the *cause* of what both the author of the *General Theory* and I describe as a fall in income.

II. THE MULTIPLIER

§ 1. The story originally told by Mr. Kahn (*Economic Journal*, 1931, pp. 173-98), if we express it in terms of income instead of employment and strip it of complications connected with the dole and foreign trade, portrays an Authoritarian act of investment of money amount N as generating a series of increments of money income—qN, q^2N, etc.—and a series of increments of saving $(1 - q)N$, $(1 - q)qN$, etc.—at later dates. We can regard the latter series as adding up to and, as it were, balancing retrospectively the original act of investment. Alternatively, if the act is repeated a sufficient number of times, we can regard the sum of the increments of saving being done in any one period of time as balancing the investment done in that period; and if, with Mr. Kahn,[2] we are prepared to forget about the period of transition, we can declare

[1] According to Mr. Keynes, that author "argued that change in the excess of investment over saving [in the *Treatise* sense] was the motive force governing changes in the volume of output." But in that work (see Vol. I, pp. 151-2) the *direction* of a change in the volume of output was regarded as depending on whether I-S was positive or negative, not on whether it was increasing or decreasing—the latter circumstance would only affect the *magnitude* of the change. There is thus a much more radical difference between the doctrines of the two books than an incautious reader of pp. 78-9 of the *General Theory* might suppose.

[2] *Op. cit.*, p. 183 *n.* 2, "I am here considering the position in the final position of equilibrium when everything has settled down.... I do not enter into the question of [the] time-lag."

the problem of the finance of the process of investment to be self-solving.

For the convenience of those who, like myself, are left uneasy by this last step, and who prefer a more explicitly temporal method of analysis, I venture to retell the story in my own language and in tabloid form as follows, taking provisionally [1] as my unit of time that interval in which on the average each unit of money enters once into income. The point to be noted by those whose methods of thought are as old-fashioned as my own is that in each period the Authority is conceived of as acting only partly (and decreasingly) by increasing the supply of money, partly (and increasingly) by maintaining the income velocity of the previously issued supply, *i.e.* by causing the savings of the public to generate income in circumstances in which they would otherwise have failed to do so.

§ 2. Mr. Keynes, while I think that like Mr. Kahn he is primarily interested in "the final position of equilibrium when everything has settled down," claims (p. 122) that formally his revised analysis, exhibiting the increment of income as a multiple $\frac{1}{1-q}$ of the increment of investment,[2] "holds good continuously, without time-lag, at all moments of time." The explanation given is that if there are temporary obstacles to expanding output in the consumption trades, q will for various reasons suffer a temporary reduction.[3] But suppose there are no such obstacles to distort q from its normal value, and expansion takes place smoothly, as in Mr. Kahn's story. Even so the process occurs in a world in which time must be regarded as real; and I find it hard to see how, *while income is*

[1] Cf. *E.J.*, Sept. 1933, p. 399.

[2] It is explained that increment of total *employment* will only be $\frac{1}{1-q}$ times increment of "primary" *employment* if the elasticity of supply is the same in the consumption trades as in the investment trades.

[3] The implications for practical policy of this concession, and of the recognition that the elasticity of supply may be less in the consumption than in the investment trades, seem to me of the first importance, but that is another story.

1 Period	2 Investment	3 "Disposable Income," *i.e.* Income Received in Preceding Period	4 Of which Saved	5 Therefore New Money Created (2 — 4)	6 Total Income Received (= 2 + 3 — 4)	7 Money at Beginning of Period	8 V = 3 ÷ 7
0	N	—	—	N	N	—	—
1	N	N	$(1 - q)N$	qN	$(1 + q)N$	N	1
2	N	$(1 + q)N$	$(1 - q^2)N$	q^2N	$(1 + q + q^2)N$	$(1 + q)N$	1
3	N	$(1+q+q^2)N$	$(1 - q^3)N$	q^3N	$(1+q+q^2+q^3)N$	$(+q+q^2)N$	1
			approaching	*without limit*			
r	N	$\frac{N}{1-q}$	N	O	$\frac{N}{1-q}$	$\frac{N}{1-q}$	1

Total "excess of Investment over Saving" = total new money = $\frac{N}{1-q}$.

(The various terms refer only to money coming into existence after the story begins.)

expanding, it can at all moments be an identical multiple of a given rate of investment.

The essential difficulty, however, of using the multiplier method to analyse the effects on employment of a given rate of authoritarian investment is that it is avowedly concerned only with the secondary employment in the *consumption* trades which is generated by the primary process of investment. In other words, the instructiveness of the story told in my table depends very largely on the strength of our reasons for supposing that, in the absence of continued activity by the authority, all the induced savings of the public would have become abortive, instead of finding a vent in real investment either directly or through the machinery of a normally functioning stock exchange. *Prima facie* the story seems too pessimistic to take as our standard of reference (at best it can be no more) if we are considering the merits of engineered reflation in time of deep depression,[1] too optimistic if we are considering the damage which might be done if the authority, mistiming its activities, carried them on into times of high boom. For the enhanced expenditure on consumption goods will normally afford a stimulus to increased investment, as well as the increased investment providing the wherewithal for increased consumption. Dogs wag tails, as well as tails dogs; and there are well-known reasons, which have figured in almost every account of cyclical fluctuation,[2] why a given percentage increase in the demand for consumption goods should stimulate a larger percentage increase in the demand for instrumental goods. The disparity in the percentage fluctuations of output in the two groups has been such a familiar feature of trade cycle history[3] that I am

[1] Though it may of course, as is generally admitted, be too optimistic if the Authority's action leads to a—rational or irrational—failure of confidence.

[2] See especially Pigou, *Industrial Fluctuations*, p. 108, and J. M. Clark, *Strategic Factors in Business Cycles*, p. 33.

[3] Cf. Cassel's conclusion, perhaps an extreme one even for the nineteenth century (his italics): "The production of fixed capital depends essentially upon conjunctures, whereas *the production of articles which pass directly into the system of consumption shows no pronounced dependence upon conjunctures*" (*Theory of Social Economy*, 1st Eng. tr., ii, p. 523).

not inclined to share Mr. Keynes' surprise (p. 127) that, even for America in 1925—33, the absolute movements in total income should not have borne a higher ratio to the absolute movements in investment.

Perhaps anything which happens can be expressed, with sufficient ingenuity, in terms of distortion of "the marginal propensity to consume."[1] But when all this is said, it seems to me doubtful whether, for the analysis of a fluctuating world, the "multiplier" constitutes much advance over more crudely "monetary" weapons of thought.[2]

[1] Which is also a *deus ex machina* for the case (p. 128 *n.* 1) in which the "investment" is not investment at all, but a Veterans' Bonus—though it is not the *propensity* but the *capacity* of individuals to consume which is increased.

[2] Cf. J. M. Clark, *Am. Econ. Review*, March 1935, pp. 14-20; D. Throop Smith, *Deficits and Depressions*, pp. 209-10; Hansen and others, *Review of Ec. Stat.*, May 1936, p. 59; Neisser, *ibid.*, Feb. 1936, p. 24, and Aug. 1936, p. 147.

X

THE TRADE CYCLE—AN ACADEMIC VIEW [1]

I

To the academic student of industrial fluctuation there were certain ironical features in the situation of last summer. In the first place, the world seems to have become more cycle-conscious than ever before—more open to the idea that good trade will not last for ever any more than bad trade has done, and more ready to "do something about it." But those who are bursting to give the world advice, and who find with surprise that there is some chance of their being listened to, are less clear in their own minds, or at all events less unanimous, than they might have been thirty years ago as to just what advice to give. Thus rather as Alice, in the White Queen's view, was in that state of mind that she wanted to deny something—only she didn't know what to deny ("a nasty, vicious temper"), so the leaders of business and politics seem to be in that state of mind that they want to avert something (a nice, virtuous temper)—only they don't know exactly what they want to avert.

Secondly, even in the democratic countries we live under a degree of authoritarianism which would have been inconceivable thirty years ago. The power of Governments over Central Banks, and the influence of Central Banks over their financial communities, have grown beyond all knowledge. Yet as a result of circumstances of various kinds, some of them perhaps fortuitous, but some the result of their own past actions, these apparently omnipotent authorities find themselves inhibited in the use of instruments of control which would

[1] *Lloyds Bank Review*, Sept. 1937.

have been applied without *arrière-pensée* in a more *laissez-faire* age. We have heard much in recent years about Poverty in the midst of Plenty. Is there some danger of our witnessing Impotence in the midst of Power?

The rest of this article will be devoted to attempting to probe a little deeper into these uncomfortable paradoxes.

II

What is the matter with periods of active trade? Is it simply that, like other good things, they come to an end, or is it that in themselves they are less good things than they look? Are we, as it has been put, just afraid of the present trade recovery fading out, or are we afraid of it exploding?

In the nineteenth century there is little doubt about what those who were responsible for such management as existed were afraid of: they were afraid of a high level of activity generating an unfavourable turn of the exchanges and a drain of gold. Nowadays, with our mobile exchanges and our Secret Sponges (*alias* Equalisation Funds) we have changed a good deal of that. Perhaps not so much of it as some people in this country expected in 1931, when, like the inspired inventor of Rugby football, we alone had learned to pick up the ball with our hands; nevertheless, there are not many nowadays who would advocate damping down prosperity solely in order to keep touch at all costs with a less prosperous neighbour. But the case for the old gold standard was not simply that it was a device for keeping step; it was also that it was a rough-and-ready device (*how* rough and ready the long tale of nineteenth-century cycles shows) for regulating the volume of home activity. It may have been silly to bother so much about the exchanges; but it was simpler than trying to bother about everything at once, and wiser than bothering about nothing at all. Reacting primarily to external situations, policy—such as it was—in fact served, so far as it went, to promote internal ends which the most hard-baked autarkist could have approved.

Is this way of looking at the matter obsolete? Ought we to have buried boom-shyness in the same grave (perhaps indeed a shallower one than it once seemed) as fixed parities of exchange? There is, I think, a general consensus of opinion that we ought not, and that even if we had got rid of our golden chains more effectively than we now seem to have done, we should have had to devise some kind of *ersatz* corsets for ourselves. Professor Robbins' words that "to avert a slump it is necessary to avert a boom" would to-day apparently win cheers (at any rate in the mild parliamentary sense of that word) in quarters where a few years ago they would only have evoked a superior smile.

III

It is when we come to selecting a pattern for the corsets that differences of opinion, or at all events of taste, begin to emerge, and that we begin to suspect that the apparent unanimity about the corsets being required veils after all rather considerable differences of attitude. Among the reasons for boom-shyness offered for our consideration it is perhaps possible to disentangle four fairly distinct strands of thought. These centre respectively round the concepts of "speculation," of "the vicious circle," of a running short of loanable funds, and of saturation in particular lines of investment. Let us examine these in order.

(1) According to this line of thought, there is no danger of "genuine" activity in trade and production being carried too far; the trouble is that as a by-product of trade activity some people lose their heads and under the influence of excitement and greed bid up the prices of materials and securities to a fantastic height, and that the buying power of these people is in the aggregate so important that their subsequent inevitable disappointment spreads general disorder and collapse. The pattern of corset to which this line of thought leads is

a discriminating one, trimmed with stock exchange controls and concerted action by the banks in respect of the quality of their lending.

(2) According to this view, the trouble begins when a hitherto healthy rise in prices leads, as in a free democracy it is apt to do, to a rise in wage-rates and so in costs of production, and this again is made the occasion for a further rise in prices, and so *ad infinitum*, or rather *ad crash*. The diagnosis, however, and the prescription which follows from it, are not altogether clear. Is it the rise in wages itself which is an evil (calling for a Hitler or a Mussolini to prevent it), because it cuts into profits and impairs enterprise, or is it the subsequent raising of prices in the endeavour to restore profits? If the latter, is it an evil because the high prices so established encounter consumers' resistance and so breed stagnation, or because their maintenance requires an elasticity in the supply of money which will ultimately lead to complete monetary breakdown?

There is room here for much meticulous argument, with curves of marginal prime costs and all the luxury of modern economic analysis. It may be said, I think, in a general way, that (in the absence of a Mussolini or a Hitler) the type of corset to which the "vicious circle" analysis points is the old-fashioned one of strict control of the supply of money. But the trouble is that if the corset is not purchased till the "vicious circle" actually develops, it may prove to be too late; for it can then only operate by refusing to re-create those excessive profit margins which have been earlier allowed to develop and to be acted upon, and have subsequently (by the rise in wages) been impaired. And to operate thus is to operate as an axe rather than a corset.

(3) Such considerations bring us to the third viewpoint—that which underlies, I think, Professor Robbins' powerful arguments for boom control in the May number of this *Review*. Investments made in a boom will tend to be bad investments. Why? Because they are made under a misapprehension about the degree in which society is really willing to refrain from present

consumption in order to construct and maintain the instruments which generate future wealth.

There is nothing in Professor Robbins' pages about the rate of interest with which in practice I disagree—neither in his defence of low money rates in the early phases of the present recovery, nor in his contention that the normal tendency of rates, both short and long, to harden as expansion proceeds should not now be resisted and may have to be actively reinforced. All the same, I am conscious of a certain difference of emphasis in my mind, both from Professor Robbins and from those who, diagnosing differently from himself, have reached precisely the opposite conclusion that an increase in interest rates should be avoided like hell-fire. For both these parties are convinced that the rate of interest is supremely important: both are concerned with averting a drying-up in the willingness to supply loanable funds. The one party finds the ultimate villain of the piece in the extravagance of the human race, the other in its passion for keeping its money safe; and their recipes for monetary policy diverge accordingly. "Let rates rise now," says Professor Robbins, "to prevent unwise planning; for the desire to spend is sure to make them rise later." "Keep rates down now," say his opponents, "lest if once you let them rise the desire to hoard prevent you from ever getting them down again." My judgment is, on the whole, with Professor Robbins; yet, even if he has his way, I hope for no great things.

(4) For, according to the fourth of the lines of thought which I am here attempting to disentangle, the phenomena of boom and slump are not primarily a matter of interest rates at all, but of something much more deep-seated, namely, of the inevitable discontinuity which attends the efforts of man to achieve material progress. It is worth noting that that very great man from whom many of the rival monetary theorists of to-day in various measure derive their inspiration, the Swedish economist Knut Wicksell, was himself at great pains to disavow the view that

his pioneer work on the relation between interest rates and prices furnished a clue to the problem of the trade cycle.[1] "My view," he wrote," ... ascribes trade cycles to *real* causes independent of movements in commodity price, so that the latter become of only secondary importance.... The principal and sufficient cause of cyclical fluctuations should be sought in the fact that in its very nature technical or commercial advance cannot maintain the same even progress as does, in our days, the increase in needs... but is sometimes precipitate, sometimes delayed."

A transcontinental railway is completed—a mercantile marine is converted from a coal to an oil basis—a steel industry has shifted its location and modernised its plant—arrears of housing or armament are made up—every American citizen has become possessed of a motor-car, wireless set and refrigerator—China or Peru after a period of chaos has resumed its place upon the economic map. Good—all to the good—man must progress. But what is the next thing, please? Whose sleeve is it up and when will it come down? It seems doubtful how much the most skilful monetary policy can be expected to do, either in flattening out the precipitous peaks of activity into long continuous tablelands, or in filling up the ravines which lie between. If we want stability of employment *at all costs*, must we not face the consequences and either turn the whole business over to Gosplan (with what faith in its competence we can muster), or make up our minds that too much progress is a bad thing, adjust the distribution of our national income accordingly, and train a larger proportion of our population to make cakes and ale, and a smaller proportion to wield those picks and shovels, to tend those cranes and steam hammers, whose willingness to be handled is so rhythmic and so temperamental?

[1] *Lectures on Political Economy*, II, pp. 209 ff.

IV

If we look at the matter in this way we shall see that, unless we are prepared to change our system altogether, it is no use getting too angry about the boom. To quote some words written nearly as long ago as those just cited from Wicksell: "We must be on our guard against condemning as over-investment what is really only unavoidable preliminary investment upon an exceptionally large scale." Fundamentally, the trouble about booms is not that they happen but that they stop. It is a pity when they explode; but even if they did not explode they would fade out, and that would be a pity too. Even at the height of the boom it is right to be thinking not only of how to prevent the explosion but of how to act—whether the explosion occurs or not—in face of the fading out.

That is really the heart of the whole difficulty when it comes to clinical treatment. There is not an exact parallelism between boom and slump. True there are things bad in themselves which happen in booms—a not negligible amount of over-work and over-strain, an intensification of industrial strife, a burgeoning of cupidity and fraud. True, too, that the increase in real enjoyable income is less than it seems to be, and to many individuals a negative quantity. But good and bad trade—and in particular high and low employment—are not *in themselves* two opposite evils like flood and drought. It is no use pretending that they are; yet a wise policy demands that we should behave in a certain measure *as if* they were.

It is, I think, because neither party to current controversies is quite prepared to swallow this crucial paradox that their words of wisdom in boom and slump respectively are apt to fall on deaf ears. To Professor Robbins' warning, it is tempting for the politician and the industrialist to reply: "Yes, that is all very well, but so far as we can see the recession is bound to come anyhow, sooner or later; why not let us enjoy ourselves while the going is good?" Such a reply is especially natural in the present boom. For the latter drew its early nourishment, to a degree for which there is no precedent, from a colossal activity in the private building of dwelling houses which bears on its face the stamp of discontinuity and non-recurrence: and its later phases are bound up with a campaign of re-armament which most people could not bear to contemplate if they did not believe that it would some day come to an end. That there has been some "bad investment" in building, that there will be some "bad investment" in connection with re-armament, is very probable: but who is prepared to say, in the former case any more than in the latter, that the fact that the thing will come to an end is a proof that it should never have been done, or that the wisest monetary policy would make much difference to the time and manner of its ending? No wonder that in its heart the business world is more impressed by the danger of fading out than by the danger of explosion.

The expansionists, on the other hand, are so conscious of the wastes and miseries of unemployment that their instinct is to cry out for the continuance of inflationary pressure right into the high boom. It is true that in practice they are prepared to make some concessions; certain measures of control, provided they are sufficiently ingenious and discriminatory, meet with their approval, and they are even prepared to express a mild preference for a balanced budget. But any general rise of interest rates or tightening up of the money supply remains anathema to them; and a whole new terminology has to be invented to make it seem plausible that dishing out unlimited money to people who want to spend it is the same thing as dishing it out to people who want to hoard it, and to invest with a halo of intellectuality the old, old policy of "letting the public act upon the circulation." [1] Right not to be too much shocked by the boom, they are too half-hearted, in my judgment, in their willingness to control it.

It is above all in the sphere of the public finances that

[1] See King, *History of the Discount Market*, p. 73.

it seems necessary to behave as though booms were more shocking than they are. It is tempting to tease Professor Robbins (who, if it came to abolishing tariffs or restriction schemes, would cheerfully, one feels, administer blows to the business world which would send it reeling against the ropes) for being content to take business opinion as so immutable a factor, and to treat business confidence as so tender a plant, when the matter at issue is the unbalancing of budgets. If it is the duty of economists to take account of public opinion, it is also their duty to attempt to mould it, as none has attempted more courageously than himself. Unless he can show that borrowing in a severe slump for unemployment relief is a stupid policy in itself he must not expect us to condemn it, any more than he himself condemns free trade, just because some business people have been brought up to think it so—they should be persuaded by the power of reason to think otherwise. Yet it must be confessed that there are excuses for Professor Robbins both in the worlds of fact and of theory, and that his critics are often their own worst enemies. Here is the United States just finishing the fourth year of recovery with a deficit of over £500 millions. And here is Mr. Harrod advocating an "equilibrating" policy of public works which turns out in the end to be a plan for the indefinite expansion of the public debt.[1] It is not surprising that Professor Robbins should insist on the State blowing in the slump only what money it has succeeded in hoarding in the last boom, and not what money it vaguely hopes to be able to cancel in the next; and it certainly seems desirable that booms, even if they do not seem to be very grand ones, should be marked by net reductions in the deadweight public debt.

V

The upshot of the matter seems to be this. In industrial fluctuation we are up against a problem very deep-seated in the nature of capitalist industry—

[1] *The Trade Cycle*, pp. 191 ff.

perhaps of all modern industry whether capitalist or not—perhaps of man himself. I do not believe myself that we can solve it. I think we can mitigate its consequences; but if we are to do so effectively those who have recently discovered that the deeper trouble is not so much that booms explode as that they fade out must not be so puffed up with pride at their discovery as to scorn altogether the use of Professor Robbins' corsets: while those who advocate the use of corsets in the boom must not try to put it across that slumps are wholly due to preventable folly and greed, or seek to limit unduly the part that collective enterprise can play in filling up the ravines which private enterprise, for all its ultimate resilience and adaptability, has not learnt, and probably cannot learn, to avoid leaving in the wake of its advance. And if some cyclical unemployment still proves to be the price of progress, the one side must try to stop using it as a stick with which to beat "the system," and the other side to abandon useless repining over any unfortunate secondary effects to which a more generous treatment of its victims may give rise.

VI

What of the second paradox with which I started? Is there anything in the suggestion that, whatever may be true of the totalitarian States, in our modern semi-authoritarian democracies the very centralisation of financial power has led to certain weaknesses when it comes to boom-control? I cannot but think that there is.

First, there is surely an increased danger that interest-policy will not really be considered on its merits from the cyclical point of view at all, but will be continuously dominated by the abiding desire of governments to borrow as cheaply as they can. To this has to be added the enormous vested interest of prestige acquired by public men in the continuance of cheap money. They have brought the rain from the skies—can they ever afford to admit that their magic powers are even temporarily in abeyance?

Secondly, the very success of authoritarian reflation has brought a technical problem, in the shape of the plethora of short-term funds, which may well seem unamenable to treatment by traditional means. Control by sermon, by taboo, by ingenious fiscal shock, has come to seem easier as well as more righteous than control by regulation of the terms of lending. And successful reflation has had another aftermath as well—the mountains of metal which threaten to turn the Equalisation Sponges into permanent dustbins and to obfuscate the long-term forces working on the rate of interest—and incidentally also to call for a good deal of ingenuity directed toward the hasty re-bunking, in the estimation of Continental Dictators, Indian peasants, Dominion Premiers and other potential baby-holders, of that Golden Calf at whose head so many bricks were heaved only a few short years ago.

In the June number of this *Review*, Mr. Henderson argues that, so far as this country and this cycle are concerned, the budgetary outlook is now so disquieting that broader considerations must be set aside, and fiscal emergency once more be given pride of place in the determination of policy. If that were true—and I confess that I am far from being convinced of it—it would seem to be a somewhat depressing outcome of six years of National Government and Managed Money. But it would not remove my suspicion that if, during the last couple of years, the Powers of Orthodoxy had been content to be a little less heretical, we might not find ourselves in the curious situation which prevails—let us hope only for the moment—as these lines are written—a situation which it is tempting to label as Panic in the midst of Prosperity.

XI

A SURVEY OF MODERN MONETARY CONTROVERSY [1]

§ 1. THERE has occurred in recent years a vast orgy of debate in the fields of the theory of money, the theory of interest and the theory of trade fluctuation. Since the writers concerned have naturally tended to work out their own ideas in their own language, the debate has turned partly on questions of the meaning of words and of the inter-relation between different modes of thought and expression. Again, since some of them, animated by a sincere desire to impress the world with the importance of their message, have been at pains to emphasise their differences with older writers, the debate has turned partly on questions of *Dogmengeschichte*, and tended at times to degenerate into a squabble about who said what first. Through the cloud of secondary disputation thus arising, it has not always been easy to see how far the parties are really at issue on matters of substance, or what the bearing of the whole discussion is on the problems of practical economic policy. To the lay public, and even to those professional economists whose main interest lies in other fields, the whole business must often have seemed, to quote from a characteristic letter of Edwin Cannan's which has recently been published, to resemble a number of Roman augurs disputing over the significance of the entrails of a goose. Latterly several helpful attempts have been made to express precisely in mathematical terms some of the points at issue. Has a stage now been reached when it is

[1] This paper was read before the Manchester Statistical Society on Nov. 10, 1937, and was printed both in the Society's *Proceedings* and in *The Manchester School*, 1938, No. 1.

possible to sum the whole position up broadly in more ordinary language, indicating in a general way what departments of the whole tangled controversy seem to be primarily concerned with words and methods, and what with more substantial issues? I do not know, but I should like in this paper to make the attempt.

The attempt, however, especially since it has to be made in cold print and not in informal talk, entails one grave risk which I must be prepared to run. The further one departs from meticulous argument, with quotation of chapter and verse, and the broader one attempts to paint the picture, the more one exposes oneself to the charge of distortion and misrepresentation. I do not know whether I shall enhance that risk or lessen it by abstaining from all quotations and from the mention of any living author by name: but that is the course which I have decided to pursue.

§ 2. I propose to begin by describing broadly in my own words the process of recovery from a depressed level of trade activity. An improved expectation of profit in the minds of entrepreneurs induces them to expand their expenditure on materials and labour, thus enlarging the total of money incomes. The monetary fuel for the expansion is provided partly by the creation of additional money by the banks, partly by the activation of money which has been lying idle in the hands of entrepreneurs themselves or of other people. It depends on circumstances whether the expansion starts in the trades making capital goods or in those making consumption goods: but in whichever it starts it will spread to the other. For the expansion of incomes in the capital trades leads to an increase of expenditure on consumption goods; and the increased profits made in the consumption trades constitute both a means and a motive for increased capital expenditure. And, of course, for similar reasons, expansion in one consumption trade spreads to other consumption trades, and expansion in one capital trade to other capital trades. The increase in expenditure tends to make prices rise, but the use of accumulated stocks, and the expansion of output, tend to prevent them from rising. Similarly the increased demand by entrepreneurs for the use of funds tends to make the rate of interest rise, but the creation of new money, and the withdrawal of old money from hoards, tend to prevent it from rising. In both cases, for whatever exact reasons, sooner or later the tendency to a rise in fact normally predominates.

I find it hard to believe that there will not be something like general agreement with this broad picture. Yet already, in filling in the details of this simple story, there is room for at least eight differences of opinion. I propose to classify these into differences of emphasis and differences of expression, and to deal first with the former.

§ 3. First, there is room for difference of emphasis as to the source of the stream of loanable funds which feeds the expansion. Some observers lay more stress on the creation of new money by the banks, others on the emergence of inactive money from its lair.

Secondly, with respect to each of these streams there is room for difference of emphasis as to how far the increased flow represents an automatic response to the increased demand, the mental disposition of the owners of the flow remaining unchanged; and how far it argues a changed mental disposition on their part—a revision of policy in the case of the banks, an improvement in the state of confidence in the case of the public. In geometrical language, are we to portray what has happened by a movement along an unchanged supply curve, or by a lowering of the whole curve? I am inclined to think that this is a matter in which mathematical habits of thought may have done some harm, by oversharpening a distinction which in the world of human motive is apt to be somewhat blurred. Yet, so far as it goes, the issue is one about psychological facts, and not merely about words: and it has a bearing upon the course of interest-rates.

Thirdly, there is room for difference of emphasis as to whether, in the mutual impact of consumable goods and capital goods trades, the more active rôle is to be assigned to the former or to the latter.

Fourthly, there is the question whether the fertilising stream of loanable funds is to be regarded as flowing mainly through the credit market for short loans or through the capital market for long loans. This question is closely bound up with the third: for while expansion in the consumption goods trades involves recourse to the former market only, expansion in the capital goods trades involves recourse to the latter as well. It is also, for institutional reasons, somewhat closely bound up with the first question—that of the source of the funds. For while an entrepreneur may draw on his own inactive money either for the purchase of plant or for the purchase of materials and labour, the inactive money of other persons is more likely to be canalised, through the security and mortgage markets, into the former than the latter use: while *per contra* the money creating banks have a traditional preference for lending, on short term, for working capital purposes.

There is, however, an institutional complication here on which some would lay much stress. The money-creating banks are not averse from intervention in one specialised department of the capital market, namely that concerned with Government debt. By relieving holders of their holdings, furnishing them instead with money which can be turned to other uses, the banks are thus able indirectly to propel a stream of long term loanable funds in the direction of those who wish to use them for the purchase of capital goods.

Fifthly, there is room for difference of emphasis as to the part played in the story by accumulated stocks of goods. On the one hand particular stress may be laid on the fact that it is on these stocks that the first impact of increased demand falls, and on the working of economic motive in the minds of the specialised merchants in whose hands they are largely concentrated; on the other hand, these things may be treated as complications of secondary importance.

In all these matters there is scope for difference of

opinion as to what happens in the real world. There is room, therefore, not only for argument but for hope, within the well-known limitations of our unhappy science, that it may become increasingly possible to put argument to inductive test. But it would, I think, be very surprising if complete knowledge of the facts were to reveal that the sequence and balance of events were the same on each historical occasion. It may well prove that the views which find expression in these differences of emphasis are complementary rather than conflicting.

§ 4. I pass to the second class of differences, those which I have called differences of expression—though I am afraid there is no doubt that some of those who recognise here their own views will resent hearing them described in this way, since to themselves their own mode of language has quite naturally come to seem the ark of the covenant, essential to the exposition of the truth as they see it.

(i) First, a choice is open to us with regard to our treatment of the monetary fuel of expansion. We can analyse objectively, in terms of the flow of short term and long term loanable funds finding their way into and out of their respective markets in successive short arbitrarily delimited slices of time. Or we can analyse subjectively, in terms of the conditions which must exist, at successive arbitrarily selected points of time, if all the actors in the drama of the exchange of money for other assets are to be satisfied with their positions on the stage. So far as this paper goes, I have, as you will have observed, already made my choice; and for the purpose in hand, which is to give an account of events in language as nearly as possible approaching that of *Reading without Tears*, I am prepared to defend it. Against the alternative method it may, I think, be urged that psychological inferences from observed facts, valid enough in the still-life photography of stable situations, have their danger when introduced into the cinematography of processes of rapid and cumulative change. For at 5 p.m. on Wednesday, November 10, the moment we hit upon for our shot, it may be far from true that all the actors *are* satisfied with their positions on the stage. Things have turned out as they *have* turned out—there is nothing to be done about it at the moment—the banks are shut—the works manager is on leave—the cornfield has been laid down to grass. Considerations of this kind cannot, I think, be neglected if our economics is to be really dynamics and not simply comparative statics. Nevertheless, there is no need to be dogmatic or exclusive in this matter of verbal machinery. A Paretian analysis in terms of preferences equated at the margin does, provided it is duly qualified to allow for the occurrence of the unexpected and the undesigned, go deeper towards the heart of things than a mechanistic analysis in terms of money flows.

§ 5. (ii) Somewhat similar considerations arise in respect of the second matter to which I turn. We have a choice as to how we shall represent the causation of the rise in prices by which, as we have seen, expansion is normally accompanied. We can say that the rise is "due to" the impact of the swollen stream of money demand on to a volume of output initially unchanged; that the rise in prices in turn, since it is not accompanied by an equal rise in unit costs, stimulates an increase in the volume of output; and that the increase in output moderates the rise in prices which gave it birth. Alternatively we can say that the swollen stream of money demand stimulates an increase in the volume of output, and that the rise in prices is "due to" the fact that increased output can only be produced at rising marginal costs. The first method of approach leads naturally to the proposition "the greater the increase in output, the smaller the rise in prices," the second to the proposition "the greater the increase in output, the greater the rise in prices." Yet, paradoxically enough, these two propositions are not in conflict; each of them, in the sense in which it is intended, is true.

Against the first method of approach, that of the traditional quantity theory of money, it may be said that it is somewhat mechanical and also somewhat incomplete, since it fails to make explicit the underlying technical factors on which the outcome depends. The second method, the extension to "output as a whole" of the ordinary short period theory of value of individual commodities, fills in the gap. The danger of the second method, as an instrument for the analysis of a dynamic process, is to my mind that, unless expressed with extreme care, it leads to an overestimate of the extent to which, at any moment, the short-period equilibrium of the textbooks is being attained. To say that price is determined by marginal cost is always bad theory; even to say that price at every moment is equal to marginal cost is a rash statement, unless the concept of marginal cost is defined with a sophistication which robs it of much of its instructiveness. We cannot, I think, in the analysis of a dynamic process, do without the supplementary Marshallian concept of *market* equilibrium, with price emerging from the mutual impact, at each moment, of the existing flows of money and of goods; and that is the concept of the quantity theory. Taking a longer viewpoint, price and output can be portrayed, if we like, as the joint determinees of the determining forces of demand and supply, their respective levels being governed by the "elasticity of supply": though even so, the causal content of the concept of elasticity is the degree to which supply will "stretch itself out" under the impulse of a given change in price, not the degree to which price will "stretch itself up" in association with a given increase in supply.

I suggest therefore that here too a battle of words has been allowed to develop between two modes of thought each of which has something to contribute towards an understanding of the real world.

§ 6. (iii) Thirdly, I turn to a more complicated issue. There runs through much of the literature of this subject a suggestion that there is a peculiar connection between the rise in prices which occurs during an expansion and the contemporary formation of material capital—a connection of such a kind that those who suffer from the rising prices may be said in some sense to be bearing the burden involved in the formation of the material capital. Attempts have been made to give precision to this notion in various ways. Thus it has been said that throughout such a period capital-formation (sometimes nowadays called, rather confusingly, by the name "investment") is outrunning saving or alternatively, that some of the saving which is being done is forced saving: or again, that a levy of real things is being extracted from certain sections of the population in the interests of capital-formation. Others, however, now denounce this whole order of ideas as nonsensical. It is true, they say, that the rise in prices will raise the real incomes of entrepreneurs and lower those of dons and Members of Parliament, of *rentiers* and of the hired workers (of all grades) already in industrial employment. But the increased saving which will be done by the entrepreneurs is perfectly voluntary, and indistinguishable from any other saving. As for the dons and the *rentiers*, they are not of much account anyway; and as for the hired workers, they are getting the full value of their work to the entrepreneur (this part of the argument depends on the attainment of theoretical short period equilibrium); and in any case, since they are willing to continue at work for the lowered real wage, there is no foundation for the idea that any kind of constraint is being put upon them. To those rational arguments it is sometimes attempted to lend support by what appears to be a verbal trick. Definitions are so framed that the amount of money saved in any interval of time is identical with the amount of money devoted to the formation of material capital; and it is suggested that this *ex definitione* identity in itself somehow discredits the notion that there is anything worthy of special comment in the process by which the formation of capital is being carried on.

Thrown thus upon the defensive, the other party rake over again the entrails of the goose. They point out that the identity just mentioned would hold equally in a period of hyper-inflation in which prices were doubling every hour and output was not increasing at all; and they therefore decline to be impressed by it. They set themselves to excogitate alternatives to the offending definition—alternatives which turn on the parcelling of time into successive phases, or on a distinction between the saving, and the capital-formation, which is planned in advance and that which actually materialises. Attempts are made to analyse the concept of "levy" or "burden" into two parts, one associated instantaneously with each upward thrust of prices, the other enduringly with the raised state of prices. As regards the hired worker it is pointed out that in a period of rapid expansion the short-period marginal product of labour may well fall below its true or long-period marginal product; so that even if the worker is receiving the former he may in a sense be receiving less than his "due," even according to the rough canons of economic pseudo-justice. And it is suggested that the argument that his actions show him to be content to work for a lowered real wage is exposed to the same danger as other attempts to reason in terms of stable psychological preferences on the basis of the phenomena observed during periods of rapid change. So the debate goes on, and the end, I fancy, is not yet.

Now in all this there is, I believe, hardly any disagreement about what happens in the real world. In a sense therefore the controversy is, like the two preceding ones, one about words rather than about things. But it is also something more; for into the rival terminologies there enters an element of commentary or judgment. The party which seeks to give precision to the idea of a levy is anxious that we should understand that you cannot make an omelette without breaking eggs: the party which pours scorn on their efforts is anxious that we should understand that by breaking a few eggs you can make a most delicious omelette. This particular piece of verbal disputation, therefore, serves to introduce us to a more fundamental issue than any we have yet considered; and to that issue I now pass.

§ 7. Is there, or is there not, in considering the relation between monetary phenomena and general economic activity, anything in the notion that there is a certain state of affairs which is to be regarded as "normal," while every other state of affairs is to be regarded as a deviation from the normal, either by way of excess or defect? Until recently there has been, I think, something like general agreement that this *is* a valid and instructive notion; and a large number of attempts has been made to give it greater precision. Efforts have been made to define the policy which is required in order that money shall be "neutral" in its effect on economic life, not of course in the sense of failing to raise it above the low level which alone would be possible if there were no money, but in the sense of failing to introduce an incidental element of distortion or disturbance. The implications of this policy have been explored in terms of the behaviour of prices, of the rate of interest and of various types of incomes. A supplementary criterion of neutrality has been sought in the degree to which the banking system succeeds in acting as a true intermediary, that is in giving effect to the thrifty intentions of the public, without either outrunning them on the one hand or allowing them to go to waste on the other. Another has been sought in the degree to which "windfall" profits, or losses, accrue to the entrepreneur at the expense, or to the benefit, of the hired factors of production.

The difficulties which have been found in giving precision to this notion of normality or neutrality in the behaviour of money may be classified into three orders. The first arises already when we try to apply the notion to an imaginary static society. Even there the relation between the various criteria and subcriteria which have been proposed is not easy to establish. It would seem, for instance, that it must be conceivable that money should behave unneutrally (*e.g.* through a governmental inflation) even in a community of small independent farmers, craftsmen and traders, in which there is no question of distortion of contracts between entrepreneurs and hired factors; and this casts doubt on the adequacy of one of our suggested criteria. A second set of difficulties arises when we go on to examine the implications of neutrality in a society which is making steady progress in numbers, in technical skill, in capital equipment or in some combination of two or more of these three things. Some writers, for instance, have argued that under certain conditions neutrality will call for progressive reductions in the money rates of reward of the hired factors of production. Others would reply that it is satisfied *ex definitione* by the avoidance of entrepreneurial windfall profit or loss in the face of a money level of factor rewards which is to be regarded as one of the given conditions of the problem. Here the difficulty arises that we cannot take the money rates of reward of *all* the hired factors of production as fixed data if the particular type of progress under analysis entails an alteration in the relative abundance of the different factors—as in the case, for instance, of a community whose capital equipment is growing faster than its population.

For these and similar difficulties it is not, I think, impossible to hope for reasonable, if somewhat rough and ready, solutions, and there has been, perhaps, some tendency to make too heavy weather about them. But a third and more formidable set of difficulties is encountered when we ask what there is left of the notion of monetary neutrality for a society which has once, for whatever reason, been thrown off the rails of steady advance, or for one which, like our own, has never really yet succeeded in adhering to them. Does it, under such conditions, imply the maintenance of the situation existing at the moment, or the restoration of some previously existing situation, or the attainment of some situation never hitherto attained? Or is it in fact not merely impossible to use it as a guide to policy but impossible even to believe that it means anything at all? And if it has no meaning in a fluctuating society, is it worth bothering about what it *would* mean in a steadily progressing one? Must not the whole line of thought be dismissed as a will-o'-the-wisp? It is this wave of scepticism as to the blessings of the golden mean, as to the validity of the Blondin[1] *motif* by which most monetary theory has been permeated, that lies behind the verbal sparrings about saving and investment and so forth, and is the real key to the controversies of the present day.

§ 8. In the light of this discussion, let us go back to the process of expansion with which we started. Penetrating as best we can behind the verbal smoke-screens, we shall find it possible, I think, to distinguish three attitudes of mind with which the expansory process is regarded. Since we have forbidden ourselves to mention names, we must find labels for these attitudes of mind; and we will call them the Optimistic, the Pessimistic and the Blondinian. But the matter is complicated, as we shall find, by the division of the Pessimists into two groups, united in little but their pessimism.

The thorough-going Optimist has cured himself of the Blondin complex, which he regards as an infantile obsession. To him the expansion is a mere process of transition from one stable equilibrium to another, from stable equilibrium at a low level which should never have been allowed to exist to stable equilibrium at a much higher level; and he sees no reason why that higher level should not be the "normal" level in what he regards as the only respectable sense of that word, namely the level at which there is virtually full employment of all the human and material resources of the community. The Optimist is no doubt aware that the expansory process takes place in time and by stages; but he is not much interested in that fact, for his eyes are on the goal. So far as he meditates on the process at all, he pictures it as convergent and irreversible—or, to speak more simply, as a lift in which a wise community may

[1] It appears, somewhat to my surprise, to be necessary to add a footnote to explain that Blondin was a famous tight-rope walker of the latter part of the nineteenth century.

voyage, almost timelessly and once for all, from the basement to the top floor.

The two Pessimists smell the seeds of trouble in the expansion from the start. To Pessimist A the processes by which it is being fuelled—the withdrawal of money from hoards, the creation of money by the banks—are sufficient evidence that it can come to no good. For in his eyes these are the very things which constitute unneutrality in the behaviour of money, bringing on to the markets for goods a one-sided stream of demand. True the output of goods is expanding; but it is expanding lopsidedly, with capital goods in alarming prominence. True also that profits are rising, furnishing entrepreneurs with the wherewithal to buy some of these capital goods, and mitigating to that extent the pressure on the banks and on the hoards; but that will come to an end by and by, as the classes who have been mulcted by the rise in prices gather strength to re-assert their claims. Then the inflated profits will shrink, the demand for capital goods fade away, and the expansion end, like all its predecessors, in collapse.

In the mind of Pessimist B the spectacle of expansion breeds a different fear. It is not the *means* for the purchase of capital goods whose drying up he foresees, but the *motive*. He resembles the Optimist in declining to be shocked at the methods by which the pump is being primed, and in laying great stress on current profits as a fertile source of funds for the purchase of capital goods; but he differs from the Optimist in seeing no secure platform ahead. For the size of these same profits gives him pause. Like Pessimist A he is concerned at their growth relatively to other incomes, but for a different reason; it is this relative growth itself, not the prospect of its reversal, which makes him uneasy. For rich people have less need to spend up to the hilt than poor people; hence sooner or later the rate of increase in the demand for consumption goods will decline, and with it will decline the incentive to purchase capital goods even on the existing scale.

The entrepreneur profits which have been the sheet-anchor of revival will creep into funk-holes and so be revealed as the *fons et origo* of collapse.

The attitude of the unconverted Blondinian is more difficult to summarise; and it is easy to deride it as a ragbag of opposing views. Like Pessimist A he detects something *outré*, something worthy at least of special nomenclature, in the process by which the expansion is being fuelled. But he insists that climbing back on to a tight-rope is a different thing from falling off it on the other side, and that ostensibly similar measures are to be viewed with different eyes according as they contribute to the one proceeding or the other. To restore profits towards normality is not the same thing, though it may entail the same actions, as to inflate them beyond the normal; and a rise in the cost of living which, while thwarting the expectations of yesterday, restores those of the day before, is not necessarily either condemnable or certain to provoke resistance. Thus like the Optimist, the Blondinian has his gaze fixed, if I may mix the metaphor, upon a platform; but the platform is both less lofty than the Optimist's and less easily to be identified. For the business man will be in no hurry to admit that profits have been restored to normal; nor, with the best will in the world, is it easy for the Trade Union leader to distinguish between the windfall element in real wages which should be surrendered in the interests of higher employment, and the increment due to secular progress which can safely be retained. Above all, the state of employment of men and plant offers no certain test for the recognition of the platform; for the distribution of productive resources between the consumption and the capital-making trades is the result of the cyclical process from which we are seeking escape, and can neither be permanently taken for granted nor altered in the twinkling of an eye. Thus in respect of fullness of employment the "normal" now speedily attainable is inferior to the normal of our dreams—the normal of the society which has never lapsed from an even rate of progress. That higher normal, so the Blondinian fears, cannot be attained through the Optimist's recipe of aiming at it directly by letting the cumulative expansion rip—that would only be to court reaction and relapse. The only hope of attaining it lies in checking the cumulative expansion at some point selected with what judgment and wisdom we can command, and then letting the slow processes of occupational adjustment get to work. If, however, some such clean-up could once be effected, and a true Blondinian policy thereafter be pursued, we might indulge a reasonable hope for the future. For the disasters envisaged by the Pessimists—both the short sharp shortages of saving which are the bugbear of Pessimist A, and the longer, more debilitating gluts of saving which are the bugbear of Pessimist B—are alike the result of attempts to force unduly the pace of material progress.

§ 9. So far I have made little explicit mention of the rate of interest; for indeed, if I have a personal heresy in these matters, it is that in recent years, alike in academic financial and political circles, we have heard rather too much about that entity in connection with the processes of trade recovery and recession. But of course many of the discussions which I have passed in review can be, and have been, conducted in terms of the nature and behaviour of the rate of interest; and I must not let my personal heresy inhibit me from saying something more about it.

As I have already hinted (§ 4), and have argued at length elsewhere,[1] one of the controversies of which it has recently been the centre seems to me to be a shadow-fight. We may start by regarding the rate of interest ruling during any short period of time as the price which equates the flow of loanable funds, which some people are prepared to put on the market during that short period of time, with the flow which other people are prepared to take off it. For this procedure it can be said that it accords well both with the ordinary language of the newspapers, and with the tendency of

[1] *E.J.*, Sept. 1937, pp. 428 ff.

modern economic theory to exhibit the hire-prices of the several factors of production as special cases of a general law of pricing. Alternatively we may start by regarding the rate of interest ruling at a moment of time as registering a momentary contentment in the breasts of the members of the community with respect to the distribution of their resources between certain rival uses. For this more recondite approach there is also, on methodological grounds, a good deal to be said. But the two approaches are complementary, not conflicting: and both of them leave a great deal still to be added.

For the real issue lies deeper. In the broadest terms it can perhaps be put as follows. How close and fruitful an approach to reality do we attain by considering the rate of interest as the resultant of two main forces—man's ingenuity in dealing productively with the forces of nature on the one hand, and his reluctance to forego the immediate consumption of the fruits of his efforts on the other? Of what order of magnitude is the difference made to the picture by taking account of two other factors—man's ability to control by means of specialised organs the supply of acceptable means of payment, and his readiness within limits to sacrifice income, whether present or future, in return for the advantages of avoiding trouble and of enjoying security against unforeseen contingencies?

The Blondinian answer to this question runs in terms of the divergence between a "natural" rate of interest, prescribed by the two major underlying forces specified just now, and an actual or market rate which is influenced also by the two minor or complicating ones. Like other Blondinian concepts, the natural rate of interest has encountered somewhat heavy weather in the course of its career. It was born entangled with probably fruitless speculations about what would happen in a world of barter, and with particular propositions about the behaviour of the price-level, from which it has had to be freed. It has tended to become entangled, too, with a different concept—that of an actually existing "profit rate" received by the entrepreneur, and differing—whether through inclusion of a risk element or on account of imperfection in the market for loans—from the rate at which he can hire loanable funds from other people. Of the two forces deflecting the actual from the natural rate, which we may call for short monetary policy and liquidity preference, it is arguable that until recently too little attention has been paid by Blondinians to the latter; while in respect of the former it is possible to detect differences of emphasis as to the degree of its deflecting power, Wicksell, for instance (for I have not forbidden myself to mention the great dead) tending at times to represent it as almost absolute, and Marshall being concerned to stress its limitations. Above all, the concept of the natural rate of interest, like that of neutral money, has been explored rather from the point of view of a traveller who desires to keep to the straight path than from that of one who has lost it and desires to regain it. All things considered, it is not perhaps surprising that a movement should have developed to throw the natural rate of interest down the sink, and to pay scant heed to the cries of Blondinians to beware lest the bath-water may contain a precious baby.

§ 10. In the ruthless hands that grip the sides of the bath, we can perhaps recognise those of our old friends the Optimist and the Pessimist type B (§ 8). The Optimist is persuaded not only of the power of the monetary authority to make the short term rate of interest what it pleases, but of the existence of channels between the various parts of the capital market so wide and deep as to give that authority effective control over the long term rate of interest as well. He does not, I think, in essence deny, though he has his own way of re-phrasing, the Marshallian proposition that the same monetary action which tends to lower the rate of interest now will set in motion forces tending to raise it again later; but he believes that the monetary authority has it in its power to keep these forces indefinitely at bay through administering repeated doses of the same medicine. Nor again does he deny that, with a given level and a given distribution of output, a relation will be found existing between the rate of interest and the degree of the community's reluctance to postpone consumption. But he believes it to be within the power of the monetary authority to establish, without risk of reversal, such a level and distribution of output that this relation is satisfied, whatever rate of interest the authority chooses to prescribe.

On the other side of the bath stands the B Pessimist (who in this connection is sometimes the same natural person as the Optimist, in a different mood). In his eyes, as in those of the Optimist, the alleged extravagance of the human race presents no insuperable obstacle to the power of the monetary authority to keep down the rate of interest: that problem looks after itself through an appropriate adjustment of the distribution of real income in favour of those who are too rich to desire to be extravagant. His bugbear is a different trait of human nature—the debilitating caution which leads the owners of wealth to prefer safety to income and so to desire to withhold their saved wealth from productive uses. It is the business of the monetary authorities to indulge this craving for security to the best of their ability, and so to rob it of its sting, by providing the owners of wealth with plenty of nice safe money in exchange for their income-yielding assets. But it must be feared that there is a limit to their powers, and that after a point, so far as the long-term rate of interest goes, against the rock of "liquidity preference" the waves of monetary expansion will beat in vain.

In this field the shades of doctrine are so subtle, and still so much in a state of flux, that an attempt to paint a broad picture is especially risky; nevertheless I must take my life in my hands. It seems to me that between the Blondinian and the B Pessimist there are certain points of agreement and certain points of difference. Both would agree that at any moment the individual tends to hold his wealth so distributed between different uses that at the margin there is equality between the satisfaction which he derives directly from the inactive part and that which he derives, through the mediation of a flow of income, from the active part. Both would agree that a change in the individual's disposition towards the holding of inactive wealth, such as might be due for instance to an impairment or a restoration of political confidence, would lead to an attempt to transfer wealth from one use to the other; so that from a short period point of view the "state of liquidity preference," like the policy of the monetary authority, can be truly represented as exercising a *causal* influence upon the rate of interest. But in the mind of the Pessimist this causal influence of liquidity preference upon the rate of interest is a persistent and independent thing, overshadowing in importance every other force; while in the mind of the Blondinian, the longer the period of time under review, the more does this force recede into the background, yielding pride of place to the more fundamental influences of productivity and thrift. For this, in the mind of the Blondinian, there are two separate reasons. In the first place it does not seem to him likely that the rate of interest equated in the mind of the money-holder with the convenience and security derived from holding any *n*th unit of money is arrived at by some kind of intuition functioning *in vacuo*, which, apart from temporary fluctuations, gives an identical answer in all circumstances; it seems more likely that it will itself depend upon the rate of return obtainable from using resources in a more active manner. Thus (to use language departing a little, I am afraid, from that of *Reading without Tears*) the schedule connecting the holding of money with the rate of interest loses its status as an independent determining force, and becomes a kind of mobile satellite of the schedule connecting the rate of interest with the active employment of resources. But secondly, even if this were not so, and the "schedule of liquidity preference" remained unchanged in the face of growing wealth, what that schedule expresses is a desire not to hold so much money, but to hold, in the form of money, command over so many real things. Temporary fluctuations either way in the rate of interest will produce in the long run such movements in the level of prices and of money incomes as to destroy themselves, and to assign to the "liquidity preference schedule," as its permanent rôle, a share in the determination not of the rate of interest at all but of the price-level.

Thus the Blondinian, less sanguine than the Optimist about the power of the monetary authority to make the rate of interest what it pleases, is also less apprehensive than the Pessimist about the power of the hoarding instinct to oppose a chronic resistance to such a secular fall in the rate of interest as the forces of thrift and productivity may dictate. That is the nearest which I can get to putting in words of (approximately) one syllable the upshot of all this pother about the rate of interest.

§ 11. My purpose in this paper has been, first, to disentangle issues of words from issues of substance, and secondly, in respect of the latter, to set forth opposing viewpoints as fairly as possible without pronouncing between them. But I am aware that to many people I shall seem in my exposition to have done something more than justice to that general standpoint which I have called Blondinian. For to many people this standpoint seems outrageously timorous in its apprehensions that to aim always at the maximum level of activity immediately attainable is to court future trouble (§ 8); and at the same time outrageously complacent in its faith that through all the manifest evils of fluctuation there persists a long-period tendency of the system to right itself rather than, as some have argued, a chronic disposition to run down (§ 10). I would like therefore to end by making it plain that I think there is much even for the convinced Blondinian to keep turning over in his mind. How far has the resilience which he detects in the system been bound up with that rapid growth of population which for the western world has now become a thing of the past? Can the authoritarian State solve that problem of periodic painless transition from a higher to a lower level of fixed capital formation which liberalistic capitalism has failed to solve, and if so is the achievement worth the price? If it is not worth the price, would a drastic redistribution of income help towards keeping the system moving forward at a pace no greater than can be continuously maintained, and if so how is it to be achieved? To suspect that from a long-run point of view Cheap Money may prove a broken reed and Liquidity Preference a bogy man is not necessarily to suppose that all is for the best in the best of all possible worlds.

XII

BRITISH MONETARY POLICY [1]

I

THE passing of the Currency and Bank Notes Act, 1939, affords a convenient opportunity to summarise the revolutionary changes which have taken place in the British monetary system in the last eight years.

On September 21, 1931, the convertibility of the Bank of England note into gold bullion, at a rate corresponding to a price of 85*s.* per fine ounce, was suspended. The price of gold rose rapidly to 120*s.*; by 1935 it had reached 140*s.*, and towards the end of 1938 it rose again to not far short of 150*s.*, *i.e.* to one and three-quarter times the old price. Though the pound has thus been detached from gold, the general set-up of the monetary system, as established by the Act of 1844 and confirmed by that of 1928, has been in appearance retained. British legal tender money is still ostensibly a "liability" of the Bank of England, duly set off (in something which, if not exactly a balance-sheet, is as near to one as such an august body can be expected to present) against "assets" which consist partly of gold and partly—*i.e* to the extent of the so-called "fiduciary issue"—of Government securities. But in reality the whole position as regards the determination of the country's supply of money has been transformed by three factors: (1) the institution of the Exchange Equalisation Account as a second holder of gold, (2) the use in a manner not originally contemplated of the provisions contained in the Act of 1928 for varying the fiduciary issue, and (3) the *de jure* recognition of the variability in the sterling price of gold.

[1] *Lloyds Bank Review*, May 1939.

The effect of the operations of the Exchange Equalisation Account in the six years which followed its birth in April, 1932, can be differently described according as we make comparison with what would have happened in its absence under a régime of free exchanges or with what would have happened under a gold standard. As compared with the former it had served to lead gold into the Bank, as compared with the latter it had served to keep it out. By the middle of 1937 it had spent sums which must have been of the order of £300 million in buying gold which it had re-sold to the Bank for £205 million, *i.e.* for the highest price (85*s.* per fine ounce), which the Bank could in those days properly agree to pay, since on entering its portals all gold shrank automatically in stature (in a manner with which the casual visitor to that institution will sympathise) to its pre-1931 value in terms of pounds. Had the fiduciary issue remained unchanged at the level of £275 million at which it stood in the spring of 1932, this would have enabled the Bank (which at that date had held only £120 million of gold) to expand the note issue from £395 to £600 million; but in fact the fiduciary issue was reduced to £260 million in March, 1933, and to £200 million in December, 1936, so that the note issue rose only to £525 million. Thanks, however, to this growth the authorities were enabled to pursue an expansionist policy, as well as to offset the hoarding of British notes by foreigners, in a manner which would otherwise, in the then state of the law, scarcely have been open to them.

Nevertheless, by the spring of 1938 the Exchange Equalisation Account itself also held some £300 million worth (at 140*s.*) of gold, which had *not* been allowed to penetrate into the monetary system, but was being held to meet a possible reversal of the process, namely a strong disposition on the part of foreigners to remit money to England for safe-keeping, which had brought it hither. As a result of the international crisis and the consequent flight of foreign capital, this gold had been reduced by the end of 1938 to a figure which has not been revealed but is commonly thought to have been less than £100 million. In January, 1939, it was augmented by a retransfer to the Exchange Equalisation Account of nearly all the gold which the latter had sold to the Bank in the course of its life, *viz.* £200 million worth at 85*s.* per fine ounce or £350 million at the then market price of 148*s.* 6*d.* The gap thus created in the assets of the Issue Department of the Bank was first filled by Government securities, the fiduciary issue being raised for the purpose to £400 million; but a little later, by the Act which became law on February 28, the fiduciary issue was lowered to £300 million, and the gap filled by revaluing the remaining £125 million of gold at the market price, *viz.* at £220 million, supplemented by a re-re-transfer of £5 million of gold from the Exchange Equalisation Account to the Bank.[1]

Thus, through their combined power of shifting gold between the Exchange Equalisation Account and the Issue Department and of altering the amount of the fiduciary issue, the authorities have been able to make the behaviour of the Bank's gold reserve conform to that of its note issue instead of the other way round. It follows that, instead of making the amount of the balances held by bankers with the Banking Department conform to the reserve of notes held by that Department, they have been able to make the latter conform to the former; and the state of the Banking Department's reserve has lost that central significance which it had possessed ever since 1844. The bankers' balances have been allowed to stand at a level higher by more than a half than that which prevailed before 1931; though since the till-money held by the banks themselves, which used to form two-thirds of their "cash" reserve, has increased very little, their total "cash reserve," and hence the total of bank deposits—which, of course, form the preponderant element in the

[1] In this narrative I have used round figures, and have omitted complications caused by the fact that on two occasions temporary expansions of the fiduciary issue have been made to meet the exceptional demand for notes at Christmas time.

country's money supply—has stood at only about a quarter above the pre-1931 level.

The meteoric changes in the volume of the fiduciary issue would seem to have robbed that venerable entity of whatever rational significance it may once have possessed. In the old days of a gold circulation and Bank notes of a minimum denomination of £5, it may perhaps have been possible to regard it as that part of the note circulation with which the business world would find it very difficult in any circumstances to dispense, and which therefore could "safely" be left uncovered by gold. With the advent of the £1 Bank note and the abolition of convertibility into gold coin, this explanation lost heavily in plausibility: nevertheless the Act of 1928 preserved some significance, if not for the absolute amount of the fiduciary issue, at any rate for the powers of growth with which it was at that date endowed. That the supply of legal tender money should be permitted to grow with the growth of population—that it should be capable of temporary expansion in emergency without recourse to a breach of the law—such innovations could be interpreted as a natural development of the old system. But what is the public to make of a régime under which, without any change in the underlying situation, it can ostensibly be the considered judgment of authority that in January £200 million of notes can safely lack a gold backing, in February as many as £400 million, while by March safety has prescribed a splitting of the difference?

The Act of 1939 has on paper increased in an important particular the wide powers of manœuvre already possessed by the authorities. For it recognises not only that the sterling price of gold has changed since 1931, but that it may change in future. The gold in the Issue Department is now re-valued weekly at the market price, any increment or deficiency of value thus revealed being handed over to, or made good by, the Exchange Equalisation Account. This procedure opens up attractive vistas of thought. Thus suppose, to take an extreme example, that by a wild inflation of credit the price of gold were driven up to 200*s*. per fine ounce; the Bank's gold would rise in value by some £80 million, and £80 million additional notes could be printed and handed over to the Exchange Equalisation Account, which could deposit them with the Banking Department, thus expanding by a like amount the latter's reserve. No need for any further skylarking with the fiduciary issue! No need for the costly business of buying gold in the market! The Bank's gold has apparently come to share with the amœba and the jelly-fish the enviable faculty of reproduction by fissure.

The British monetary system, as it has emerged from the furnace of the last eight years, is thus on the face of it a somewhat eccentric contraption. Between some enquiring Socrates from another planet and an economist instructed to explain its nature some such dialogue as the following might well take place:—

Socrates: I see that your chief piece of money carries a legend affirming that it is a promise to pay the bearer the sum of one pound. What is this thing, a pound, of which payment is thus promised?

Œconomist: A pound is the British unit of account.

Socrates: So there is, I suppose, some concrete object which embodies more firmly that abstract unit of account than does this paper promise?

Œconomist: There is no such object, O Socrates.

Socrates: Indeed? Then what your Bank promises is to give me another promise stamped with a different number in case I should regard the number stamped on this promise as in some way ill-omened?

Œconomist: It would seem, indeed, to be promising something of that kind.

Socrates: So that in order to be in a position to fulfil its promises all the Bank has to do is to keep a store of such promises stamped with all sorts of different numbers?

Œconomist: By no means, Socrates—that would make its balance-sheet a subject for mockery, and in the eyes of our people there resides in a balance-sheet a certain awe and holiness. The Bank has to keep a store of Government securities and a store of gold.

Socrates: What are Government securities?

Œconomist: Promises by the Government to pay certain sums of money at certain dates.

Socrates: What are sums of money? Do you mean Bank of England notes?

Œconomist: I suppose I do.

Socrates: So these promises to pay promises are thought to be in some way solider and more sacred than the promises themselves?

Œconomist: They are so thought, as it appears.

Socrates: I see. Now tell me about the gold. It has to be of a certain weight, I suppose?

Œconomist: Not of a certain weight, but of a certain value in terms of the promises.

Socrates: So that the less each of its promises is worth, the more promises the Bank can lawfully make?

Œconomist: It seems, indeed, to amount to something of that kind.

Socrates: Do you find that your monetary system works well?

Œconomist: Pretty well, thank you, Socrates, on the whole.

Socrates: That would be, I suppose, not because of the rather strange rules of which you have told me, but because it is administered by men of ability and wisdom?

Œconomist: It would seem that that must be the reason, rather than the rules themselves, O Socrates.

II

What are the considerations by which the "men of ability and wisdom" are guided in steering this curious car along the crowded and perilous roads of the contemporary world? That is a question whose full answer is known only (if at all) to themselves. But it would seem that they must be supposed to pay regard to at least four major factors, which can conveniently be thought of as four *prices*, and the inter-relation between which is by no means always simple. These are the prices of commodities, of Government securities of various dates, of dollars and of gold.

When the new system was coming to birth in 1932, it was generally recognised that the prices of commodities stood at so low a level as, in view of the burden of charges fixed by legal agreement or powerful frictional forces in terms of money, to constitute a strong discouragement to enterprise and employment, and indeed to imperil the whole structure of business relations. It was accordingly the avowed object of British monetary policy, as set forth at the Ottawa Conference of 1932, and again at the abortive London Conference of 1933, to promote their recovery to a more remunerative level. The subsequent rise, as indicated by the advance of the Board of Trade wholesale index number from 60 per cent. of the 1924 level in the autumn of 1932 to 70 per cent. in the autumn of 1936, may thus be presumed to have been wholly in accordance with their aims. Subsequent events have, however, enveloped in a certain mistiness the concept of a given behaviour of prices as the primary objective of monetary policy. The sharp rise of the index to 80 in the summer of 1937 reminded even those who had found it convenient to forget the teachings of history in this respect that once industrial activity has attained a certain level it may prove very difficult to raise it further except to the accompaniment of a price-rise so pronounced and so uneven as to generate instability and subsequent relapse; and the forgotten concepts of the bottle-neck and the vicious circle crept back into the vocabulary even of the prophets of expansion. In 1938 the sharp recession in trade and employment, accompanied by a fall of the price-index back to 70, restored a strong presumption in favour of reopening the throttle; and the decision to finance £350 million of the armament expenditure of 1939-40 by loan was an indication that the powers that be were alive to the strength of that presumption. But it may be conjectured that they would find it considerably harder to-day than they did in 1932 to give a clear and succinct account of exactly how they wish to see the level of commodity prices behave in the coming years. Judicious phrases about balance and stability would, it seems, of necessity replace the old claims that the snapping of the gold link has cleared the way for full steam ahead along the exhilarating road which leads through the Land of Rising Prices to the City of Prosperity.

If the level of prices in 1932 was by common consent too low for comfort, so the level of interest rates was by common consent too high; and the most spectacular apparent achievement of the new régime has been to bring down rates in the money market to little above zero and the yield on long term Government debt from the region of 5 to the region of 3½ per cent. (not to mention the consequential breach in that time-honoured dyke, the minimum rate of 5 per cent. for bank advances). Indeed, it is on this homely medicine of cheap money, by contrast with the more sophisticated drugs employed in other lands, that the authorities have, until recently, placed almost exclusive reliance for restoring health to the economic body. Here again, however, experience and reflection have led to the emergence of a certain scepticism. The fall in rates from the inflated level of the 1920's is seen in retrospect to have been a development entirely consonant with the underlying conditions of demand and supply in the world markets for capital—a development which it was in the power of monetary policies to ease or to retard, but for which we may be excused for hesitating to accord them exclusive credit. Furthermore, in spite of the debauch of the short term market, the ground won between the parallels of 3½ and 3 per cent. in the gilt-edged sector has hitherto proved impossible to consolidate: and economists have amused themselves by enshrining in curves and equations the apparent unwillingness of the investor to be persuaded by the flood of cheap money that human inventiveness on the one hand, and human extravagance on the other, have vanished for ever from the earth. Finally, the heretical doubts long nurtured by the present writer as to whether in the lecture-rooms alike of Vienna and of Cambridge, in the pronouncements alike of Fleet Street and of Whitehall, we were not hearing rather too much about the rate of interest as the arbiter of industrial activity have not remained unechoed. Comparable with the famous strife in Lilliput between Big-Endians and Little-Endians, there has emerged in the economic world a lively battle between Long-Raters and Short-Raters, each, indeed, claiming almost magical powers for his own specific but each pouring well-argued ridicule on the pretensions of the other. The business man, called in to arbitrate between the parties, has shown a disconcerting tendency to belittle the claims of both. One way and another the rôle of the rate of interest in economic affairs has come to seem less plain a matter than it did in 1932, when Humpty Dumpty was crying aloud to be helped or hustled off his 5 per cent. wall.

In guessing at the mind of the powers that be in this matter of the rates of interest, it is necessary to remember that they are inevitably endowed in this connection with a dual personality. As controllers of the monetary system, they must be supposed to desire that such rates of interest shall at any time prevail as are likely to prove consistent with the objectives at which they are aiming in the domain of production and prices: but as guardians of the public purse they are likely to desire that the rates shall at all times stand at the lowest level that can possibly be contrived. There are certain phases in the cyclical ebb and flow of trade in which these two laudable desires may come into conflict. Thus, while it may be accepted that the establishment of a low rate at the bottom of a slump is conducive, so far as it goes, to industrial recovery, the very process of recovery tends normally to bring a hardening of the rate; and there is some danger that the fear of this consequence, and the desire to keep the market sweet for the Government at all costs, may prompt the authorities to discourage enterprise on the part of Local Governments and similar bodies just when, from the industrial point of view, it most needs encouragement. To keep down the price of bread by prohibiting its sale makes no great contribution to the relief of starvation.

Conversely, if pressure in the markets for capital, labour and materials has reached an advanced stage, there is some danger lest the claims of the Budget should hamper the Head Cooks in their handling of a homely utensil which, if its selective virtues as a sieve have been somewhat overpraised, is perhaps after all not to be despised in its cruder aspect of a damper for the kitchen stove. Such considerations are especially relevant if, for urgent reasons of national defence, the Government must come on the market for fresh borrowing at a time of fairly pronounced industrial activity: and it is natural to enquire whether the authorities can or ought to hope to finance the present rearmament programme without permitting a rise in interest rates. The shibboleth (now escaped from the lecture-rooms into the columns of the higher-browed press) that "investment (*i.e.* capital outlay) creates its own saving" does not really take us very far. In one sense, indeed, it means no more than that the pounds spent by the Government in any week will be found at the end of the week in somebody's pocket or bank account—a comforting if not very profound reflection. In another sense, however, it may be taken as a useful reminder of the proposition, enunciated by a very conservative economist many years ago,[1] that when industry is active profits are high, and when profits are high the capacity to save is large. But the ease with which these saved profits can be shepherded into the gilt-edged market remains a matter for examination in each particular case: and the evidence of what has occurred in totalitarian lands is of limited value as a guide to what can be done in the absence of more drastic substitutes—limitation of dividends, prohibition of plant extensions, Jew-robbery and the rest—for a mobile rate of interest.

Nevertheless, up till the rape of Bohemia, the immediate outlook for the Government—that is, for the

[1] Cassel, *Theory of Social Economy*, 1st Eng. tr., p. 598. Since this passage was written, however, the tendency of high profits to generate high *consumption* by the wealthy classes has perhaps increased.

taxpayer—seemed to be comparatively favourable. To begin with, whatever exactly happens to the *rate* of interest, the *aggregate* interest burden on the Budget is presumably made less than it otherwise would be by the removal of the need to pay interest on the cost of storage of some £200 million of barren gold. But there was a further technical point, which had been driven home by a number of expert writers. The money received by the Exchange Equalisation Account from the sale of gold had been used mainly to take up three months' Treasury Bills, leaving fewer of these desirable objects for other people to scramble for: and since the banks regard these bills as not far removed from "cash," the difficulty of obtaining them had apparently led them—or some of them—to desire to strengthen the proportion of their cash to their total liabilities, and so to become less willing to hold longer-dated Government issues. Hence the issue of Treasury Bills to finance armament expenditure could be expected, somewhat paradoxically, to increase rather than diminish the appetite of the banks for other kinds of Government securities, and so to lessen the demands which would have to be made on other types of investor. No doubt there were limits, both as regards the amount and the date of maturity of the issues which the banking lions would be prepared to swallow; but the fact that they had been kept a bit short of rations in recent months had equipped them with a useful hunger, of which the warders could be expected, by dangling before them suitably prepared morsels at suitable intervals, to take full advantage.

To some extent these considerations remain valid to-day. The revolution of national policy in the last few weeks has however changed the outlook to an extent of which the Chancellor's Budget proposals afford perhaps only a preliminary recognition. Even those who are more convinced than the present writer of the propriety of sitting on the head of the interest rate in all circumstances are concerned to warn us that such a policy may require as an accompaniment a direct repression of consumption, and a control of the markets both for free capital and for capital goods, on a scale much more drastic than has hitherto been envisaged in this country except during actual war.[1]

So much for the prices of commodities and securities: what of the prices of dollars and gold? As a first approximation we may treat these as twins, with the price of dollars as the elder; for normally the policy of the authorities as regards the purchase and sale of gold appears to be ancillary to their management of the dollar exchange. If they desire to support the pound in the face of a drain of funds to New York, it makes little difference in principle whether they sell dollars themselves, obtaining them by the surrender of gold to the American Treasury, or whether they sell gold to enterprising persons who can be relied on to send it to the American Treasury for conversion into dollars which *they* will desire to sell. Increasingly the latter seems to have been found the more convenient course; and the price of gold has normally stood very close to the "American shipping parity," *i.e.* at a figure which just affords the enterprising persons a profit on transactions of this kind. Thus, as under the old gold standard, the actual gold movements necessary to ensure the maintenance of a given rate of exchange are largely left to private enterprise to initiate. The survival in the present system of this element of "automatism" requires, however, as was shown in 1937, the fulfilment of certain conditions. On the one hand, if confidence were again to be impaired, as it was in the spring of 1937, in the willingness of the American Treasury to continue to buy unlimited quantities of gold at a fixed price, the price of gold in London would fall below the "shipping parity," unless steps were taken to maintain it. On the other hand, if trade or capital movements were to turn the exchanges, as they did in the autumn of the same year, against the United States, the price of gold in London would not automatically fall to match. For in the first place

[1] See M. Keynes, *The Times*, April 17 and 18. [But see also *ibid.*, May 4.]

there is a range (of something under 1½ per cent.) within which the price of dollars could fall without making it possible for anyone to ship gold *from* the United States to London without loss. Secondly, even when this point were reached, it would not be open to the enterprising persons above mentioned to obtain gold from the American Treasury for shipment—a privilege reserved to the authorities themselves; and since in the autumn of 1937 this point was not reached, we have no basis for certainty as to how the authorities would act if it *were* reached. The present situation, however, is not such as to threaten an early recurrence of the embarrassments of 1937: and we may allow ourselves here to treat the price of gold as a by-product of the price of dollars.

What then has been the policy of the post-1931 régime with regard to the dollar exchange? It would be indelicate at this time of day to enquire too closely how far the 30 per cent. depreciation of sterling which prevailed till the spring of 1933, when Mr. Roosevelt decided to go one better, represented a "natural" position; indelicate, too, to enquire whether the American counterstrokes, culminating in a 40 per cent. write-down in the gold value of the dollar, constituted a shining example of the behaviour of a good neighbour. For these things are now ancient history: and since the autumn of 1936 the authorities of both countries have been pledged to behave like little gentlemen in their dealings with the exchange.[1] And whether we look at the price indices of the two countries or at their balances of payments on current account, it seems fair to conclude that the flurried boom and recession of 1936-38 left the dollar value of the pound definitely too high, so that its subsequent decline by the modest figure of 6 per cent. represented a reasonable readjustment to which no exception need be (or has been) taken. But there are some who would go further than this, and

[1] Though there are six parties to the Old School Tie Convention, it is still commonly known as the *Tri*partite Agreement—perhaps because we must *try* to remember it is still in force even when we see the exchange of one of the signatories depreciating by nearly 60 per cent.

who have severely criticised the authorities for not making more unbridled use of their powers of monetary expansion in the last twelve months without regard to the consequences to the dollar exchange. To let the exchange slide as a result of expansion at home, they point out, is a very different thing from giving it an unprovoked jog downwards in illicit stimulus to the export trade; for the former is, what the latter is not, part of an integrated policy which may help to ward off trade recession from the world at large. To this argument, valid within its own field, it may nevertheless be replied that pronounced instability of the exchanges, from whatever cause arising, makes havoc of tariff schedules and breeds trade restrictions. After so much clucking and so long an incubation, to have addled that handsome egg the Anglo-American Trade Treaty by precipitating a marked decline in the dollar value of the pound would scarcely have been a very bright stroke of business. And the urgent need to press ahead with clearing away the brambles which choke the path of international trade inevitably imposes upon the authorities the necessity of exercising restraint in the use which they make of exchange freedom, and of interpreting fairly strictly the somewhat nebulous obligations of the O.S.T. Convention. Armed with the formidable panoply of powers described in the first section of this survey, it is still not open to them, or to any man, to secure continually the best of all worlds. But I think we were justified in replying to our solicitous visitor from another planet, "Pretty well, thank you, Socrates, on the whole."

XIII

REVIEWS

ROBBINS: THE GREAT DEPRESSION[1]

In this remarkable tract of 200 pages Professor Robbins offers a condensed narrative and a coherent interpretation of the greatest depression in history. His brief epitome may be even more briefly epitomised as follows. The slump of 1929 was, like its predecessors, the inevitable result of an over-expansion of credit, leading to an over-development of the industries producing capital goods. Centring in America and the countries fed by American capital, this over-expansion was, nevertheless, largely the result of Britain's failure, after 1925, to bring herself into international equilibrium. The slump has been made peculiarly severe, and recovery peculiarly difficult, by the attempts made to maintain consumption at a high level: by State-supported rigidities in the markets for commodities, capital and labour—themselves the product of a philosophy of "interventionism" dating largely from the war: and by Britain's destruction of the international gold standard. For the restoration of lasting prosperity there is required not merely an abstinence from reflationary policies and the restoration of an international standard of value, but the complete reversal of the whole tendency towards State interference with industry and so-called "economic planning."

Thus, in the course of his survey, Professor Robbins is led to pronounce judgment on many of the most hotly disputed subjects of present-day economic controversy: the proper objectives of monetary policy and

[1] *Economica*, 1935.

the causation of the trade-cycle: the effect of restriction-schemes on total purchasing-power, and of reductions in money wage-rates on employment: protection and free trade, fixed and moveable exchanges: the feasibility or otherwise of steady progress under Capitalism and of rational accounting under Socialism. It would be an unwise critic who would attempt, in the brief space of a review, to dog his author's footsteps over so vast a range of thickly wooded country. It must suffice to offer one or two reflections on the book as a whole, and then to select one or two of its central topics for special discussion.

First, there can be no two opinions about its high intellectual and artistic quality. If its self-imposed limits preclude elaborate development of its numerous themes and sub-themes, it contains an amazing amount of solid argumentation. Lucid narrative and illuminating comment are interwoven with extraordinary skill. The style, pungent and pugnacious, eschews bitterness and vulgar abuse, and ascends at times into realms of sincere and moving eloquence. Books on economics which have also the stirring quality of a work of art are not so common but that all economists should join to give them welcome; while the adherents of the austere school of thought which finds expression in this work owe Professor Robbins a special debt for proving that the devil, or what they deem such, has not collared all the best tunes.

Secondly, Professor Robbins naturally presents his judgments as they exist in his own mind—bound together into an interconnected whole by—I dare not say a doctrine, but at least a point of view. This unity, indeed, is part of the secret of the book's appeal. It is perhaps the more legitimate for a reviewer to point out that the reader is under no moral or intellectual compulsion to swallow the menu as a whole, but is at liberty to dine *à la carte*. It seems to be quite possible, for instance, to agree with Professor Robbins' diagnosis of the primary phase of the depression without agreeing that no monetary action can usefully be taken to counter its secondary phases: or again, to agree that the prime necessity is to restore the confidence of the business world, but to draw an exactly contrary inference as to the effectiveness, for this purpose, of the introduction of a scheme of protective tariffs or of regulation of output: or again, to agree that under certain conditions wage-rates should be reduced, but to hold that mass purchasing power should nevertheless be sustained by measures which do not involve the maintenance of industrial costs. For such eclecticism there seems to be warrant in Professor Robbins' own words. In an interesting passage towards the end of the book he expressly denies that his conclusions are inspired by any metaphysical theory of the limits to the sphere of State action, and claims in effect that his objection to each particular piece of "interventionism" discussed has been established on its own merits. It is this claim which the conscientious reader of this book must test for himself in detail, undrugged by the atmosphere of a unifying philosophy which breathes through its pages, and which, if he does not take care, will lead him to accept the next proposition of Professor Robbins simply because he has accepted the last.

I must content myself with indicating one or two trains of thought which may be set in motion by this stimulating book. Has Professor Robbins really shown that the Austrian theory of "over-investment" is adequate to account for the phenomena of 1929 in the United States? In particular, will the survival of moderate activity in the consumable goods industries through 1930—a feature which can be paralleled from many previous depressions—bear the interpretation which he puts upon it—that it was this activity which, by attracting to the trades concerned the lion's share of a limited stock of the factors of production, retarded recovery in the capital-goods industries? Is it not natural that after an orgy of construction there should be a high level of output from the newly created capital instruments, and would a policy which compels existing instruments to work far below capacity really be the best method of evoking a demand for new ones? But, indeed, even if Professor Robbins' diagnosis is right, does his prescription really follow logically from it? For, according to that diagnosis, it was the orgy of capital construction that was the "artificial" thing, and the subsequently enhanced demand for consumable goods which represents a return to "natural" preferences. Is not the advice to sacrifice everything to the restoration of profitability in the capital-making trades, tarred, for good or evil, with the same brush as efforts to achieve the same end through "monetary manipulation" of the rate of interest? In an interesting passage on p. 178, Professor Robbins advocates the recrudescence of foreign investment, especially for Great Britain, largely on the grounds that it will give the capital-making industries plenty to do. Such an argument comes naturally enough from those who hold that "structural rigidities" are so ingrained in our system that policy must humour them: does it come so logically from one who is never tired of asserting that there must be no "bolstering up" of situations which do not accord with consumers' present desires?

In championing the claims of the consumer to cheapness at all costs, Professor Robbins writes with even more than his usual punch. "It is all very well for the dilettante economists of wealthy universities, their tables groaning beneath a sufficiency of the good things of this world... to say, 'Food is cheap enough... We have enough of plenty. Let us safeguard security.' It is for the millions, to whom a slice of bacon more or less... still matters, to make the decision. It is not so certain that if the issue were clearly and honestly explained to them, they would choose the maintenance of existing capital values. For as yet the issue has not been put either honestly or clearly." But is it putting the issue fairly or clearly to represent all attempts at mitigating the rigours of industrial transition as conceived in the interests of existing *capital*? Are they not often also conceived (whether well or ill) in the interests of *employment*? Is it so certain that the consumer, who (unless we confess to a special tenderness for the *rentier* or for the dilettante don just so dexterously debunked) is also for the most part the labourer, will ever as a class endorse the nineteenth-century social accountancy by which slight gains of comfort to the many were held to outweigh total loss of livelihood to the few? That, acting as an individual, he snatches with avidity at the slight gains, proves nothing: for by failing to do so he could no whit diminish the chance that he will himself be the next victim of the arrow of industrial change. It is comparatively easy to show, as Professor Robbins has certainly done, that many actual attempts at "planning" have failed to achieve the stability at which they aimed: it is less easy to prove, as he also attempts to do, that the whole notion of stability and progress as in some measure alternatives is a chimera, and that the maximum of *both* is to be attained under a system of individual enterprise, unhampered and unbuttressed by State intervention, yet rigidly debarred by central banking control from indulging in those escapades of inflationary capital-creation which have seemed to some observers to have been in the past among its most effective, if also its most callous, methods of adding to the world's material wealth.

Thus one lays down the book with the feeling that if the world is less simple than it seems to our high-hearted Planners of the Right and Left, it is also less simple than it seems to Professor Robbins and his friends. But one's chief emotion is gratitude that so forcible and eloquent an exposition of a case which is often gravely mishandled by its adherents is now available for the candid consideration of all the dilettante dons and prancing politicians, all the greedy entrepreneurs and purblind Labour leaders, against whom Professor Robbins has launched such an exhilarating covey of thunderbolts.

RÖPKE: CRISES AND CYCLES[1]

THE position developed by Professor Röpke in this vigorous and stimulating book is an interesting and individual one. In his general outlook he remains an uncompromising Liberal in what I must venture to call the Continental sense. He regards the troubles of the world as due largely to ill-judged interference with the free working of the capitalist—identified perhaps too easily with the *competitive*—system ("very rarely has a monopoly come to life in the absence of more or less violent engineering on the part of the State"): as a long run policy he demands a diminution not an increase in the part played by the State in economic life. In the field of cyclical fluctuation he remains faithful to the view that the fundamental trouble is "over-investment" during the boom, and that once this has been allowed to develop a period of recession and readjustment is inevitable and should not be resisted. But the experience of recent years has convinced him that after a point this salutary process may, if we do not take care, deteriorate "into a process of murderous and ferocious destruction," "devoid of every necessary function... and therefore without sense." Since Professor Röpke holds all his views with decision and expresses them with élan, his trouncing of the "cleaning-up" enthusiasts and economy campaigners (pp. 181-2) is no whit inferior in energy to those which have emanated from very different quarters. And against the "secondary depression" thus distinguished and condemned he is ready to use the weapons not merely of monetary policy but of governmental borrowing to finance public works or even (from some points of view, preferably) deficits on current account. Such things may be described as "conformable intervention" and do not come under the condemnation of "Planning." But they should be conducted with as little fuss as possible. "The less we hear of 'reconstruction' and 'new epochs,' the more we avoid creating the impres-

[1] *Economica*, 1936.

sion that we need a new money or credit system, a new State, a new philosophy and newer and better economics, the greater will be the prospects of success." In particular, devaluation is almost always naughty and unnecessary.

It is not denied that this policy involves two difficult problems of timing—when to start and when to stop. How are we to know just when the primary depression has become secondary? "No cut-and-dried answer to this question seems possible, since a more or less broad period of a doubtful nature divides the two phases"; but the persistence of mass unemployment, and the engulfment of the *consumption* industries in depression, may be a guide. How are we to know when the "compensatory and balancing" phase of the upswing is passing into the "self-inflammatory and unbalancing" phase? This question I think Professor Röpke, in his eagerness to reassure his fellow-anti-interventionists that "expansion" does not mean "inflation," at times tends to over-simplify. He is emphatic that, since there are unused productive resources, effective expansion can be carried out without any perceptible rise in the price-level (this conclusion, incidentally, is used to give somewhat dubious support to his argument against the need for exchange depreciation; it is by no means clear that, just because a country's price-level does not rise, the generation of an increased stream of buying-power therein will not exert a pressure on its exchanges). But it is all, surely, a question of degree: in most countries, on most occasions, the level of activity adjudged on general grounds to be the best may well entail a price-level substantially higher than that touched in the depths of the slump; in this matter as in others we cannot as a rule hope to get the best of both worlds. Professor Röpke is on safer, though still—as he sees—sufficiently debatable ground when he makes the "sudden and excessive increase of investment activity" his criterion for a reversal of the engines.

This brings me to the theoretical heart of the book—

the pages (97-119) in which Professor Röpke attempts to give precision to the concept of the "over-investment" which does the damage during the boom. His "over-investment" is not the same as that of Professor Hayek and of the Mr. Keynes of the *Treatise on Money*, *i.e.* it is not merely investment which in some sense outruns the spontaneous thriftiness available, feeding instead on the precarious fuel provided by credit expansion. It is true that in the actual capitalist world it *is* credit expansion which extracts the fuel: but whereas under capitalism the coercive machinery "is represented by the banking system with its cheques and overdrafts," in Russia it "is represented by the G.P.U. with its rifles and dungeons." Further, even if the fuel were provided with unambiguous spontaneity, over-investment would be over-investment none the less: hence Professor Hayek's remedies are no remedies ("if the increase of investments has taken on pathological dimensions a further increase of capital can only postpone the turn, and this only at the expense of a later and all the more severe reaction"), and his "over-investment" only the commonest species of a larger genus.

What then is "over-investment" or "over-saving" in this extended sense? Fundamentally it is a product of the "principle of acceleration"—of the fact that, when capacity is reached, an increase of x per cent. in the demand for a finished good or service will involve an increase of more than x per cent. in the demand for new instruments of production, while any slackening of the rate of increase of the former demand will entail an absolute fall of the latter below its enhanced level. Hence, failing an infinite and inconceivable mobility of resources between different branches of production, there occur periods of indigestion in which investment (however financed) turns out to have outrun the adaptive powers of the economic system. Such a phenomenon is quite consistent with the absence of any *chronic* tendency either for investment to exceed what is socially desirable, or for the system to run down through a leakage of thrift (pp. 105, 131). Indeed to some extent "over-investment" thus conceived is an inevitable feature of economic progress: and it is ultimately a question of political judgment (pp. 138-9) how much of it we want to have, *i.e.* what is *over*-over-investment and what is not.

The present reviewer, to whom (if he has interpreted them correctly) these somewhat intricate ideas are particularly sympathetic, is inclined to wish that Professor Röpke had devoted more of his 220 pages to their elucidation, to the exclusion of a certain amount of general polemics which he finds less interesting and persuasive! But the book as it stands is not only a compact and useful survey of a wide field, but a sincere and courageous contribution to constructive thought.

HARROD: THE TRADE CYCLE[1]

THE main thesis of this closely-reasoned and stimulating book is that the causes of the trade cycle are deeply seated in certain "real" features of the modern economy, the part played by money being that of a passive accomplice rather than an active ringleader, and the prospects of control by monetary policy less favourable, therefore, than is sometimes supposed.

For the working out of this proposition, Mr. Harrod employs a somewhat formidable company of familiar spirits (three Primary Stabilisers, three Capitalist Stabilisers, a Destabiliser, five Dynamic Determinants, a couple of Multipliers, and a Relation), the drilling of which affords full scope for his remarkable powers of analysis and exposition. With their aid we are conducted through a severely rational and frictionless world in which nobody ever loses his head or makes mistakes or finds himself in a bottle-neck, in which the capitalist producer is at every moment successfully striving to equate an ascertainable marginal revenue with an estimable marginal cost, in which even the non-capitalist farmer could instantaneously reduce

[1] *Canadian Journal of Economics*, 1937.

output in the face of a falling demand, though he is wise enough to do the opposite (p. 32). At times we are impelled to cry "But this is *not* so! Such assumptions are in place in other connections, but not in the hugger-mugger of the trade cycle." And, indeed, Mr. Harrod sometimes seems to me somewhat arbitrary in what frictions he assumes away and what he allows to remain: thus at one point we find ourselves instructed to forget the imperfect mobility of producers between occupations, but not the imperfect mobility of consumers between shops (pp. 13-14). Nevertheless the hugger-muggerness of fluctuation is no excuse for not attempting to analyse it; and so strong is my own sympathy with Mr. Harrod's desire to show that it is not *wholly* a matter of error or minor frictions that I am willing to let him lead me by the hand—provided my right to squeak "But this is *not* so" later on is not forfeited.

"Imperfect mobility of consumers between shops." This is Mr. Harrod's surprise rabbit. It appears already in the introductory chapter, in which, abstracting from what is to be his main theme of the phenomena of growth, he explains how the determinants of the level of economic activity change as we pass from a Crusoe to a capitalist, from a barter to a monetary economy; and it plays a prominent part later on. Competition, Mr. Harrod thinks, will become more imperfect as output expands, because consumers, being richer, will take less trouble to buy in the cheapest market. Here is a factor limiting the increase of output, since the individual producer will come up against a law of diminishing elasticity of demand for his own product (pp. 19-21). Mr. Harrod is modest about forcing his rabbit down our throats, but it evidently occupies a warm place in his own mind and heart. Frankly, I find it hard to swallow. To begin with, if the rabbit is real, is it so clear that it is the behaviour of total output which regulates its activities? On Mr. Harrod's own showing those who become better off in an expansion are the profit-makers, who save a large part of their gains, and those who are regaining lost employment—not a great step on the road to affluence; the great mass of already employed workpeople, salary-earners, and *rentiers*, become worse off. Is it certain, even if allowance is made for the behaviour of firms (p. 87), that on balance the sensitiveness of purchasers to price-differences diminishes? But, secondly, the rabbit has to be confronted with a very formidable snake in the shape of the virtual certainty that, however consumers behave, producers behave more monopolistically in bad times than in good.[1] I have my fears for the rabbit.

Mr. Harrod's central thesis (Chs. II, III) is a combination of the familiar "principle of acceleration," according to which changes in the rate of output of capital goods depend *ceteris paribus* on changes in the *rate of increase* of output of consumption goods, with the proposition that (owing largely to a shift of distribution in favour of profit-makers) as output increases a decreasing proportion of the money income representing it will be spent on consumption. Hence, even if we start with full employment, a steady rate of advance of x per cent. in total output can never be maintained; for the rate of increase of consumption will fall below x per cent., the absolute level of the output of capital goods will therefore decline, which in turn will lead to an absolute decline in the output of consumption goods, until eventually the need to make capital replacements in excess of available depreciation allowances permits a turning-point to be reached and passed (pp. 88-101). And if we start with unemployment the position is still worse; for the absorption of the unemployed involves a rate of increase of consumption which, even apart from the tendency of the proportion of income saved to increase, cannot be maintained when once the unemployed have been absorbed (pp. 57, 106).

[1] Pigou, *Theory of Unemployment*, p. 135. Why does Mr. Harrod say that "it is generally believed" that in a depression the prices of goods produced under imperfect competition fall more than their marginal costs?

Thus after an advance there sets in a process of hoarding, in which firms as well as individuals participate (pp. 125-45), and in face of which monetary policy may be relatively powerless. For the level of the long-term rate of interest at any moment depends partly on what its level is expected to be over a fairly long future, so that its movements are not nimble enough to solve the problems set to it both by the behaviour of the principle of acceleration and by fluctuation in the rate of invention (pp. 110, 125).

I find myself in agreement with Mr. Harrod that the principle of acceleration deserves pride of place (p. 54) in any analysis of the trade cycle. But the next most important thing to be said is perhaps that some of the principal forms of investment in the modern world—the instruments of power-production, of transport, of office activity—are, after all, very loosely geared to the visible demand for particular types of consumption goods and depend rather on fairly vague estimates of the future progress of whole areas and populations. From this it follows, I think, that the working of the principle, especially in its interplay with the discontinuous phenomena of invention, would often give trouble even in the absence of that chronic tendency to over-saving which is implied by Mr. Harrod's analysis of the obstacles to a steady rate of advance—an analysis in which, it must be noted, what I have called the rabbit is called upon to play a prominent part (pp. 85-7). Thus the way is opened up on the one hand for even worse situations of temporary saturation than he discloses, but on the other perhaps for greater possibilities than he admits of controlling the tempo of advance. I cannot but think that he carries too far his acquiescence in the elasticity of the credit machine in the face of the demands made upon it in the name of the principle of acceleration during an upswing—his attitude in this matter being perhaps unconsciously influenced by his choice of a set of definitions which would enable the most outrageous credit inflation to be represented as a mere act of beneficent midwifery for the community's unborn thrift (p. 145). In other words, the degree of that "shift to profit" which in his eyes is immediately so useful and ultimately so damaging is surely less inexorably "decreed," to use one of his favourite words, than he would have us suppose. Nevertheless, his reminder that in a society in which fluctuation has become endemic the very effort to absorb unemployment evokes a spectre of future unemployment, is justified and timely.

If the gearing of the capital trades to the consumption trades is looser than in Mr. Harrod's scheme, and if the credit machine in the end offers greater resistances to expansion than he contemplates, it follows also, I think, that the actual mechanism of relapse may on occasions be quite different from that which he describes, and may be connected, as many writers have asserted, with a decline in profits and in saving in the later phases of the boom. Nevertheless, even on these occasions it would remain true that the acceleration principle, in one or other of its manifestations, is the ultimate obstacle in the background to steady progress.

In his last chapter Mr. Harrod discusses possible remedies for the trouble which he has diagnosed. Though he examines also other possibilities, he pins his faith chiefly to a policy of Government borrowing, initiated at the very onset of recession, to finance both a carefully prepared plan of capital works and also if necessary the maintenance of consumption. This policy is at first presented as merely a means by which we may bridge the transition between a situation requiring a given rate of private investment and a situation requiring a somewhat smaller rate, without going through a full cycle of depression and recovery; so soon as the transition is effected, the borrowing policy is to be reversed. It is not easy to square this pious programme with the pessimism of Mr. Harrod's central analysis; and indeed in the end he admits that he feels bound to contemplate the possibility that the Government debt may on balance continually increase. After all, he consoles us, there are worse things than debt, *alias* the ownership of claims to income by poets and other worthy people; and fortunately it will be possible to combine the apotheosis of the *rentier* with his euthanasia (p. 222).

It is, naturally, in considering Mr. Harrod's practical proposals that one is most conscious of the stripped nature of his analysis. In particular, his insistence that action to be effective must be taken immediately, comes into conflict with a widespread opinion that, if the boom has contained large elements of disproportionality and error, immediate attempts at reflation will delay essential readjustments and do more harm than good. This, however, applies doubtless rather to general ease of credit conditions than to a plan of specialised construction such as Mr. Harrod advocates. His proposal for a Public Works Commission to work out such a plan deserves the careful attention of Cabinet ministers: but perhaps they had better not be told too much at present about the apothenasia of the *rentier*.

BRESCIANI-TURRONI: THE ECONOMICS OF INFLATION [1]

It is a matter for great satisfaction that, thanks to the enterprise of the Halley Stewart Trust and other persons, this monumental study of the decline and fall of the German mark has now become available in English. Founded on personal observation and enquiry as well as on elaborate documentation from official and unofficial sources, and ordered by theoretical acumen and social insight, the book will long stand as a masterly record and interpretation of the most spectacular episode in the history of the world's monetary affairs.

The first half of the book is concerned with the analysis, period by period, of the mutual relations of the conspicuous phenomena of the inflation—the growth of the floating debt and of the note issue, and the rise in the prices of foreign exchange, of foreign goods, and of the various categories of home-produced

[1] *Economica*, 1938.

goods and services. On the vexed question of causal sequence the author's judgment is firm and uncompromising. It is true that during certain phases the external value of the mark fell more rapidly than the internal, and that some of its spectacular plunges must be connected with "autonomous" events and not with any immediately preceding burst of currency expansion. It is true, too, that when in the final phases of the catastrophe the external and internal values came together again, it was because the latter came to be immediately adjusted to the former through the growing habit of reckoning in gold values, ending in the virtual "rejection" of the local standard of value. And it is true, finally, that the rise in internal prices thus generated provoked both a further increase in the issue of Reichsbank notes and that speeding-up in their velocity of circulation which caused their total real value progressively to decline, and so, by revealing a "shortage of money," stimulated the creation of substitute moneys of various kinds. Nevertheless, *in the sense that most matters*, the causal sequence must be pronounced to start with the note issue and to end with the exchanges. Or rather, it must be pronounced to start with the budget deficits financed by the discounting of Treasury Bills with the Reichsbank for new notes. For not only did these new notes directly provide continuous fuel for the flight of capital over the exchanges: the key to the whole causal tangle must be sought in the consideration that, as the event ultimately proved, the whole complex cumulative process could at any time have been stopped and reversed if the determination of the authorities to restore the public finances and control the money supply had been placed beyond a doubt.

In hammering in this side of the truth, Professor Bresciani-Turroni deals as they deserve with the naïve sophistries of those Helfferichs and Havensteins by whom it was so long denied. He deals, too, as they deserve with those powerful and sinister influences which, acquiring a vested interest in the depreciation of the mark, opposed their whole strength to a drastic treatment of the disease. But does he deal as they deserve with those victorious Powers whose blind rapacity helped to impose on the leaders of the young Republic a task so manifestly beyond their strength? I for one feel that he does not, and that in this single but important respect his book lacks balance and fails of achieving the definitive picture of the events which it records. "I willingly admit," he says at one point, "that the Treaty of Versailles created psychological influences unfavourable to the mark." Surely that is almost as though a historian of more recent events were to record that the rise of National Socialism "created psychological influences unfavourable" to the Jews!

From causes Professor Bresciani-Turroni turns to consequences, and in a series of penetrating chapters analyses the effects of the inflation on the volume and character of production, on the structure of industry, on the financial position of various types of enterprise, on the distribution of wealth and income between social classes and on the broader aspects of social and political life. He gives it due credit for the stimulus afforded to employment during the world depression of 1920-1, and due blame for the distortion of productive activity ("Germany offered the grotesque, and at the same time the tragic, spectacle of a people which, rather than produce food, clothes, shoes and milk for its own babies, was exhausting its energies in the manufacture of machines or the building of factories"), and for the ultimate collapse of employment and production in 1922-3. The depression of real wages, the ruin of the intelligentsia, the birth of industrial monstrosities of the type associated with the name of Stinnes, the "process of continual centralisation of the social income by a small minority of inflation profiteers," the consolidation of "the dictatorship of heavy industry—an industrial feudalism pitted against the nation"—all are depicted with a wealth of illustrative detail and a remorseless pen.

An account of the monetary reform of November 1923 ("the miracle of the rentenmark") fitly brings the main narrative to an end. But the epilogue on the post-stabilisation crisis, continued in an appendix which carries the story on to the crisis of 1931, contains some of the most valuable material in the book—material which will bear much reflecting on by students of the theory of industrial fluctuation. I can here do no more than call attention to the illuminating discussion (pp. 359-69) of the nature of the "shortage of capital" whose existence was revealed after the stabilisation, and of the different fortunes experienced in the ensuing years by different groups both of consumption goods industries and production goods industries (pp. 376-83). May these latter pages, and especially the often-neglected distinction drawn on p. 383 between cases where the dependence of constructional activity on consumption activity is direct and intimate and cases where it is remote and speculative, be earnestly studied by all those who feel the allure of a simple schematic treatment, in terms of Multipliers and Acceleration Principles, of very complex relations!

The translators have performed an exceedingly laborious task with few blemishes save a chronic tendency to misuse the English word "even" (pp. 66, 88, 210 *n*). On p. 48, line 22, and in three obvious places on p. 53, "millions" should be "milliards."

HAWTREY: A CENTURY OF BANK RATE[1]

In this book Mr. Hawtrey marshals his rich knowledge of financial history, reinforced by some most laborious *ad hoc* statistical investigations, in support of his well-known thesis that the manipulation of Bank rate, working through the decisions of merchants to alter the size of their stocks, can be an almost completely effective instrument for controlling the level of economic activity.

The purpose of the book is "to show how the Bank-rate tradition grew up, what was in the minds of those who originated it, to what extent their intentions were

[1] *E.J.*, 1939

realised in the experience which followed, and what is its virtue in the circumstances of the present day and the future." In my judgment the first and third of these aims are most successfully accomplished, while the pursuit of the second leads to somewhat indecisive results, and that of the fourth reveals some blind spots, as well as great powers of penetration, in Mr. Hawtrey's organ of vision.

By citations from the Parliamentary enquiries between 1832 and 1858 Mr. Hawtrey has no difficulty in showing that the "Fathers and Prophets" of that era looked toBank rate to exercise its effects upon the exchanges and the Bank of England's reserve mainly through modifying the level of domestic activity. But to claim them as preachers of the strict gospel of the *modus operandi* through merchants' stocks would entail, I think, placing an excessive strain on an apparently isolated dictum of G. W. Norman (pp. 33, 62, 224). If it were possible to line them up in the witness-box to-day, I cannot help suspecting that as a group they would testify more readily to the vaguer formulations of Marshall (p. 228) than to the strait Hawtreian thesis.

Anyway, as Mr. Hawtrey illustrates with a profusion of historical detail, somehow or other the instrument worked, though not so smoothly as it might have done. Some of the imperfections in its working are now, thanks largely to Mr. Hawtrey's own previous writings, an old story; but he lays most illuminating emphasis upon a hitherto neglected one. Just as a high Bank rate would attract gold from abroad, thus adding fresh fuel to the expansion which it was its function to damp down, so it would stimulate country bankers to send idle currency to London with similar results in provoking a premature relaxation of the rate. And conversely a low rate might lead to an accumulation of idle currency in the provinces, depleting the Bank of England's reserve and compelling a rise in rate though trade was still depressed (pp. 64-5).

Two chapters are devoted to examining the relation between long- and short-term rates of interest. With the aid of some instructive history Mr. Hawtrey expounds and illustrates the principle (familiar to readers of Pigou and Lavington[1]) that the repercussion on the long rate of a change in the short rate which is expected to be reversed before long is likely to be relatively small; and emphasises well (pp. 158, 168, 185) that such community of movement as exists between the two rates is chiefly to be explained by their exposure to common influences. He also lays welcome stress on those imperfections and rationings in the capital market which are so apt to be neglected in certain modern trains of reasoning which appear to assume that the money required for "investment" can be picked like blackberries in a hedge.

Is he too optimistic in his view that "only occasionally" (p. 177) is the condition of the capital market other than one of pressure, regulated by rationing? Does his very financial *expertise* blind him to deeper technical and distributional forces making for fluctuation? Does his very historical learning lead him to deal too perfunctorily (p. 262) with certain secular structural changes which have swollen the investment portfolios of the banks, impaired a convenient but perhaps somewhat fortuitous liaison between the desire of the public to keep money on hand and the desire of entrepreneurs to borrow for working capital purposes, and so brought the long-term rate of interest nearer to the centre of the financial stage? On the other hand, once the emphasis is shifted from the rate of interest itself to the ease or stringency associated therewith (pp. 61, 202), is not the door thrown open to a more catholic interpretation of the working even of the short-term market than that which concentrates almost exclusive attention on the route through merchants' stocks of finished goods?

On these and many other controversial matters raised towards the end of the book there is more to be said than can be said in a review. Among the authors who

[1] *Industrial Fluctuations*, p. 276; *Economica*, 1923-4, p. 299.

have contributed to their discussion Mr. Hawtrey is not, indeed, the least dogmatic: but he is by common consent among the most learned, scrupulous and urbane.

GUILLEBAUD: THE ECONOMIC RECOVERY OF GERMANY, FROM 1933 TO MARCH 1938[1]

THE purpose of this important book is to give, for the benefit of the general reader as well as the economic specialist, an orderly and objective account of economic developments in Germany under the Nazi régime. There is no doubt of the learning and skill which Mr. Guillebaud has brought to his task. The book is well arranged and extremely readable. The main facts of the struggle with unemployment and subsequently with labour shortage—of the progress towards autarky and the present peculiar system of foreign trade—of the extension of control over the markets for commodities, labour and capital—of the new organisations in agriculture and industry—are clearly and interestingly set forth. And a place is found too for mention of several less-known features of the régime, such as the attempts to guide consumers' demand in response to the vagaries of the seasons (p. 163), and to bring latent industrial capacity to the fore (p. 196).

Nor can there be any doubt of Mr. Guillebaud's intention to paint an impartial picture. In estimating that the standard of life was about the same in 1938 as in 1929, he does not omit to warn us that the official cost-of-living figure does not reveal the whole truth (p. 186): nor does he conceal the nuisances and vexations imposed by the régime (p. 222), nor the inner contradictions to which it has been subject, especially as regards the position of the peasant (pp. 116-17) and the small industrialist (p. 246). Yet it is arguable that in his laudable desire to be fair to the Nazi system, and also to dispel a mischievous belief in the inevitability of its early breakdown, Mr. Guillebaud has some-

[1] *E.J.*, 1939.

times been tempted, like vaulting ambition, to o'erleap himself and fall on the other.

Thus he would have us think charitably of Germany's treatment of her foreign creditors; and to this end (p. 62) performs or reproduces a curious calculation by which the outflow of gold and foreign exchange in 1932-4 is *added* to the outward movement of capital instead of being treated as its vehicle: "it is to such figures as this that the Germans point when they contend that they were doing their utmost to meet their foreign obligations." He gives no hint of the extent to which the halving of the foreign debt (pp. 213, 282) has been due to the fact that Germany could apparently afford exchange to buy up at default prices the bonds on which she could not afford to remit the interest; and his estimate (p. 100) of the interest actually remitted in 1935 appears to be more than double that given by Dr. Eicke at the time (*Economist*, May 2, 1936, p. 245).

Again, is it, I wonder, the sign of a very bigoted Free Trader to feel that the defence put forward on economic grounds (p. 106) for the pursuit of autarky in respect of raw materials requires a little more critical dissection than it receives? On these lines it would seem that England might be able to improve her standard of life enormously by growing all her cotton at prodigious cost in glass-houses at home; for she would then be free to import a great deal more French wine and Russian caviare instead.

Again, Mr. Guillebaud is more concerned (pp. 86, 105 *n.*, 237) to warn us against over-estimating than against forgetting the part played since 1935 by re-armament, as compared with other kinds of "investment," in the process of expansion. In appraising his treatment of this matter it is indeed necessary to bear in mind the inevitable time-lags between composition and publication, between publication and review. Had he been writing in April 1939, he would probably have forestalled one of his critics (*Economist*, April 1, 1939, p. 4) by elevating to a more prominent position the caution, now blushing modestly in a footnote near the end of the book (p. 268), that "the German economic system under present conditions has many of the characteristic features of a wartime-economy." *Per contra* he might have felt compelled to withdraw his concession (p. 236) that armaments are an "unproductive" form of investment: for from Germany's point of view why should a war-machine designed to extract juicy slices of *Lebensraum* from her neighbours by a succession of threats and acts of violence be denied the attribute of economic productivity? In any case the problem of how far Germany's achievement of full employment has been due to her being a Planwirtschaft and how far to her being a Wehrwirtschaft is likely, I think, to remain obscure. The fact that (if the above-mentioned critic is to be believed) she has not been conspicuously more succesful than Britain in creating industrial employment does not indeed alter the fact that she *has* been conspicuously more successful in eliminating unemployment. But equally the fact that she *has* eliminated unemployment does not prove that she *would have* done so if her energies had not been canalised towards the over-riding aim of intimidation and annexation: even sloppy old Britain can stumble into labour shortage in war-time.

In assessing the stability of the German system, Mr. Guillebaud implicitly adopts (to the natural pleasure of the present reviewer) a double-headed theory of the possible causes of the onset of depression in a *laissez-faire* economy. From a Hayekian crisis due to "shortage of saving," Germany has so far been preserved by her rigid controls of the markets both for money capital and for capital goods, and by the stabilisation of basic money wage-rates at depression levels—supplemented, Mr. Guillebaud believes (p. 254), by the inveterate thriftiness of the German people. Against a Keynesian slump due to "excess of saving" he believes her to be fore-armed by the mass of constructional work—industrial reconditioning and replacement, canal-making, house-building—waiting to be taken up when the pressure of rearmament ceases: and in the background there remain possibilities of orderly transition to enhanced consumption (p. 261). Certainly a totalitarian economy, with its direct controls over the occupational distribution of free capital, entrepreneurship and labour, is theoretically in a much stronger position than a *laissez-faire* economy to cope with the problems of demobilisation. But the German machine, as Mr. Guillebaud half admits (pp. 243, 263), seems to be subject to peculiar pressures and momenta of its own: and at the moment of writing (April 26, 1939) it remains uncertain whether its nature is such as to permit the phase of demobilisation ever to be reached, before involving itself and the rest of the world in irretrievable ruin.

XIV

NOTES ON INTERNATIONAL TRADE

I. THE TERMS OF TRADE [1924][1]

IN the *Economic Journal* for December, Mr. Keynes restates his reasons for supposing that in the decade before the war the real ratio of international interchange was turning in favour of agricultural and against manufacturing countries, in such wise as to yield year by year a decreasing quantity of the products of the former to a given expenditure of effort in the latter. In *Economica* for February Sir William Beveridge gives his reasons for rejecting this view. In this controversy I do not intervene. My concern is with the second section of Mr. Keynes' article, in which, having admitted that after the war the ratio of interchange swung violently in England's favour, he proceeds—a raven not thus easily to be baulked of his croak—to draw disquieting inferences from this apparently encouraging fact. In brief, he suggests that "we are asking too much for our exports, and will have to ask less if we are to sell enough to pay for our necessary imports": in other words, that stable equilibrium in our trade can only be secured at the cost of a further reduction in real wages. I think this suggestion may correctly indicate the best policy which, in the circumstances, it is open to us to pursue; but I think also that it is somewhat misleadingly phrased, and that its highly paradoxical nature deserves further comment.

The phrase "asking too much for our exports" seems to me to cloud the issue by suggesting that the price in question is an artificial one, out of accordance with the conditions of current demand and supply. It is by no means clear to me that this is the case. Let us take a

[1] *E.J.*, 1924. See Preface, p. vii.

simplified instance of the time-honoured kind. Anglia is exchanging cotton-goods for Transmarina wheat. As a result of good harvests Transmarina's demand schedule, in terms of wheat, for Anglian cotton-goods is raised throughout—the ratio of interchange alters in Anglia's favour. But Anglia's demand for wheat has, let us suppose, an elasticity less than one, with the result that Anglia, importing at least as much wheat as before, exports fewer cotton-goods. She is potentially richer than before, for she finds herself with a surplus of productive power, no longer required for obtaining imports but theoretically divertible into other uses. But in so far as that surplus is stereotyped in the form of cotton-stocks, cotton-mills and cotton operatives, those stocks will accumulate, those mills be idle, and those operatives unemployed: there will occur all the recognised symptoms of "trade depression." There are now two alternative policies for Anglia. She may attempt to convert her resources to other uses: or she may, in order to prevent distress among particular groups of capitalists and workpeople, deliberately degrade her standard of life below that to which the conditions of reciprocal international demand entitle her. Which policy she will be wise to adopt depends (like the wisdom of accepting an idemnity [1]) partly on the difficulty and expense of the process of conversion, and partly on how far the original alteration in the ratio of interchange may be expected to be permanent. But the second policy, if adopted, is at best a *pis aller*, and it is the new alteration thus effected in the ratio of interchange, not the original alteration, which is contrived and artificial.

This instance seems to represent fairly the essential features of the post-war slump in British trade. Agricultural production had continued relatively undisturbed: industrial production had been gravely dislocated, and its fruits were in keen demand for reconstruction and restocking purposes. The defection of the German and Russian markets compelled overseas agricul-

[1] Cf. J. M. Keynes, *A Revision of the Treaty*, pp. 152 ff.

turists to force their wares on the rest of the world. Whether or no normally inelastic, our demand for raw produce became so in face of the great reductions in real price flung at our heads. So the Argentine, Indian and other oversea exchanges crashed: the grower of raw produce found himself deprived of his power to purchase our goods, and "depression" overtook our export trades. The improvement in the ratio of interchange, which should have been for our wealth, became unto us an occasion of falling.[1] The process is seen at work in the quarterly figures (extracted and calculated from the *Board of Trade Journal*) exhibited in Table I. Perhaps in 1921 it really went too far, owing to the continued export of manufactured goods, made out of materials bought at the higher price-level and priced accordingly, and to the artificial paralysis of export by the coal dispute. But it looks as though in 1922-4 something like a true equilibrium has been attained: though, of course, it is still open to anyone to argue that this equilibrium is not likely to be permanent.

To this interpretation of recent history one obvious objection may be made. The argument of our simplified example requires that the volume of Anglia's *imports* shall not be diminished by the improvement in the ratio of interchange. Even if her demand for wheat is completely inelastic, she will not import *less* than she did before. But the volume of British imports is seen to have been less by one-ninth in 1919 and 1920 than in 1913, and by one-quarter in 1921 than in 1919 and 1920. Here indeed is an odd result of cheapening—that we should actually buy less of the cheapened thing! Must we conclude then after all that the post-war ratio of interchange is not a genuine register of a change in the conditions of reciprocal demand, but is in some manner spurious and uneconomic? I think

[1] Normally, as Mr. Keynes remarks, an improvement in the real ratio of interchanges is associated with an industrial boom in this country (for further instances see my *Study of Industrial Fluctuation*, pp. 168-9). His inference that boom conditions are secured "at the expense of" agricultural countries is, I think, unfortunately phrased. If the lowered price of raw produce is due to the bounty of Nature, *everybody* concerned may gain.

not, for a reason which can best be made plain by another example. Let Anglia now import from Transmarina not only wheat but the raw cotton which she transforms into cotton-goods for export: thus the wheat is in effect payment for her manufacturing effort. Let there occur an alteration in her favour of the ratio of interchange. Her demand for wheat being inelastic, she will find it worth while to expend less cotton-manufacturing effort than before, and will therefore export fewer cotton-goods, and will therefore, in spite of its lowered real price, import less raw cotton. In the following numerical illustration, it is assumed that as a result of war the price of Anglia's imports, in terms of her own labour and of her own currency, is reduced by 20 per cent., and that her demand for wheat is completely inelastic. The item "wheat"

TABLE I

(Corresponding period of 1913 = 100.)

	Average Value of Imports	Average Value of Exports	Average Value of Imports in terms of Exports	Volume of Imports	Volume of Exports required to purchase actual Volume of Imports	Actual Volume of Exports
1919	240	277	87	88.4	76.6	54.9
1920-1 ...	284	326	87	95.2	82.9	71.3
2 ...	285	358	80	96.6	76.9	73.5
3 ...	289	376	77	90.6	69.6	73.6
4 ...	283	373	76	73.1	55.5	65.4
1921-1 ...	220	334	66	71.3	47.0	53.5
2 ...	192	283	68	75.5	51.2	38.4
3 ...	182	241	76	78.6	59.4	46.4
4 ...	170	226	75	72.3	54.4	60.7
1922-1 ...	149	218	68	79.7	54.5	67.1
2 ...	152	196	78	91.5	71.0	65.0
3 ...	155	196	79	86.9	68.7	69.9
4 ...	153	189	81	85.5	69.2	73.3
1923-1 ...	146	196	74	95.3	71.0	74.4
2 *..	148	188	79	94.8	74.6	77.6
3 *..	151	192	79	88.8	69.8	68.7
4 *..	152	184	83	92.8	76.7	77.5
1924-1 *..	150	193	78	99.3	77.1	74.6

* Approximate correction made for exclusion of Irish Free State.

may be taken to include cotton worked up by Anglia *for her own use.*

The post-war position is seen to be one of real equilibrium, and essentially more favourable to Anglia than the pre-war position, in spite of the diminished volume not only of exports but of imports.

Imports (£ millions Anglian).		Exports (£ millions Anglian).	
(1) *Pre-war Trade.*			
Raw cotton	25	Cotton in goods	25
Wheat	20	Manufacturing effort	20
	45		45
(2) *Post-war Trade.*			
Raw cotton	16	Cotton in goods	16
Wheat	16	Manufacturing effort	16
	32		32
(3) *Post-war Trade at Pre-war Values.*			
Raw cotton	20	Cotton in goods	20
Wheat	20	Manufacturing effort	16
	40		36

This example suggests that our diagnosis of the essential nature of the post-war slump in British trade is not necessarily invalidated by the decline exhibited in Table I in the total volume of imports. It suggests too that we need not be unduly scared by Mr. Keynes' demonstration (*E.J.*, 1923, p. 482) that the aggregate of our manufactured exports would command (he says rather confusingly "are now buying") 12 per cent. less food-stuffs than the aggregate of our manufactured exports before the war. It would be alarming indeed if we were, in fact, buying less food; but we are actually buying more.[1] (In the above example, Anglia's post-war total of manufactured exports would only command $\frac{8}{9}$ as much wheat as her pre-war total of manufactured exports: yet she is buying just as much wheat as before—it is her raw material imports which she has

[1] One per cent. more, if we take a similar average of triennial averages to that from which Mr. Keynes derives his 12 per cent. figure: 14 per cent. more, if we compare 1923 directly with 1913, itself a year of maximum.

found it advisable to restrict.) Table II exhibits in more detail, from this point of view, the course of events in the critical years 1920-1.

The general conclusion is that if a country's resources in capital and labour were completely mobile between different occupations, an improvement in the ratio of interchange would be an unmixed blessing, even though it led to a reduction in the volume both of exports and imports. If we could costlessly erect a vast sausage-machine which would grind shipyards into cottages and cotton-spinners into plasterers, we should be wise to do so. I am not sure that even as it is we ought not, so far as labour is concerned, to take a leaf out of Germany's book, and make a far more decisive move in that direction than we have yet done. But if the difficulties are too formidable, or if we take view that the present situation is too transitory to make the attempt worth while, we may have in practice to fall back on the expedient advocated by Mr. Keynes—a contrived fall in the ratio of interchange, just as it may be right in certain circumstances to break windows in order to save glaziers from starvation. There is indeed a third alternative, to which we have already had some recourse—

TABLE II

(Corresponding period of 1913 = 100.)

	Retained Food Imports		Retained Raw Material Imports		Manufactured Exports	
	Average Value	Volume	Average Value	Volume	Average Value	Volume
1920-1	275	106	346	89	314	72
2	288	90	329	111	350	80
3	308	84	283	112	375	81
4	336	69	247	78	375	72
1921-1	246	92	181	62	344	55
2	216	99	150	66	298	40
3	183	88	186	64	251	46
4	181	84	174	58	234	62

an artificial stimulation of the export of goods on credit, that is, of foreign investment. I do not gather that Mr. Keynes sets much store by this [1]; but it seems more sensible to get something for our goods, even if only bits of South American paper, than in effect to give some of them away, by selling them cheaper than we need.

To sum up, we are buying adequate food for our growing population, paying £30 million a year interest to the United States, and sending abroad £100 million worth a year of new savings sorely needed at home; and still we have a surplus of export-producing power. I do not know whether Mr. Baldwin had these considerations in mind when, to the bewilderment of friend and foe, he advocated a restriction of exports; but I think he might have had.

II. THE TRANSFER PROBLEM [1929] [2]

§ 1. THE reparation problem seems to be still unsolved in practice; nor (which is perhaps of less interest to the world at large) do economists yet appear to be agreed on its theoretical aspects. Does the need to make reparation payments impose on a country a "transfer-burden" or "transfer-difficulties," apart from the budgetary difficulty of raising the necessary sums by taxation? Or are those who suppose this neglecting the "increase of purchasing-power abroad" which comes about as a result of the payments? And, incidentally, how valid is the analogy often taken for granted between such payments and the export of capital?

Discussion of these matters [3] is apt to be carried on at cross purposes, for two reasons. First, it is not always clear whether the disputants are discussing the methods by which adjustment is brought about when reparations begin to be paid, or whether they are discussing the

[1] See his exposure of the disadvantages of Protection from this point of view, *The Nation*, Nov. 24, 1923.

[[2] This matter has lately been further discussed between Prof. Viner and myself in *Q.J.E.*, 1938 and 1939.]

[3] See Keynes, three articles in *E.J.*, 1929, and *A Treatise on Money*, vol. i, pp. 329-42; Ohlin, articles in *Index*, April 1928, *E.J.*, 1929 and *Zeitschrift für Nationalökonomie*, 1930; Haberler, two articles, and Machlup, one article, in the same *Zeitschrift*, 1930.

features of the new state of equilibrium which prevails while they are being continuously paid.[1] It is perhaps to the former that the phrase "transfer-difficulties," to the latter that the phrase "transfer-burden," is appropriate; and it is with the latter that I propose to deal. Secondly, the champions of "transfer-burden" write with a vision firmly planted on their retina of the familiar Marshallian curves of real demand-and-supply, from which they usually deduce that the pressure to remit reparations from one country to another will turn the real ratio of interchange in the first country's disfavour, by an amount which may be great or small in accordance with the respective elasticities of real demand, but cannot be less than zero.[2] This result they usually regard as self-evident and inevitable, whatever the nature of the monetary happenings in which it is enshrined; but they have nowhere, so far as I know, explained clearly the reactions of a reparation payment on the shape and position of the Marshall curves.[3] Their opponents, on the other hand, think entirely in terms of monetary demand curves; and, on the ground that the position and perhaps the shape of these curves will change as a result of the reparation payment, are prone to deny the validity of appeals to "elasticity-analysis."[4] And their modes of expression frequently leave one uncertain whether they are, or are not, making some statement which is incompatible with the fundamental proposition of the opposite party.

§ 2. The deniers of "transfer-burden" correctly point out that if, as it is natural to assume, the reparation-money is raised by taxation in the paying country (to be called Germany) and used for remission of taxation in the receiving country (to be called America), the net annual flow of money devoted to the purchase of goods is less in Germany, and greater in America,

[1] Cf. Keynes, *op. cit.*, i, 332.
[2] Taussig, *International Trade*, pp. 109-15; Pigou, *Essays in Applied Economics*, p. 153.
[3] Except, apparently, for an unfortunate attempt by Marshall himself, in connection with an analogous problem: see below, § 7.
[4] See especially Haberler, *Zeitschrift*, Aug. 1930, p. 101.

under the new conditions than under the old. But this statement by itself throws no light whatever on the question whether a "transfer-burden" has been imposed on Germany, *i.e.* whether the real ratio of interchange has moved against her. It is compatible both with the existence and with the non-existence of such a burden.

In order to illustrate this matter numerically, let us make certain assumptions. First, let us assume that a rigid gold standard technique is in force in both countries, *i.e.* that in each country the relation between the gold stock and the total quantity of money remains the same under the new conditions as under the old. Secondly, let us assume that the representative man in each country needs to hold the same money balance in connection with a given annual expenditure on goods as he does in connection with an equal annual expenditure in payment of taxes: so that in each country the number of times in a year that a representative unit of money becomes income is the same under the new conditions as under the old. From these two assumptions it follows that in each country the proportion of aggregate incomes to gold stock has remained unchanged. Call this proportion V. Thirdly, let us suppose for simplicity that all taxes are direct; that there were no taxes in America other than those which have been newly remitted; and that there are no taxes in Germany other than those which have been newly imposed. Fourthly, let us suppose, again for simplicity, that Germany's consumption of American goods is completely unchanged, *i.e.* that she makes the reparation transfer entirely by increasing her exports.

Then consider the following tables:—

Germany.	*America.*
I. *Original situation:*	
Total income of £1,500 buys 1,300 *g* goods + 100 *a* goods.	Total income of £1,600 buys 900 *a* goods + 100 *g* goods and pays £600 taxes.
Gold stock £1,400. V = 1.	Gold stock £1,600. V = 1.
Price of *g* goods = £1.	Price of *a* goods = £1.

II. *New situation, on assumption of unchanged ratio of interchange:*

Germany.	*America.*
Total income of £1,400 buys 700 *g* goods + 100 *a* goods and pays £600 taxes.	Total income of £1,600 buys 900 *a* goods + 700 *g* goods.
Gold stock £1,400. $V = 1$.	Gold stock £1,600. $V = 1$.
Price of *g* goods = £1.	Price of *a* goods = £1.

III. *New situation, on assumption that ratio of interchange is moved against Germany, becoming* $\frac{5}{7}$:

Germany.	*America.*
Total income of £1,200 buys 560 *g* goods + 100 *a* goods and pays £600 taxes.	Total income of £1,800 buys 900 *a* goods + 840 *g* goods.
Gold stock £1.200. $V = 1$.	Gold stock £1,800. $V = 1$.
Price of *g* goods = £$\frac{6}{7}$.	Price of *a* goods = £$\frac{6}{5}$.

The champions of "transfer-burden" are, I think, sometimes tempted to argue as though the fact that reparations are being paid proves that there *must* have been a gold flow from Germany to America and an alteration in the relative size of gross money incomes in the two countries. Table II shows that this is not the case, and that, so far as monetary factors go, the relative flows of "net purchasing-power" *might* alter without the relative size of gross money incomes altering. On the other hand, Table III shows that an alteration in the relative flows of "net purchasing-power" is perfectly compatible with the existence of a severe "transfer-burden," so that to assert the existence of the former is by no means to disprove the existence of the latter.

§ 3. We may turn aside at this point to enquire how far, so far as the matters dealt with in § 2 are concerned, there is analogy between the payment of reparations and the export of capital. The answer seems to be that the analogy is partial and incomplete. In the lending country, the diversion of annual spending-power from expenditure on goods to expenditure on foreign securities furnishes a pretty exact analogy to the payment of new taxation; but in the borrowing country the expansion of buying-power does not come about in a manner analogous to the remission of taxation. In attempting to analyse how it does come about, we are, as so often in economic analysis, brought up against the difficulty of reconciling the conception of economic equilibrium with the phenomenon of the growth of capital. But, broadly, we can either regard the expenditure of the proceeds of the annual flow of loans as forming an annual flow of spending-power *additional* to the money income of the borrowing-country; or we can regard it as being distributed, in the form of wage-advances, among the members of a new increment of population, and so forming *part* of an enhanced total of money income: or we can adopt a mixture of the two methods. But in any case, on the assumption of rigid gold standard technique, the following conclusion emerges. In the case of capital export, unlike the case of reparations, even supposing the real ratio of interchange has remained unaltered, a flow of gold must have taken place in order to implement the expansion of "buying-power" in the borrowing country; and from the fact that such a flow of gold has taken place it cannot be argued either that there has, or that there has not, been a change in the real ratio of interchange and in the relative levels of the representative man's money income in the two countries.

Germany.	*America.*
I. *Original situation:*	
Total income of £1,400 buys 1,300 *g* goods + 100 *a* goods.	Total income of £1,000 buys 900 *a* goods + 100 *g* goods.
Population 20, representative income £70.	Population 20, representative income £50.
Gold stock £1,400. $V = 1$.	Gold stock £1.000. $V = 1$.
Price of *g* goods = £1.	Price of *a* goods = £1.
II. *New situation, on assumption of unchanged ratio of interchange:*	
Total income of £1,120 buys 700 *g* goods + 100 *a* goods + £480 *a*-securities.	Total income of £1,280 buys 900 *a* goods + 700 *g* goods.
Population 20, representative income £56.	Population 32, representative income £40.
Gold stock £1,120. $V = 1$.	Gold stock £1,280. $V = 1$.
Price of *g* goods = £$\frac{4}{5}$.	Price of *a* goods = £$\frac{4}{5}$.
III. *New situation, on assumption that ratio of interchange is altered against Germany, becoming* $\frac{8}{9}$:	
Total income of £1,050 buys 612½ *g* goods + 100 *a* goods + £506¼ *a*-securities.	Total income of £1,350 buys 900 *a* goods + 787½ *g* goods.
Population 20, representative income £52½.	Population 32, representative income £42$\frac{3}{16}$.
Gold stock £1,050. $V = 1$.	Gold stock £1,350. $V = 1$.
Price of *g* goods = £$\frac{3}{4}$.	Price of *a* goods = £$\frac{27}{32}$.

In the foregoing examples it is assumed that the loans are used, and are sufficient, to draw into employment at current rates of pay a new increment of population which is not immediately productive of saleable goods, and the state of affairs portrayed is that during the *first* period of the new "moving equilibrium"—we cannot, as in the case of reparations payments, construct an example which will be valid year after year. And it is assumed, though of course this may not be the case, that the aggregate gold supply at the disposal of the two countries has remained unchanged.

§ 4. Now let us return to reparations, and examine Table III of § 2, in which the ratio of interchange turns against Germany. The turn of the ratio takes the form partly of a diminution of gross money incomes (as well as of "net purchasing-power") in Germany, but partly also of an increase of gross money incomes (as well as of "net purchasing-power") in America. To demonstrate, therefore, that gross money incomes (as well as "net purchasing-power") have been raised in America, is not (as seems sometimes to be thought) to demonstrate that a transfer-burden does not exist. It is true that for various practical reasons that burden may be more conveniently borne if it takes the form predominantly of an absolute rise of money incomes in America rather than of an absolute fall of money incomes in Germany. It is true also that, given the alteration in the real ratio of interchange, the sacrifice of consumption involved by the reparation payment itself (assumed to be fixed in gold) will be smaller the more the value of gold is diminished in America. But the champions of "transfer-burden" are right in maintaining that the degree of burden depends primarily not upon the *absolute* movement of gross incomes in Germany but upon their *relative* movements in the two countries. They are also, I think, justified in pointing out that since in practice the amount of money in "America" is likely to be large as compared with that in "Germany", the proportionate rise in gross incomes in "America" will, in fact, be small as compared with the proportionate fall in gross incomes in "Germany."[1]

§ 5. We may next consider the possibility that, concurrently with the beginning of the reparation payments, one or both of the countries will have relaxed the rigours of gold-standard technique, in such wise as to permit an alteration in the factor V. Thus Mr. Keynes (*Treatise*, i, 337) discusses the two cases in which Germany is determined (i) to keep her gold stock unaltered, (ii) to keep the level of her gross money incomes unaltered, being prepared in either case to adopt such a banking-policy as will bring about the requisite relation between gold stock and money income: while America is assumed to adhere to her old rules. Mr. Angell, on the other hand, in discussing the case of a foreign loan, assumes that the banking authorities in *both* countries will be ready to alter their policy about reserve-ratios in such wise as to implement the loan. Thus he argues (*The Theory of International Prices*, pp. 402-12) that if borrowers in B are raising a loan in A, their representatives will, with the proceeds of the securities sold in A, buy bills upon B held by the banks in A, who will thus find their assets and deposit liabilities diminished, and will (apparently) be able to think of no way of increasing them again; while banks in B will be glad to expand the scale of their operations by buying the bills thus remitted to B from A. If we are considering a steady flow of capital-export lasting over a series of years, I am not clear either that this is a plausible account of the behaviour of either banking-system, or that the matter can be satisfactorily treated without recourse to analysis of the behaviour not of bankers but of income-receivers, on the lines set out in § 3. Nevertheless, we can so far adapt Mr. Angell's assumptions to the matter of reparations as to allow ourselves to consider a case in which the banking policy of *both* countries (and not one only, as in Mr. Keynes' case) is so modified as to obviate the necessity for any transfer of gold.

[1] See especially Keynes' *Treatise*, i, 341.

In all the three examples below, the real ratio of interchange is turned against Germany by $\frac{2}{7}$, and a "transfer-burden" of this magnitude consequently exists, whatever has happened about the stock of gold. It will be noted that, as explained in § 4, the total sacrifice of consumption by Germany is greater the smaller the rise in the American price-level. The situation from which we start is that of Table I, § 2.

Thus we see once more that many statements can be made about the "flow of purchasing-power" in the two countries which are quite irrelevant to the question of whether there is, or is not, a "transfer-burden" in existence.

§ 6. It is, however, one thing to show that the champions of "transfer-burden" are not proved wrong

Germany.	*America.*
IV. *Angell-change* (gold flow unnecessary, both banking policies flexible).	
Total income of £1,200 buys 560 g goods + 100 a goods and pays £600 taxes.	Total income of £1,800 buys 900 a goods + 840 g goods.
Gold stock £1,400. $V = \frac{6}{7}$.	Gold stock £1,600. $V = \frac{9}{8}$.
Price of g goods = £$\frac{6}{7}$.	Price of a goods = £$\frac{6}{5}$.
V. *Keynes-change, i* (G. holds gold stock rigid, A.'s banking policy unchanged).	
Total income of £1,000 buys 420 g goods + 100 a goods and pays £600 taxes.	Total income of £1,600 buys 900 a goods + 980 g goods.
Gold stock £1.400. $V = \frac{5}{7}$.	Gold stock £1,600. $V = 1$.
Price of g goods = £$\frac{5}{7}$.	Price of a goods = £1.
VI. *Keynes-change, ii* (G. holds incomes rigid, A.'s banking policy unchanged).	
Total income of £1,400 buys 660 g goods + 100 a goods and pays £600 taxes.	Total income of £2,000 buys 900 a goods + 740 g goods.
Gold stock £1.000. $V = \frac{7}{5}$.	Gold stock £2,000. $V = 1$.
Price of g goods = £1.	Price of a goods = £$\frac{7}{5}$.

by certain statements about monetary purchasing-power, and another thing to show that they are right. Is it not at least *possible* that these monetary happenings should veil an underlying change in the conditions of *real* reciprocal demand? Most champions of "transfer-burden" will, I think, concede that it *is* possible; for they will admit that under modern conditions the desire-schedules of populations for foreign goods are to some extent susceptible to manipulation, and that a reparation payment may be accompanied by organised attempts to manipulate them—for instance, by creating a collective desire in America for public works using German materials, or by propaganda in Germany against the use of foreign bread-stuffs. So far as this occurs, they will admit the effect of the reparation payment on the real ratio of interchange cannot be considered in isolation, since there is an influence at work on the other side, operating, as the case may be, through a raising of the American real demand-and-supply curve or a lowering of that of Germany. They will, however, go on to point out that this is one of the matters in which the analogy between reparations and capital export is apt to be most treacherous. For in the nineteenth century at least (apart from the definite stipulations about the mode of expenditure of foreign loans which in some countries were common) it seems to have been something like a law of nature that the countries whose investors were rich enough to want to lend abroad were also the countries whose industrialists were ingenious enough to need, and enterprising enough to find, an expanding market for the products of large-scale industry; while the countries which were poor enough to want to borrow were also the countries which were sufficiently simple in economic structure to have a high demand for the specialised products of factory industry. Thus the needs of exporters, of importers, and of borrowers and lenders walked for the most part hand in hand in apparently pre-ordained harmony. It would be rash to make the same assertion about the post-war "reconstruction" borrowing of European countries; and it would be rasher still to make it about the payment of reparations. Where reparations are concerned, such compensatory movements of real demand are not indeed impossible; but they require more deliberate organisation, about which in practice many difficulties may arise. Further, there may well be a counter-influence working in the opposite direction—namely, an organised distaste in the reparation-receiving country for buying the goods of the defeated enemy.

§ 7. Apart from such concessions, it seems to be usually implied by the champions of "transfer-burden" that the old real demand-and-supply curves must be thought of as remaining in force, and that the degree of the "transfer-burden" will depend on their relative elasticities at the original point of intersection. Only, it is tempting to add, in the extreme cases in which *either* the elasticity of German real demand for American goods *or* the elasticity of American real demand for German goods is infinite, can Germany escape *some* turning of the ratio of interchange in her disfavour.

So far as I know, however, only one attempt has been made to illustrate precisely the effect of payments of this kind upon the behaviour of the Marshall curves—an attempt by Marshall himself in discussing the effect, not indeed of reparations, but of annual interest payments; and it is, I am afraid, quite clearly unsuccessful. For Marshall deals with the matter geometrically (*Money, Credit and Commerce*, p. 349, fig. 19) by shifting the starting-point of the curve of only one of the countries—that making the interest payment—by a distance from the origin representing the amount of the interest payment, while leaving the shapes of both curves unchanged. His construction exhibits the paradoxical results that (with "normal" elasticities—*viz*. greater than unity) imports into the interest-paying country are *increased*, and the terms of trade inevitably turned in its favour. Clearly this construction is not acceptable; but what are we to substitute for it?

The solution—largely suggested by Professor Pigou [1] —appears to be broadly as follows. To speak geometrically, *both* curves must be shifted to a new common

[[1] See his subsequent formulation in *E.J.*, 1932, pp. 532 ff.]

starting-point, and there is a general probability that both must be not only shifted but *distorted* inwards towards one another. This represents the probability that Germans, having in effect parted with some of their goods for nothing, will not be willing to trade away a given quantity of German goods on such easy terms as before; while Englishmen, having in effect received some German goods for nothing, will not be willing to offer so many of their own goods as before for a given quantity of traded German goods. The fate of the real ratio of interchange depends on the relative degree of distortion of the curves, and it seems at first sight as if nothing more could be said about this—as if the deniers of "transfer-burden" were right after all, and the ratio of interchange were as likely to move in Germany's favour as against her. But this turns out not to be true, for a reason which may be expressed briefly by saying that in all probability German goods have more nearly the character of money [1] to Germans than they have to Englishmen, and English goods have more nearly the character of money[1] to Englishmen than they have to Germans. Hence there is a considerable balance of probability that the willingness of Englishmen to trade will be reduced more than the willingness of Germans, and so that the ratio of interchange will be turned against Germany. But it appears that, contrary to common opinion, the degree of the change cannot be expressed in terms of the elasticities of the original curves, though it *can* be expressed in terms of the utility and disutility schedules from which those curves are built up.

The position, then, can be summed up as follows. Even apart from changes of the type discussed in § 6, it is not *impossible* that the real ratio of interchange should move in Germany's favour; and some of the statements that are made by those who call attention to the "increase of purchasing-power abroad" are

[1] Which can be surrendered or gained without leading to a change in its marginal utility.

probably to be interpreted as assertions that the underlying utility and disutility schedules in the two countries are such as to permit this to occur. But it is *not* true that there is no presumption against the schedules being of this kind; and many of the statements that are made about the "increase of purchasing-power abroad" are irrelevant to the question of whether they are or not.[1]

[1] This conclusion seems to correspond broadly with that of Mr. Keynes, as re-stated in the *Treatise*. But I am not sure that his method of treatment distinguishes clearly between the possibility that the American utility schedule is changed in a direction favourable to Germany (§ 6), and the possibility that t is, to start with, of a character abnormally favourable to Germany (§ 7).

XV

THE FUTURE OF INTERNATIONAL TRADE[1]

§ 1. THE question to which I am seeking an answer is—What is the future of international trade? Will it ever play again the same dominant part in the economic life of the world that it played in the nineteenth century?

Let me put the question another way. Consider two well-known sets of facts. Ever since the war, and especially since 1931, the course of international trade has been throttled by an incredible maze of obstacles and restrictions, culminating in that startling bid for economic self-sufficiency, the German four-year plan. Yet in 1929 the volume of world trade was greater by more than a quarter than in 1913; even in the trough of 1932 it did not sink below three-quarters of its 1929 level: and it has now come near to regaining that level. Which of these two sets of facts represents the true mind of the world for the future—the apparent determination of Governments, egged on by their citizens (for it is no use pretending it is all the fault of the Governments), to strangle international trade, or the obstinate determination of trade not to be strangled? Or are the two sets of facts reconcilable in terms of some intelligible trend, some fumbling purpose to which the nations will one day learn to give fruitful effect?

§ 2. Forgive me if I go back to the beginning. The case for a large volume of international trade rests on the different endowment of nations in respect

[1] A lecture delivered to the Liverpool Economic and Statistical Society on October 13, 1937, and printed (with the embodiment of some helpful criticisms) in *E.J.*, March 1938.

of natural resources, human quality and skill, and acquired equipment. Where these differences are great, it is to the immediate economic advantage of all parties that a large volume of trade should take place. The fact that Utopia *can* grow wheat, even the fact that she can grow more wheat per acre or more wheat per man than Ruritania, is not in itself an argument against her importing wheat from Ruritania if she can turn her resources to the production of other things in which her advantage over Ruritania is greater still. The volume of profitable trade depends on the width of these gaps in the *comparative* advantages of different countries for the production of different things.

Let us first put ourselves back in the first decade of this century, endow ourselves with ordinary economic foresight but not with prevision of the war and its consequences, and ask ourselves what the future then seemed to hold in store as regards these gaps in Comparative Advantage. It was, I think, fairly evident that they were tending to become narrower. The sharpness of the outline between the granaries and the workshops of the world, to put it briefly, was already becoming blurred. In the first place, it was becoming plain that proficiency in the arts of mechanised industry could not remain for ever the monopoly of the nation, or even of the group of nations, that had first learnt to use them. Secondly, electricity was already promising to release the factory from the pull of the coalfields and pointing both to a different, and to a less intense, localisation of manufacturing industry. Thirdly, to turn to the other side of the picture, the exploitation of virgin soils in the new countries appeared to be reaching its limit, and agriculture there too to be coming up against its old enemy, the law of diminishing returns. Thus the long-term prospect seemed to be that of a world in which the international exchange of goods would play a smaller part relatively to total production, and would be conducted on terms progressively more disadvantageous to the teeming industrial populations of western Europe.

§ 3. Now let us demand of ourselves a great feat of the imagination, and picture ourselves living indeed in 1937, but in a world in which there has been no war. Have the forces which we descried at work thirty years ago worked themselves out as we expected in reducing the advantages of international specialisation, or have they been modified in any way? Has any new force made its appearance?

As regards the first two forces, there is no doubt, I think, as to the answer. The diffusion of industrial capital and of industrial skill has proceeded even more rapidly than most people would have prophesied. In particular it has become evident that the simpler processes of textile manufacture can be carried on with approximately equal efficiency by almost any kind of population in almost any part of the world. The oil-engine and the hydro-electric plant have continued to press home their assault on the sovereignty of coal. From this side the narrowing of the gap of comparative advantage has proceeded apace.

§ 4. When we turn to the other side, the conclusion is not so clear. There are three far-reaching factors to be taken into account, and it is by no means evident how their net effect is likely to work out. The first and most obvious is the astonishing achievements of science in the domain of agriculture. These achievements fall into two main groups, the mechanisation of agricultural operations and the improvement of the breeds of animals and plants; I have neither the time nor the knowledge to appraise them in any detail. Their most spectacular effect has been to cheapen the cost of the products of agriculture in terms of the products of industry, so that one of the tendencies which we thought we saw at work thirty years ago—the tendency of the terms of trade to turn against the manufacturing countries—has been dramatically reversed. To step for the moment into the real world (since for the hypothetical warless world which we have agreed to explore we dare not invent figures), the price of Britain's imports in terms of her exports was in 1931 some 30 per cent., and is even now some 20 per cent., lower than in 1913.[1] But for the purpose of our main problem what we want to know is, not how much scientific progress has cheapened the products of the earth, but whether it has increased or diminished the economic advantages of international specialisation. And in spite of some confusing cross-currents, there seems at first sight to be no doubt about the answer. It is on the side of the large prairie wheat-factory, not of the fragmented countryside of the Old World, that the tractor and the combine weight the scales. It is in outlandish regions in the cold north or the drought-ridden desert rather than on the rich soils of temperate zones that the Mendelian plant expert confers his richest gifts. And it is not only in the field of the production of raw things but also of their transport that science, on the whole, still seems to fight on the side of regional specialisation and long-distance trade. Man has learnt to control temperature, and therefore the good fairies of ripening and the demons of decay; meat that is no worse than chilled can at last voyage safely from the Antipodes, and the most telegonous fruits appear in our shop-windows at the most unlikely seasons.

True, nothing in this world works only one way; and scientific invention, which can thus confer its blessing on the localised producer, can also suddenly turn round and smack him in the face. In the warless world in which we are still moving in thought, we can perhaps forget about Buna rubber; but we can hardly think away synthetic fertilisers and artificial silk. Air and wood are more widely diffused over the globe than nitrate deposits or fibrous annuals,

[1] These figures, it is true, reflect not only the relative movement of *costs* in agriculture and industry, but also the relative change in ability to control production by monopolistic methods.

as water is more widely diffused than coal; at the bid of science a Chile yesterday, a Texas or Bengal to-morrow, may wake up to find its occupation gone.

§ 5. Furthermore—and this is the second of the far-reaching factors to which I alluded a few minutes ago—there hangs over the populations of the new countries, or some of them, a cloud of which they were scarcely aware thirty years ago. It is being increasingly borne in upon them that their vast specialisations of the late nineteenth century were to a certain extent bogus specialisations, founded on reckless mining of the soil, on natural but disastrous ignorance of the cyclical misbehaviour of sun and cloud, on improvident sacrifice of the leisurely tree to the crop which is here to-day and gone to-morrow. Behind the restriction schemes of Secretary Wallace and the financial junketings of Mr. Aberhart looms the enormous spectre of the Dust-Bowl. The same charge of living on capital lies, of course, ultimately against specialisations founded on the exploitation of mineral wealth, though the pigeon takes longer to come home to roost—*how much* longer the South African in particular does well from time to time to ask himself. But whether it work slow or fast, we have here a factor tending, like the diffusion of manufacturing skill, and on the whole *unlike* the factor of agricultural improvement, to limit the advantage of international specialisation and the growth of international trade.

§ 6. Thus even for the peaceful 1937 of our imaginings, the picture is already somewhat complex and confusing. But perhaps we can fairly sum the argument, so far as it has yet gone, by saying that on the balance the tendencies which we descried thirty years ago towards the curtailment of long-distance trade have received a moderate check. It is true that the overseas populations have become cleverer at twisting and hammering things; but they have also become cleverer at their old game of growing things: so that if the gap of Comparative Advantage has been encroached upon from one side, it has also been widening out on the other.

Is that, still barring war and the mentality begotten by war, a picture which, however sketchy, is complete as far as it goes, or have we left something vital out? Yes, I am afraid the answer is that, apart altogether from war and the rumour of war, we have left out something of great importance—the third of the far-reaching factors which I mentioned some minutes ago. When we try to introduce it, the picture becomes more complex still; and I think on the whole the balance of the argument changes.

The specialisations of the nineteenth century were not simply a device for using to the greatest effect the labours of a given number of human beings; they were above all an engine of *growth*. Their most spectacular effect was to hold at bay for a century the devil which Malthus had unchained, so that, just as the Red Queen was five times as rich as Alice *and* five times as clever, so the inhabitants of these islands in the pre-war decade managed, according to a commonly quoted though obviously not very reliable computation, to be four times as well off as their ancestors of a hundred years before *and* four times as numerous. And then, just as we were wondering whether the devil of population pressure could be kept at bay much longer, we looked over our shoulders, and lo and behold!—he was gone. But he has left a curious smell behind, and we are none of us quite sure whether it is brimstone or roses. So far as the future of international trade is concerned, there is at present a strong disposition among thoughtful persons to believe that the brimstone predominates.

It is important, though it is not always quite easy, to make out exactly what these thoughtful persons are saying. Let us try to give definiteness to the problem by supposing that the populations of the whole world, at any rate outside Soviet Russia and eastern Asia, become stationary within the next few years, and continue practically stationary for, let us say, the next half-century. Naturally we shall not expect the aggregate either of world production or of world trade to grow as fast as they did while population was still increasing smartly; we should expect production to grow, for instance, by an annual average of say 2 per cent. instead of 3 per cent. But are there any reasons to expect that in such circumstances world *trade* will grow more slowly than world *production*, and indeed perhaps will cease growing at all?

Yes, say the thoughtful persons who smell brimstone, there are such reasons. As people become richer they spend a smaller proportion of their income on food of any kind, and a smaller proportion still on the simpler and cheaper kinds of food. Now, as long as the industrial populations were still increasing at a brisk rate, it was possible to rely on a constantly expanding market for the simpler foodstuffs. Anything which cheapened their cost of production in the overseas countries was an unequivocal blessing to their farming populations; even falling prices were compatible with rising profits and increasing employment on the land. But if the increase in aggregate world output has to be absorbed entirely in the form of increased consumption of goods per head, that is no longer true. The combine and the tractor and the researches which produced Marquis wheat and P.O.J. 2878 have come in a sense too late. For they bring with them now not only lowered costs, but glutted markets, and a formidable problem of occupational transfer for the farming populations of the overseas lands. And even if that problem could be solved quickly and without friction, which is not the case, it seems likely that it would be solved in ways that tend to close rather than to widen the gap of Comparative Advantage, and so to limit the scope for international exchange.

§ 7. There is, say the thoughtful persons, one outstanding reason why this process of readjustment should lead to a relative decline in international trade.

The Great Specialisation of the nineteenth century was not simply an exchange of industrial products for agricultural products. Following Mr. Hartley Withers, we may visualise it as in part an exchange of capital goods for pieces of paper called securities, followed at a later date by an exchange of other pieces of paper, called interest-coupons, for agricultural products. Thus the volume of trade was kept at a high level by two closely connected facts—first, the fact that the new countries keenly desired a type of goods, which we may think of for short as steel rails and girders, which the older countries were peculiarly fitted to supply, and secondly, the fact that the old countries did not demand immediate payment for these goods, but were willing in effect to supply them on tick, so that the volume of trade was continuously larger than it would have been had it depended solely on the opportunities for simultaneous barter.

Now this process of foreign investment, so the argument runs, was bound up with the growth of population rather than of production. In whatever exact form a stationary population elects to take its rising standard of life, it is not likely to be a form which entails the same hectic construction of railways and harbours and bridges in distant lands as did the clamour for bread and shirts which rose in the last century from the growing millions in the factory towns. Thus three consequences will follow, all of them damaging to the volume of international trade. In the first place, the imports of overseas countries will tend to be confined to what they can pay for out of their current output. In the second place, their demand will shift away from those things in which the gap of Comparative Advantage between agriculture and manufacture is widest—for when all is said and done there is stronger reason why steel should be forged in Sheffield than why cotton should be spun in Oldham or saucers baked in Staffordshire. And thirdly, so far as the overseas countries still *do* desire to borrow and to import capital goods, they will tend to make their interest payments in subsequent years not by expanding their exports but by curtailing their imports—a method equally satisfactory, perhaps, to the foreign creditor, who is concerned only to receive his money, but by no means equally satisfactory to those whose livelihood is bound up with the processes of international trade.

Now I think myself that there is at present a little too much disposition to smell brimstone rather than roses in the wake of the vanished devil of population pressure. It would seem as though we ought to be able to make the roses predominate if we really wish. But as regards the problem immediately in hand, the probable behaviour of the volume of international trade in the next half-century, I think there is much force in the argument which I have just tried to set forth, and that it goes a long way to cancel the argument on which I laid stress earlier—the argument, namely, that the progress of agricultural improvement has lowered agricultural costs more in the new than in the old countries, and so on the face of it favoured a still higher degree of international specialisation.

§ 8. Let us now enlarge the range of our enquiry by asking a further question. Granted that we must learn to accommodate ourselves permanently to a smaller relative volume of international trade, does it also follow that we must learn to accommodate ourselves permanently to a more restrictionist trade policy throughout the world? Or is the tangle of restrictionism in the midst of which we live the result not of the deep-seated economic forces which we have so far been attempting to analyse, but of the factors which we have been deliberately trying to think out of the way—of the war and its unhappy aftermath?

The logical connection between trade *shrinkage* and trade *restriction* is not, I think, immediately self-evident. The mere fact that the balance of advantage is on the side of having a smaller relative volume of international trade than in the past is not *in itself* an argument for taking steps to make that volume smaller still, for the benefit of particular groups of producers, any more than it is an argument for trying to keep the volume uneconomically large, for the benefit of the owners of ships or dockyards. It is good fun for the Protectionist to be able to catch the Free Trader out, as he sometimes can, adopting the posture of a defender of vested interests and the *status quo*—shedding over laid-up ships and closed bill-brokers' offices those tears which he would condemn as unmanly weakness if they were allowed to flow over derelict wheat-fields and idle cotton-mills. But to cry *Tu quoque* is not the same thing as to prove one's case. Why should the fact that the scope for advantageous exchange between nations is narrowing be an argument for putting increased obstacles in the way of such exchange as still remains advantageous? Is it not rather an argument for sweeping away those obstacles which exist?

Something like a rational answer to this question can perhaps be put forward on these lines. A narrowing of the gap of Comparative Advantage will not only diminish the volume of advantageous foreign trade, but will tend to produce a state of affairs in which there is a relatively large volume of foreign trade trembling, as it were, on the margin of advantageousness, and liable to be blown to one side or the other of that margin by small changes in the wind of circumstance. If, having been for some time just outside the range of profitableness, it is suddenly blown just within that range, great dislocation and distress will be caused to those who have laid their plans on the expectation of its remaining outside that range; and at the same time the benefit conferred on the community as a whole will be relatively small. To take an extreme example, the exchange of ice for coal between North Polia and Infernia not only yields a large measure of benefit to consumers, but is also likely to remain very stable, since a violent change in climatic conditions would be needed to disturb it. But the exchange of black shirts and red shirts between Fascia and Bolshevia is liable to ebb and flow in the most confusing fashion in accordance with minute technical changes; to eliminate it altogether would confer a great boon of security upon the shirt-makers of the two countries, at a cost to the shirt-wearers negligible compared with the sums of which they are already being mulcted for the benefit of their respective party funds.

It is very difficult to make up one's mind how much weight *ought to be* attached to this argument in any particular case. We must not overlook the fact that specialisation by different countries even in what look to the outsider like very similar branches of the same industry may bring great advantages, owing to the economies of production on a large scale, and may remain fairly stable over decades. But I think we can be certain that great weight *will* be attached to this argument from stability whenever it can be made to seem at all plausible to do so. And we can therefore affirm as a fact, so to speak, of natural history, that a relative shrinkage of world trade due to a narrowing of the gap of Comparative Advantage *is* likely to be associated with a further shrinkage due to policy, since it tends both to make more prominent the evils of instability and insecurity and to lower the real cost to the community of attempting to mitigate them.

§ 9. So far as the prospective relative shrinkage of world trade is due to the agricultural revolution and the flight of the Malthusian devil, the connection with increased restrictionism appears to be of a somewhat different kind. For, as we have seen, the agricultural revolution has not diminished the relative advantage of the overseas countries in the production of food, but rather increased it. To the urban populations, therefore, the cost of agricultural protectionism, in the sense of the benefits now within their reach which it forces them to forego, is not less but greater than it was. But since they have benefited absolutely from the agricultural revolution, they are not too acutely aware of this; and it proves politically feasible, in various countries in various degrees, to extract from them the sacrifices necessary to accord to the home agricultural populations some protection against that instability of livelihood which results from the recurrent tendency to world-wide agricultural glut. Indeed, it proves feasible in some countries to go further, and to hold in check, perhaps indefinitely, that migration from the soil which the agricultural revolution and the flight of the Malthusian devil prescribe. Thus it becomes possible to indulge in a certain measure those deep non-economic instincts—in part military, in part social, in part æsthetic,[1] in part apparently sheerly mystical—which instruct all of us, in greater or less degree, that a country whose agriculture is "too small" (whatever exactly that may mean) is a country not fit to live in.

§ 10. Now once more the prime object of my enquiry is not how far these developments of policy are justifiable, but how far they were in any case to be expected as a by-product of fundamental economic change, as distinct from being merely the spawn of war and the atmosphere of war. It is, I think, quite extraordinarily difficult to determine. One cannot lay one's finger on this duty, that quota, that piece of exchange control and say that one is due to the check to the growth in population, the second to currency disturbance and the third to political ambition or military precaution. As our British tariff conspicuously illustrates, the arguments by which a measure is defended do not always bear much relation to the pressures which have led to its imposition; and the reasons for which it remains in force may differ widely both from the real and from the avowed reasons for its original introduction. But it may perhaps serve to throw some light on the prospects for the future if we attempt to distinguish three phases in the progressive orgy of restrictionism in which the world has in fact indulged since the end of the Great War. The first, taking principally the old-fashioned form of tariff protection, may be said to have arisen fairly directly out of the war itself: for its chief motive force was the desire of individual industries in

[1] My own ideal agricultural policy would make the payment of a subsidy on the production of wheat conditional on the sowing of a handsome quota of poppies in among it.

numerous countries to perpetuate the natural protection which they had enjoyed, with the end of the submarine and the blockade, during war-time. Sir Arthur Salter has vividly described how the great difficulty in making head-way against the "cumbrous, complex and provocative" tariff system which thus grew up in the twenties lay not in any "real conflict between divergent national interests and national policies," but in the fact that "there were no genuine national policies conceived as a whole but only a series of national systems improvised under pressure." [1] It would be difficult, I think, to argue that this system, at any rate as it actually developed, represented any real or rational attempt on the part of the world to adjust itself to long-term changes in the underlying conditions of international economic relations.

The second wave of restrictionism, extending far beyond mere tariff protection into the jungles of quantitative regulation of imports and control of exchange dealings, was of course associated with the rush for cover from the depression of 1929 and the financial crisis of 1931. In the case of every country the primary and ostensible object of intensified restrictionism was the protection of its balance of payments, endangered, as the case might be, by the collapse of the market for its exports, by a drying up of the long-term loans on whose continuance it had based its economic life, by a flooding of its market with dumped imports, by a withdrawal of short-term loans which had been incautiously woven into the fabric of its monetary system—or by some combination of these various misfortunes. Now since in every country this wave of restrictionism had its immediate origin in a crisis of currency and exchange, there has been a tendency to hope that it would recede automatically as, by one expedient and another, the various countries got their currency and exchange position into some sort of order; and the Tripartite Monetary Mouse of October 1936 was loudly acclaimed as heralding a return towards what seems in retrospect

[1] *World Trade and its Future*, p. 39.

the economic liberalism of 1929. This has turned out to be an over-optimistic view; for, apart from the special troubles of the French, and from that darkening of the political atmosphere to which I will come in a moment, the truth seems to me to be that, so far as one can now distinguish between them, the post-1929 restrictions, whether justifiable or not, were more in the nature of a genuine reaction to a long-period change in underlying conditions than was the hugger-mugger tariff-building of the nineteen-twenties. For it was in the crisis of 1929-33 that the world first woke up to the long-term problems created by the agricultural revolution and by the precariousness of the whole system of foreign lending. Whatever measure of recovery has been achieved since, these problems still remain unsolved; and the refusal of the post-1929 restrictions to disappear is therefore less surprising, if not less annoying, than is sometimes pretended.

In the third and latest era of restrictionist policy, we must, I think, detect a different strain. For though in a sense it dates from the fall of the dollar and the breakdown of the World Economic Conference in 1933, and thus represents an intensification of the crisis policies of 1929-31, in another and deeper sense it is, it has lately been suggested,[1] more instructive to connect it with two slightly earlier events, the Japanese seizure of Manchukuo and the inauguration of the Ottawa System of Empire trade. Each of these events, however different otherwise in character, represented the deliberate use of political power for the attainment of exclusive economic advantage, and in turn foreshadowed the sacrifice of economic well-being to the consolidation of political power. With the closure of Germany for rearmament and repair, with the breakdown of the world peace system in the face of aggression, with the exhibition of the inconvenience which even half-hearted economic sanctions could inflict, with the tardy re-arming of the British Empire, the Economics of Crisis have tended to pass insensibly into the Economics of War. And in

[1] PEP *Report on International Trade*, p. 223.

the Economics of War the subtleties of Comparative Advantage become a foolish irrelevance. *A* must grow, not what he is most fitted to grow, but what will save most shipping space. *B* must make, not what he is most fitted to make, but what can be made most easily out of local sawdust and mud.

Confusingly enough, this final efflorescence of economic nationalism has been accompanied by a striking expansion of world trade, and even by a slight tendency towards the relaxation of certain trade restrictions. But we must not, I think, be too much uplifted by these facts. For in the first place the rise in the price of raw materials on which the trade recovery has been largely based has increased the economic pressure on the hungry Powers, and reinforced their motives for achieving ultimate self-sufficiency. And secondly, a temporary governmental thirst for deadly metals is not a very firm foundation on which to base our hopes of freer trade.

§ 11. We have now, I think, at last, however summarily, taken all the elements of the confused story into account. What kind of picture emerges? It is, I am afraid, neither a very clear nor a very cheerful one. But it seems to be a picture of a world in which a volume of international trade, relatively diminished as compared with pre-war or even pre-crisis days, will continue to be conducted by mechanisms more cumbrous, in the face of hindrances more severe, than then prevailed. In some degree, whatever political appeasement may achieve, these restrictive policies will continue inevitably to be coloured by the Economics of War. But in some degree they will be based on conceptions of national advantage, expressed in terms like "stability" and "balance," which would not be unintelligible or unworthy even in a world where peace was assured. So vague, however, are these concepts, so difficult of measurement are the advantages claimed, that there will be constant danger of the whole system degenerating into a struggle of interested groups, and constant need for initiative and endeavour to prevent the volume of international trade from being constricted beyond what is necessary or reasonable.

What particular courses of action does it behove a wise man, who wishes to keep his feet upon the earth, to advocate in this situation? That is what I wish to learn. For my own part, I can only pass on, in my own grouping, the thoughts which I have picked up from better instructed persons than myself—I have in mind particularly Sir Arthur Salter, and the anonymous authors of that remarkable production, the PEP *Report on International Trade*, on which I have already freely drawn. I propose therefore to end by flinging down, without argument, six propositions to serve as bones of contention.

(1) We should do our best to widen and exploit such gaps in Comparative Advantage as remain. The broad dichotomy between agriculture and manufacture does not exhaust the truth; there is agriculture and agriculture, manufacture and manufacture. In agriculture, the deflecting menace of war obstructs, perhaps fatally, the full exploitation of the economically obvious specialisation—durable foods from the prairies, perishable foods from the home acres: but subject to its pressure, we must do what we can. In manufacture there is still room for specialisation between the simple and the complex, the low grade and the high, the goods for consumption and the machine that makes the goods. If, say the PEP experts, manufacturing industries abroad are assisted to grow on sound lines with active participation by United Kingdom manufacturers, the inevitable decline in the export of directly competitive goods should be accompanied by increasing exports of capital and other specialised goods. How much is there in this idea?

But I think the event may show that sooner or later we must go further, and reconsider in some measure that wholesale lopping off of manufactured imports from Europe which constituted, together with the depreciation of the pound, our main contribution to the international beggar-my-neighbour of 1931. For the wiseacres who sneer at three-cornered trade have not appreciated, I think, the full dimensions of the world agricultural problem.[1] For reasons already emphasised, we are not in a position to make up to the primary producers overseas for the loss of those European sales which gave them pounds with which to buy from us—pounds which they can no longer obtain because the European manufacturer is hindered by our tariffs from earning them by the sale of his goods in our markets.

(2) National complexes about the balance of payments, while less acute than they were, still exist among creditors and debtors alike; they are not wholly irrational, and we must take account of them. Thus we must be prepared for a time to see foreign investment largely take the form of the export of machinery and the like, financed by credit of a few years' duration, rather than of the old long-term untied loan; though the opportunities for that may return some day. In a different field, here is another interesting suggestion of the fertile PEP. In the old days, they point out, the balancing of imports and exports was not left so wholly to chance as we are sometimes taught to believe. For the merchant who sold British goods abroad frequently did a two-way trade, providing a market for the wares of his customers. This the big manufacturing firm, who has learnt to dispense with the merchant's services, fails to do; and the opportunities for trade are curtailed accordingly. There is room, suggests PEP, for a new type of trading company to fill the gap.

(3) We must be thankful for small mercies. Bilateral agreements are better than nothing to start with; so perhaps even are the despised exchange clearings with which the continent of Europe is honeycombed. Groups for the mutual expansion of trade would be better still. Our rigid insistence on the maintenance of our most favoured nation rights hampers their formation; it is also, in view of the Ottawa system, something of an impertinence.

[1] I owe recognition of this point particularly to Mr. P. K. Debenham.

(4) In the light of what is now known about the nutrition of the people, it is not tolerable that we should chatter for ever, as I have been chattering, about there being too much food in the world, though too much of *some* foods there may from time to time be. The recent report of the League of Nations Committee on Nutrition has given some striking illustrations of how far, even in the richest countries in the most prosperous years, the diet of large sections of the people falls below what is reasonable. If increases in direct taxation are needed to implement a nutrition policy which shall reap the fruits of modern dietetic knowledge and at the same time go some way towards reconciling the conflicting claims of Wiltshire, New Zealand and the Argentine, sooner or later they will have to be forthcoming.

(5) A detached matter, but one of great importance. It is our bounden duty to contribute to political appeasement by the reversal of the policy of discrimination in favour of British goods in the Colonial Empire—a policy which has been indifferent economics, bad morals, and shocking diplomacy—though it may not be an economist's business to say so. The recent stirrings of Government policy in this direction are much to be welcomed, though it does not look as if Lancashire is going to allow them to go very far.[1]

(6) To relax import control in booms and tighten it in slumps is a bright thought as far as it goes: the trouble is that it is likely to occur to other people as well, and that spoils half the fun. The truth is, commercial policy is not enough. Unless we can work towards international control of the cyclical movement of trade, sooner or later we shall all be back in the gutter playing beggar-my-neighbour. But that is another story.

[1] Between the delivery and printing of the lecture, the quota system in Malaya was further extended.

XVI

A VISIT TO THE LACCADIVE ISLANDS[1]

THE *Lady Nicholson* is, or was (because I'm speaking of four years ago), a neat little ship of about 100 tons who for the most part leads a blameless life fishing for pearls in the harbour of Tuticorin, in the south-east corner of India. But once a year she has an outing: for it is her proud privilege to carry an officer of the Indian Civil Service on the annual tour of inspection of the Laccadive Islands—some of the most out-of-the-way fragments of the British Empire, which lie, as I'm sure I needn't remind you, in the Indian Ocean, about 200 miles due west of the port of Calicut.

In the year in which I had the good fortune to take part, as a visitor, in this important fixture, *Lady Nicholson* was in a bad temper: and when she finally arrived, five days after the appointed time, at Calicut, the two British officers who had been bringing her round the coast from Tuticorin used language about her which was in the best traditions of the Indian, or any other, Marine. Her compass, it seemed, had no lights, so it was not easy to be sure where one was going at night; the petrol engine by which her sails were assisted was fitful and wheezy; there was an ominous crack down the middle of the mainmast: and worst of all, they could not get a rate for their chronometer. My I.C.S. friend and I, being hopeless landlubbers, suggested we should wire for one to Madras—only to learn that such things cannot be bought for gold, and that the uncertainty whether *Lady Nicholson's* great watch was ticking at the right speed meant that while we should be all right about latitude we should never be able to be very sure

[1] A broadcast talk given in 1931, and printed in *The Listener*.

about our longitude. This, it was thought, would matter the less because, as I've already told you, the islands are due west of Calicut, so that if we sailed west for long enough we should be almost sure to hit one or other of them. I say *almost* sure, because history records that on two previous occasions the Laccadive Islands have had to remain uninspected, for the simple reason that the navigating officer failed to find them.

Well, we set out, and after thirty-six hours of such tossing as I hope never to experience again, we did indeed, to our great relief, sight the first of the islands. All the inspecting officer's large retinue, from his two fox-terrier puppies up through his sweeper and his cook and his clerk to his English friend, were unashamedly and profusely sick. So were most of the crew, the nucleus of which, itself only accustomed to the calm waters of Tuticorin harbour, had been augmented for the occasion by a sprinkling of cab-drivers, who were more used to the dusty roads of Madras than to what Homer calls the wet ways of the sea—and who, moreover, could only understand Tamil while their officers (who came from the north) could only give them orders in Hindustani. Nevertheless, somehow or other we reached Ameni, the central island of the northern group, and anchored successfully outside its rocky reef.

Anchoring off a Laccadive is no mean feat of seamanship. For the islands are coral atolls of the approved *Treasure Island* pattern, most of them consisting of a more-or-less crescent-shaped stretch of habitable land, the tips of which are united by a reef containing one or two gaps through which a boat—though not of course so large a ship as the *Lady Nicholson*—can find a safe passage into the still lagoon. Outside the reef the ocean-floor drops precipitously away, so that, to quote the official manual, "There are only one or two places on each reef where a ship can safely anchor, and even at these it is no unusual occurrence for the anchor to slip off a terrace in 6 fathoms into perhaps 20 fathoms." Thanks to the skill of the Indian Marine, I am glad to say that no mishap of this kind befell *Lady Nicholson*.

I only visited three of the islands: for there were other things to see in India, and when, after a week, the *Lady Nicholson* made her first trip back to the mainland for stores, I came with her. The whole tour of inspection lasts about five weeks. The islands I saw have the delectable names of Ameni, Chetlat and Kiltan, and each of them has an individuality of its own: but as I cannot hope to make you see them separately as I still see them, I shall only try to tell you in a general way what a Laccadive is like and how we spent our days.

The islands vary of course in size—a mile or two in length and a few hundred yards in breadth will give you the right idea. They are made of shining white limestone coral, imperfectly covered by a coat of sand. The vegetation is, to anyone brought up on romantic stories of Pacific coral islands, disappointing and dull; for it consists chiefly of coco-nut palms. But I won't bother you much about fauna and flora: I will only say that the first night you spend on a Laccadive you will probably think that you must be drunk or mad. For as you walk along the beach in the moonlight, it will suddenly seem to you that all the stones are alive and are scurrying rapidly in all directions. But in truth the coral does not move: it is only that it is strewn with countless shells, many of them marked with the most beautiful and sophisticated geometrical patterns, and each containing a particularly nervous and nimble hermit-crab.

Nobody quite knows when the islands began to be inhabited, but it was many centuries ago, and it was probably in the fourteenth century that the inhabitants were converted to Mohammedanism and in the sixteenth that they passed under the yoke of powerful overlords on the mainland. Towards the end of the eighteenth century they were grossly misgoverned by a lady called the Bibi of Cannanore, and there can be little doubt that their fortunes have greatly improved since they came about 1800 under British rule.[1] The islanders

[1] Of all this and much else you will find an admirable account in the official account of the islands written by Mr. M. H. Ellis, of the Indian Civil Service, to which I am much indebted (Madras Government Press, 1924).

have a magnificent physique, as one would expect of people who spend much of their life in boats, and a good deal of the rest of it walking up coco-nut trees as if they were staircases. This is an astonishing operation to watch: on most of the islands the tree-climbers use a short rope held between the hands to give themselves a purchase; but the climbers of one island reject such artificial aids and trust to the bare hands, being under the special protection of a private saint, who is said never to have allowed one of them to fall. The question of food presents some difficulty, for no rice can be grown upon the islands and it all has to be brought from the mainland in the magnificent ocean-going boats called odams, made of planks sewn together with coir (coco-nut hair), which are the most striking product of the islanders' craftsmanship. For months together the 400-mile double voyage is impossible because of the winds, so a large store of rice has to be kept on each island under the supervision of a minor official called a Karani. On the island of Chetlat we found the Karani in great disfavour, being suspected of unduly favouring his relatives in the distribution of rice: and one of our duties was to sack him and appoint a successor. The choice appeared to be rather limited, since one only of the applicants (an intelligent-looking youth) could read or write. But the appointment did not appear to give the satisfaction which was expected, and just before we left the island the terrible truth emerged—the new Karani had been convicted only a few weeks previously of stealing coco-nuts. The appointment had to be cancelled, and the islanders subjected to the terrible indignity of committing their rice to the care of a foreign Karani imported from a neighbouring island where the standard of education was higher.

This rice is not bought for money, but is bartered by the Government, at a fixed rate of interchange, for the coir or coco-nut-hair which is the staple product of the islanders, and over which the Government has a monopoly. This arrangement serves as a substitute for taxation, and has many conveniences: but it is not free from difficulty, among other reasons because, in apparent defiance of the laws of physics, a given mass of coir is apt to have different weights at different times, in accordance with the state of the atmosphere. It was one of our duties to attempt to resolve some of the problems arising out of this peculiar form of international trade.

But to return to food. Some of the islanders keep poultry, and there are many varieties of fish and other sea-creatures—we dined one night on chops of turtle, and another on a rather woolly sword-fish. But the northern islanders are said to have grown lazy about fishing, and to trust too much for their diet to the ubiquitous coco-nut. For the coco-nut is the central institution of the islands. It can be eaten and drunk; and after it has been duly shorn for the benefit of the Government, it can be traded on the mainland for clothes and other superfluities of life. It is the symbol of wealth and respectability: for the idea of property in land is still unfamiliar, and a man's status is reckoned by the number of trees that he possesses. This tradition has led to an overcrowding of trees which much distressed the gentle little Indian agricultural expert who had been trying to raise the standards of silviculture among the islanders. Talking of property, the Laccadiveans have anticipated a modern school of reformers by drawing a sharp distinction between inherited property and property acquired during a man's lifetime. But they have no occasion for making this distinction a basis for different rates of taxation, in the way that these modern reformers suggest. The only distinction is that one form of property passes to one's own children, according to ordinary Mohammedan law, while the other passes to one's sister's children, according to the law of Malabar. You will easily believe that this complication gives rise to a pretty crop of problems for the attention of the inspecting officer.

The coco-nut is also at the root of the very deep class

division which prevails on the islands between the Koyas, or patricians, who own the trees, and the Melicheries, or plebeians, who climb them. The division is marked in a number of ways: Melicheries may not wear coats or carry umbrellas, and it is doubtful whether they may have singing at their weddings. So far as I remember, when I visited the islands a compromise hit on by a previous inspector was still in force, by which Melicheries might sing on their way to a wedding, but not at the actual ceremony. Some of the islands are inhabited entirely by Melicheries, who have settled there in the past, fleeing, like so many colonists of all ages, from oppression at home. But even there, I am sorry to say, such is the innate snobbishness of human nature that new class divisions have tended to grow up, based on ability to read the Koran, which carries exemption from the climbing of trees.

I needn't say that on a Laccadive island the visit of the inspecting officer is the great event of the year. Strong arms rowed us through the gap in the reef and across the crystal-clear lagoon to the accompaniment of songs and shouting; and on the shore, where the whole population was drawn up to receive us, we were welcomed with the discharge of fireworks, and, in one case, of an aged gun. Even in the neat little white limestone court-house, with its quasi-Doric pillars and its geometrical decorations in the latest Bloomsbury style, where we dined and slept, we were generally conscious of the bright eyes of the island children fastened upon us out of the darkness. Our official day comprised three main events. First, the court, at which the kind of question to which I have alluded and many others were settled by my friend, sometimes under the guidance of the twelve Mopans—a kind of Greek chorus of village elders, who are dressed rather more grandly than their neighbours, and whose business it is to interpret island custom to the inspecting officer. Secondly, but hardly less serious, the official rat-hunt! For it was one of my friend's duties to prevent the islanders from growing slack in their warfare against the rats which dwell in the tops of the coco-nut trees and do great damage to the fruit: and there is a special clause in the Indian penal code, as modified for use on the islands, which imposes a fine of 2 rupees on any person who fails to attend a rat-hunt when called upon to do so by a properly constituted authority. The rats are chivvied by the tree-climbers out of their leafy lairs, and kept moving along their overhead roads until they miss their footing and fall with a thud to the earth, when they are dispatched with sticks. Thirdly, the official baby-show, at which a prize was given for the plumpest Laccadivean born since the last official visitation.

On Chetlat we had another strange duty to perform—to visit the Primrose Tomb. Primrose was the ship's carpenter of the ship *Vizier*, which was wrecked off the islands in 1853. He died on Chetlat while waiting to be taken home, and some other shipwrecked sailors built him a rough coral tomb, which it is the duty of the islanders to keep in decent repair. It is odd to reflect on the destiny of this obscure man, who probably hoped to lie in some English churchyard, but whom Fate has singled out to be, for nearly the whole of every year, the only white inhabitant of the Laccadive Islands, his rude grave the sole visible symbol of the imperial power.

In the evenings, the islanders sometimes devised an entertainment for our benefit. On Kiltan, we were privileged to witness a Zikkar—a religious dance peculiar to the islands, though no doubt its parallel is to be found in other Moslem lands. I wish I could make you see the two lines of swaying bodies, arranged as for Sir Roger de Coverley, but worked up into two sonorous masses of rhythmic ecstasy, while up and down the lane so formed there pranced, faster and faster, the chief actors, men of proved and especial holiness, who shouted and leapt into the air and beat their breasts with great clumsy instruments of wood and iron. The climax was reached when, in the course of one of these frenzies, a youth was pinned through the cheeks with a rusty skewer to the wall of the court-house, within a few feet of my face. No blood—apparently no pain: and after the deskewering and a very little rubbing from a very holy old man, no trace of damage to be seen.

It was on Kiltan too that the little girls came one evening to sing a hymn of welcome to my friend—one of them leading with impromptu verses, the rest taking them up in chorus. And I will end these memories by giving you a translation, which was furnished me at the time, of the hymn they sang. "Praise be to God, and to Mahomet the prophet of God! Praise be to the redskinned man, the lord of Tellicherri. He has beautiful eyes and beautiful ears: he is followed by a crowd of policemen: his teeth are white, and he wears trousers. We are poor folk, and our hands are tired with beating out the coir: but he is our protector, and has come to redress our grievances."

I saw more famous and splendid places in India than the Laccadive Islands, but none which has left me with kindlier memories either of the folk of India or of the British Raj; and I wish that to-night, when I leave this building, I could take a walk under Canopus and the Southern Cross along one of those shining beaches, putting to flight those uncanny armies of perambulating shells, and myself pursued by the bright eyes of the island children.